RETHINKING COLONIALISM

UNIVERSITY PRESS OF FLORIDA

Florida A&M University, Tallahassee
Florida Atlantic University, Boca Raton
Florida Gulf Coast University, Ft. Myers
Florida International University, Miami
Florida State University, Tallahassee
New College of Florida, Sarasota
University of Central Florida, Orlando
University of Florida, Gainesville
University of North Florida, Jacksonville
University of South Florida, Tampa
University of West Florida, Pensacola

RETHINKING COLONIALISM
Comparative Archaeological Approaches

Edited by Craig N. Cipolla and Katherine Howlett Hayes

University Press of Florida
Gainesville · Tallahassee · Tampa · Boca Raton
Pensacola · Orlando · Miami · Jacksonville · Ft. Myers · Sarasota

Copyright 2015 by Craig N. Cipolla and Katherine Howlett Hayes
All rights reserved
Published in the United States of America

This book may be available in an electronic edition.

First cloth printing, 2015
First paperback printing, 2020

25 24 23 22 21 20   6 5 4 3 2 1

LIBRARY OF CONGRESS CATALOGING-IN-PUBLICATION DATA
Rethinking colonialism : comparative archaeological approaches / edited by
Craig N. Cipolla and Katherine Howlett Hayes.
pages cm
Includes index.
ISBN 978-0-8130-6070-5 (cloth)
ISBN 978-0-8130-6802-2 (pbk.)
1. Colonization—History. 2. Imperialism—History. 3. Nationalism—History.
4. Social history. I. Cipolla, Craig N., 1978- editor. II. Hayes, Katherine
Howlett, editor.
JV105.R48 2015
325'.3—dc23
2014048348

The University Press of Florida is the scholarly publishing agency for the State
University System of Florida, comprising Florida A&M University, Florida
Atlantic University, Florida Gulf Coast University, Florida International
University, Florida State University, New College of Florida, University of
Central Florida, University of Florida, University of North Florida, University
of South Florida, and University of West Florida.

University Press of Florida
2046 NE Waldo Road
Suite 2100
Gainesville, FL 32609
http://upress.ufl.edu

Contents

List of Figures   vii
List of Maps   ix
Preface and Acknowledgments   xi

1. Introduction: Re-Imagining Colonial Pasts, Influencing Colonial Futures   1
   Katherine H. Hayes and Craig N. Cipolla

PART I COLONIAL STRUCTURES PAST AND PRESENT

2. Colonial Consumption and Community Preservation: From Trade Beads to Taffeta Skirts   17
   Craig N. Cipolla

3. Globalizing Poverty: The Materiality of Colonial Inequality and Marginalization   40
   Paul R. Mullins and Timo Ylimaunu

4. Indigeneity and Diaspora: Colonialism and the Classification of Displacement   54
   Katherine H. Hayes

5. Cultural Colonization without Colonial Settlements: A Case Study in Early Iron Age Temperate Europe   76
   Peter S. Wells

6. Colonial Encounters, Time, and Social Innovation   99
   Per Cornell

7. Rethinking Colonialism: Indigenous Innovation and Colonial Inevitability   121
   Stephen A. Mrozowski, D. Rae Gould, and Heather Law Pezzarossi

8. Materializations of Puritan Ideology at Seventeenth-Century Harvard College   143
   Christina J. Hodge, Diana D. Loren, and Patricia Capone

9. Working with Descendant Communities in the Study of Roman Britain: Fragments of an Ethnographic Project Design   161
   Richard Hingley

10. The Archaeology of Slavery Resistance in Ancient and Modern Times: An Initial Outlook from a Brazilian Perspective   190
    Lúcio Menezes Ferreira and Pedro Paulo A. Funari

   PART II LOOKING BACK, MOVING FORWARD: COMPARATIVE COLONIALISM AND THE FUTURE

11. Comparative Colonialism and Indigenous Archaeology: Exploring the Intersections   213
    Stephen W. Silliman

12. Comparative Colonialism: Scales of Analysis and Contemporary Resonances   234
    Audrey Horning

    List of Contributors   247
    Index   249

Figures

2.1. Benjamin Garret Fowler I's house and grave marker and the shared grave marker of Benjamin Garret Fowler II and his wife, Hannah, Brothertown, Wisconsin   27
2.2. Brothertown ballroom, Brothertown, Wisconsin   34
3.1. A seventeenth-century silver spoon from the town of Oulu   45
3.2. The town of Tornio at the end of the seventeenth century   46
4.1. Wampum (shell beads) produced at Sylvester Manor   58
4.2. Clipped and reworked brass items and obsidian flake recovered at the Little Round Hill site   66
4.3. Interpretive sign, including artist's renditions, at the Little Round Hill site   67
7.1. Magunco Hill site, foundation of Magunkaquog meeting house, Ashland, Massachusetts   128
7.2. Foundation of the Sarah Burnee Phillips–Sarah Boston farmstead, Grafton, Massachusetts   133
7.3. Cisco Homestead, Hassanamisco Reservation, Grafton, Massachusetts   136
8.1. Commemorative *wetu* at the location of the Harvard Indian College built in 1655   155
9.1. *Agricola* by J. Goldar   166
9.2. The Living Frontier event at Corbridge, Northumberland, England, on May 30, 2009   170
9.3. One of the commemorative stones from Coventina's Well, now at Chesters Museum, Northumberland, England   178
9.4. Offerings on the Roman altar at Carrawburgh, Northumberland, England, in 2012   179

Maps

2.1. Locations of both Brothertown settlements and the seven ancestral reservation communities   18
3.1. Fennoscandia   42
4.1. Eastern U.S. site areas   57
5.1. Principal sites discussed in the chapter   81
6.1. Major sites in the southern Calchaqui highland valley, northwestern Argentina   107
6.2. El Pichao sites, Argentina   109
7.1. Location of the "Praying Indian" communities of Natick, Magunkaquog, and Hassanamesit in Massachusetts and Connecticut   125
7.2. A 1727 land redistribution map showing the Sarah Robins and Peter Muckamaug lot and the Moses Printer lot   132
9.1. Frontiers of the Roman Empire   163
9.2. Britain, with the locations of Hadrian's Wall, the Antonine Wall, York, and London   165

Preface and Acknowledgments

As archaeologists, we know that tracing origins of ideas and materials is challenging, especially when searching for a finite beginning. Tracing the origins of this volume is more like a genealogy. In certain ways, we might push the "prehistory" of this collaboration to 2002, when we first worked in the field together at Sylvester Manor, New York. A few of the themes highlighted in this volume were at least on the peripheries of our discussions of the complicated material culture, features, and overall layout of the plantation site; however, we had not yet a full appreciation of how complex the nature of colonialism was (and is) there. As we each headed off in different directions to complete various degrees, these discussions continued via email and conference meet-ups.

The project's more immediate roots materialized as each of us began working on comparative colonialism in new settings. Kat joined the anthropology department at the University of Minnesota in 2008, and in 2012 Craig took a job overseas, in the University of Leicester's School of Archaeology and Ancient History. Each of these places brought new awareness through new comparisons. For example, the colonial histories of New York and New England have radically different trajectories than those in Minnesota, and these differences are stark in terms of the contemporary political circumstances of American Indian tribes. When teaching a course titled Archaeologies of Colonialism with an explicitly comparative approach, moreover, Kat found that many undergraduates had difficulty even recognizing the United States as "colonial" beyond the struggles of colonists against the British crown authority. What sparked the students' willingness to rethink the grounds of American colonialism were the comparative perspectives on Greek and Roman colonization, the Inca Empire, or the trade diaspora of Uruk. The contemporaneous contexts of Africa, Australia, and South America, with the complicated discourse of indigeneity, opened considerations of whether there are common practices for imposing or resisting colonial power and whether there are common outcomes.

In Leicester, Craig engaged with his new colleagues and was struck by the rich and diverse set of approaches that the School of Archaeology and Ancient History employed in studying the human past. The interdisciplinarity of the dialogues and debates that emerged on a regular basis in the department inspired him to consider the relevance (or lack thereof) that his work on colonialism in Native North American had for his new English colleagues working all across the globe, particularly those who studied colonialism, defined broadly. Some were reluctant to accept the definitions and theories that circulate in North American archaeology and especially the engagement with descendant communities. This made for a lively and arguably productive set of debates.

In January 2012, we began planning a large conference session devoted to comparative colonialism to draw on these insights. The occasion that presented itself was the 2013 Society for Historical Archaeology meetings, held at the University of Leicester. The location offered the opportunity to bring together scholars working in and on Old World and New World contexts. The session was designed to encourage direct engagement among scholars working on very different times and places but with potentially comparable interpretive themes, such as consumption, diaspora, critical approaches to temporality, stakeholders and descendants, and slavery. The symposium, titled "Entangling Colonial Narratives New and Old," took place on January 10, 2013. It included papers by Craig Cipolla, Paul Mullins and Timo Ylimaunu, Per Cornell, Stephen Mrozowski, Katherine Hayes, Lucio Menezes Ferreira and Pedro Funari, Jane Webster, Richard Hingley, Christina Hodge, Diana Loren, and Patricia Capone, with Audrey Horning and Kent Lightfoot as discussants.

As the project moved toward the publishing phase, several participants had to drop out. Luckily, Peter Wells and Steve Silliman each agreed to join the project later and contribute to the book. Additionally, Rae Gould and Heather Law Pezzarossi agreed to co-author a chapter with Steve Mrozowski. We very much wanted the published chapters to continue in the spirit of comparative approaches by encouraging authors to engage with one another's work. To that end, all the draft chapters were circulated among all the authors, not just the editors. As our authors revised, we saw that the original thematic pairings multiplied into connections across many chapters. The remnant of the thematic dialogues resides in the order of the volume chapters, but it became impossible to confine chapters to thematic sections. This, we felt, was part of the point. It has been an enormously satisfying process, and we hope to encourage this type of scholarly collaboration in future projects.

We each owe thanks for support and help in the unfolding of this volume. Craig received copyediting funds for this project from a European Commission Marie Curie Career Integration Grant (grant number 333909). Any findings and conclusions or recommendations expressed in this material are those of the editors and authors and do not necessarily reflect the views of the European Commission. Both editors are grateful to Kelly Ferguson for painstakingly copyediting several drafts of each chapter. We also thank all session participants and chapter authors, Peter van Dommelen, and an anonymous reviewer for suggested improvements on the complete manuscript, along with Meredith Babb and Sonia Dickey at the University Press of Florida.

Craig thanks Kat for providing enthusiasm and hope when his was running low, his colleagues at the University of Leicester School of Archaeology and Ancient History for general support, and the Brothertown Indian Nation for participating in—and supporting—some of the research reported on in chapter 2. Special thanks are due to Kelly, Maya, and Pete for making England a home.

Kat thanks the University of Minnesota American Indian Studies Workshop and the Sociocultural Anthropology Brownbag group for critical comments on her chapter. She is also grateful to Craig for keeping the conversation going all these years and to John Matsunaga for keeping her going.

1

Introduction

Re-Imagining Colonial Pasts, Influencing Colonial Futures

KATHERINE H. HAYES AND CRAIG N. CIPOLLA

Twenty years ago, the Columbian quincentenary inspired archaeologists to initiate conversations and debates about colonialism that extended well beyond Columbus specifically and modern European expansion in general. These conversations were particularly poignant and fraught among archaeologists in the Americas. Not only did they touch upon the raw nerve of the newly passed Native American Graves Protection and Repatriation Act (NAGPRA), they also brought attention to the gaping ontological and epistemological divides in our discipline over temporality and subjectivity. In the years that followed, we turned more attention to the question of colonialism and have found not one but many processes and historical outcomes and found not two categories of people involved (colonizer and colonized) but a vast plurality of variously gendered, racialized, aged, and occupied peoples of a multitude of faiths, desires, associations, and constraints. Perhaps one of the most important lessons learned in these investigations is that colonialism is not a phenomenon of limited historical duration, a phase or era in our chronology, but is ongoing. This we learn when we try to identify a finite end point of the process and do not find it and especially so when we learn from contemporary descendant communities. The impacts of colonialism, if not in some instances the same processes set in place by the likes of Columbus, are ongoing.

How are we to take on this challenge of interpreting ongoing circumstances? The comparative project of this volume, in which we engage archaeologists of the New and Old World in dialogues on the subject of colonialism, is an effort to compare the practices of the past while also drawing attention to the unfolding consequences or futures in colonial circumstances. Unlike previous volumes on the archaeology of colonialism that draw upon ancient and modern cases from Old World and New World contexts (among them Gosden 2004; Lyons and Papadopoulos, ed. 2002; Stein, ed. 2005; Voss and Casella 2012), this volume gives explicit attention to the relevance of colonialism to contemporary communities regardless of the temporal spans under consideration. How do these themes and concepts resonate from settler societies to postcolonial societies, from the deeper temporal histories of Roman, Greek, or earlier empires to the making of the modern world? What frameworks have circulated across all of these contexts, and to what effect? Perhaps most importantly, how do these approaches help us to critically engage with the ongoing impacts of colonialism today, whether they lie in the federal recognition process for Native American nations or in the heritage representation of a Roman past? In this introductory chapter we explore the ways in which entangling colonial narratives, that is, the critical comparison of archaeological case studies from a wide variety of geographical and temporal contexts, can foster rethinking colonial pasts and influencing colonial futures.

Frameworks for Comparison

The approach in this volume draws together several frameworks for archaeologies of colonialism with the aim of highlighting the significance of colonial pasts to contemporary communities. First, we follow the example of Stein's work (1999, 2002, ed. 2005), which has shown that broadly comparative cases help to identify generalizable or cross-cutting processes of colonialism: a "nuanced, holistic understanding of the complexities of colonial encounters" (Stein 2005:18) via comparative colonialism from a wide variety of historical contexts. When we engage in comparative approaches, we are faced with a series of scalar tensions: the specific versus the general, the historical versus the anthropological, the practical versus the theoretical, and the broad-brush perspective on human history versus the local and individual experiences constituted and oftentimes lost therein (Gosden 2004; Lightfoot 2005a, 2005b; Rothschild 2003; Stein 2005; Stein, ed. 2005; Voss and Casella, ed. 2012). The scale of archaeological perspectives provides interesting and productive entry points into colonial histories. Recognizing the valuable insights that archaeology's on-the-ground perspective offers, researchers (Casella and Voss 2012:2; Lyons and Papadopoulos 2002:9) often frame archaeologies of colonialism—comparative or not—as upending, or at least complicating, standardized approaches to colonial history, which tend to begin with archives and the global or national scale. These disciplinary and scalar tensions reflect that a comparative approach can identify common concepts and categories but can also be used to deconstruct common (received) concepts and categories. The dual roles of comparison are particularly apropos in studying colonialism, a process that relies on the construction of new social categories and hierarchies, often through material culture (Gosden 2004). Moreover, these constructions are still in circulation as we design our research.

For example, Horning (2006a, 2006b, 2007) while focusing specifically on her research in Northern Ireland and on her efforts to compare English colonialism on both sides of the Atlantic, has voiced concerns with global historical archaeologies that reduce complex colonial contexts to universalized, black-and-white portrayals of the oppressive, agentive colonist on the one hand versus the oppressed, passive colonized on the other (top-down models). She has pointed out the ambiguities or "grey areas" in such contexts (2006a:188), noting that we must take "the agency of transcultural actors, skilled in the translation and mediation of multiple identities" into account when drawing comparisons rather than reifying the same old dichotomous tropes. This point resonates with other colonial researchers concerned with issues of agency (as in Stein 2005). In this volume we build upon such studies to recognize the delicate balance between the "powerful" and the "powerless," using great care to avoid the trappings of neoliberalism, which run the risk of framing the potential of the "weapons of the weak" (Scott 1985) as limitless and fully liberating for colonized peoples despite the overarching colonial power structures in which they were or are enmeshed. An example of this balanced approach can be seen in the work of Kent Lightfoot, who has engaged in comparative colonialism for the purpose of identifying common factors while recognizing that those factors relate at least as much to indigenous histories as to colonizers' strategies. These factors include colonial programs impacting native communities as well as political, subsistence, and settlement practices of those communities prior to colonization (Lightfoot 2005a, 2005b; Lightfoot et al. 2013; Panich 2013).

Common Themes

As we began the dialogues featured in this volume, we focused on a broad range of themes or processes that may be traced across cases: consumption, representations of temporality, slavery, diaspora, and the entanglement of descendant communities with archaeology. However, in drawing connections across case studies we realized that our comparisons converged on two main concepts: critical temporalities and critical geographies. By this we mean that compared cases radically challenge or lay bare the assumptions we have regarding the way archaeological subjects understood time and place. We find that an unexamined belief in the inevitability of colonial outcomes leads us to a flat and fixed view of temporality. Instead we could be open to a multitude of imagined futures and memorialized pasts (Colwell-Chanthaphonh 2010; Colwell-Chanthaphonh and Ferguson 2006). Critical temporalities take on the concepts of innovation, creativity, continuity, and tradition and ask that we trace how and when they are deployed rather than treating them as ahistoric processes. Too often we find that innovation is assumed to be the province and power behind colonists and tradition seen as the shrinking haven of the colonized. Critical temporalities highlight false distinctions between continuity and change or traditional and modern and assert the value in pondering perception and intention even when we know they may be empirically irretrievable.

Critical geographies similarly challenge our assumptions about fixed or objective boundaries, borders, belonging and exclusion, and centers with margins.[1] Such a challenge might implicate specific places or landscapes, but more often we find they lie in the geographic metaphors that underwrite colonial relations. The term "native" can operate on both levels, in some cases referencing a literal homeland yet also making a statement of place and belonging by calling out its opposite in "foreigner," "immigrant," or "colonist." The ethnonym "Pequot" demonstrates this point precisely. Now native to southeastern Connecticut, the Pequot Indians are thought to have originally come from the middle Atlantic region of what is now the United States, making their way northwest to upstate New York before settling in Connecticut sometime before European contact. The precise meaning of the Algonquian name "Pequot" is still debated, but many gloss the name as "invader" or "destroyer" (Brooks 2006:9; Cave 1996:183), and most agree that it was a name imposed upon the group by neighboring tribes already settled in the area at the time of the Pequots' arrival. In this case, European colonialism overwrote more distant forms of pre-European colonialism and cultural exchange in North America, making both invaders and locals "native" to European "newcomers."

We see also how material culture may be used to mark (and mask) those distinctions of insider and outsider but that such meanings are subject to change as the scope of our local geography shifts, even to the point of globalizing, and can even reference multiple scales of geographic membership. The same may be said for the materiality of poverty that, as Mullins and Ylimaunu point out in this volume, is often framed in geographic terms of "mainstream" and "margin." These too can be framed at a multitude of scales, as a global comparative perspective on poverty demonstrates. Critical geographies, in other words, are frameworks in which we must trace how "the local" is constructed. In this regard we follow Latour (2005), who attacks the problem of scale head-on by noting that global phenomena only exist as they are assembled locally, a point that many anthropological linguists have known for some time. For example, the rules of grammar (often conceived as overarching or large-scale) are created via local interactions by agents simultaneously aware and unaware of the rules they are enforcing, changing, and sometimes creating as they interact and communicate.

Second, drawing inspiration from debates over the interpretive impacts of generalization (Horning 2006a, 2007; Orser 2004, 2011; also Meskell 2002), authors in this volume acknowledge and explore acts of creativity, resilience, and resistance to colonial impositions as well as the broad structural violence of those impositions. In part this debate in interpretive focus stems directly from growing attention and accountability to political standpoints and self-reflexive attention to the standpoint of most scholars in archaeology. We would be irresponsible if we did not detail the suffering that occurred both in daily experience and in long-term prospects of those who did not wield control of colonial encounters. We would be equally remiss to frame disenfranchised populations—indigenous communities, enslaved or conscripted laborers—as utterly lacking in any craft or adaptability to survive such conditions. Worse, we subscribe to the trope of inevitability when we do not attend to such capabilities. But we argue that these do not have to be mutually exclusive perspectives on the past. Given the nature of the evidence and its articulation with archives, heritage, and oral histories, the power of archaeology lies in the capacity to tell multiple stories. In contemporary practice, we acknowledge the assertion of different stakeholders to choose the stories that do work for them. Christopher Matthews has written, for example, about his community-engaged work in Setauket, New York, where he wished to explore the nature and experience of poverty in a nineteenth- to twentieth-century community of black and Native American heritage. He found, however, that community members were quite resistant to this portrayal. They were familiar with that story, but they were instead interested in telling a story that would encourage their younger generations to stay in the community despite the lack of local opportunities (Matthews 2011). In this instance, poverty was obliquely addressed in the present-day concerns of a community dealing with structural inequality. There is a difference between conflicting versions of a story and complex stories that cause communities that have lived with them to choose strategic essentialism.

Finally, following the example of Lightfoot (2005a; Lightfoot et al. 2013), our comparative frameworks aim to indicate the impacts of colonial circumstances on both disciplinary assumptions and contemporary political and/or heritage struggles. An excellent corpus of interdisciplinary research has given us a broad understanding of the kinds of colonial programs that were deployed by British, Dutch, Spanish, French, and Russian colony administrators in North America, yet the outcomes of those programs varied greatly. Lightfoot reminds us that it was not only the aims and programs of colonizers but the histories and social-political structures of indigenous groups that shaped those outcomes. Such a perspective highlights the tensions discussed above, between representing the violence of colonial programs and the agency of the impacted peoples. A significant contribution of Lightfoot's approach lies in specifically tracing the unfolding consequences of colonialism as a counter to the static representation of cultural identity used in contemporary legal or policy discourse. The value of a comparative approach is to demonstrate that a one-size-fits-all policy, whether related to sovereignty struggles or the control of heritage resources, cannot be applied despite similar colonial programs. Contributors attend to the ways in which colonialism is still experienced, how descendant communities appropriate colonial histories, and how our narratives change when we engage with public perceptions. This is a unifying theme for the various forms of colonialism discussed, whether from several hundred or several thousand years ago.

The unique and significant contribution in this volume is to bring all of these frameworks together, drawing upon the lessons of the past two decades of archaeological work in the charged political atmosphere of ongoing colonial consequences. The comparative aspect of the volume allows contributors to extend the relevance of these lessons well beyond their respective areas of expertise and to do much more than to explore the complexities of past colonial encounters in one region and time period. Instead contributors expose the commonalities and idiosyncrasies of their respective colonial contexts by juxtaposing and entangling them with other colonialisms, old and new. Case studies and synthesis pieces in the volume likewise critically analyze the discipline of archaeology as a means of engaging various publics, including indigenous and local communities (Atalay 2012), while also considering the impacts that public engagement has on archaeological interpretation, scholarship, and pedagogy. In short, we bring our interpretations of the past into critical dialogue with the present and future.

Contemporary Consequences and the Futures We Imagine

As noted above, critical temporalities help us think beyond the events and processes of the past and consider the future as well within the purview of archaeology. One way in which we can do so is to consider the colonial legacies we have inherited and the ones we imagine leaving behind us. In other words, the ways in which we represent colonialism in our work speak to the interventions we hope to make moving forward. These legacies are perhaps most conspicuous in the federal recognition process that Indian communities must go through in the United States in order to restore tribal sovereignty. For instance, certain types of evidence are given preference (written records), and issues of cultural authenticity, miscegenation, and race (as imposed on Indian peoples) are implicitly entangled in the evaluation of such cases, as are monolithic conceptions of colonial history, marginalization, and cultural evolution. This is one contemporary issue that American archaeologists have only recently begun to take seriously in their efforts to make differences in the world that extend beyond the ivory tower (Cipolla 2013; Lightfoot et al. 2013; Mrozowski et al. 2009). But these efforts draw upon the broad precedents and contemporaneous efforts in feminism, community-engaged research, and the recognition of archaeology's role in nationalism (Little 2002; Spector 1993; Schmidt and Patterson 1995).

The use, protection, and representation of heritage resources is an important part of North American recognition cases but also plays a role in community identity across a broad spectrum of political circumstances. In the emergent field of heritage studies, the temporal component is key. Harrison (2013:4) notes, "Heritage is not a passive process of simply preserving things from the past that remain, but an active process of assembling a series of objects, places and practices that we choose to hold up as a mirror to the present, associated with a particular set of values that we wish to take with us into the future." This does not merely mean assembling those aspects of the past in which society takes pride; it may also refer to heritage that is painful, that which cannot be forgotten in order to avoid its repetition, or to conflicting values that can elicit much-needed dialogue. The heritage of colonialism acts in both these senses and highlights the assertions of pluralistic colonial communities as to their place with regard to and relationship with a larger society, whether within, separate from, or in control of that society. These are the narratives of present or past actors to which our contributors draw attention.

One type of narrative concerns how our archaeological subjects could or did act in the face of colonial oppression. As discussed above, these narratives attend to agency and creativity on the one hand and the constraining power of colonial systems on the other. Our authors ask not whether past subjects could or could not act but rather how and where and to what end within an oppressive colonial structure they could do so. Two chapters addressing the issue of consumption frame these perspectives; while Cipolla explores Pequot and Brothertown Indian purchasing practices in relation to their broader cultural priorities and the prevailing market system, Mullins and Ylimaunu focus on the pervasive structural inequalities that underlie the particular acts of consumption for Finnish communities that are labeled "marginal." In each case, the authors illustrate that neither systemic oppression nor the agency of the disenfranchised is fully comprehensible without a broadly contextualized and comparative perspective. Mrozowski, Gould, and Law Pezzarossi remind us that both agency and colonial structures have histories, varying through generations, and the significance of creative acts must be interpreted within historically contingent contexts. They offer the example of Nipmuc practices and material culture in colonized Massachusetts using the lens of social memory through which tradition is maintained in evolving circumstances.

Cornell discusses the concept of "innovation" as an aspect of agency, but he reminds us that the context of our interpretations is shaped by the long-term outcomes of colonialism. Thus before we may even take on the choice of focusing on oppression, agency, or the negotiations between them, we must critically unpack the perspectives and epistemological traditions in their use. This is another type of narrative or, if you like, metanarrative that our contributors explore that draws particularly on critical temporalities and geographies as alternative ways of knowing. Cornell juxtaposes indigenous and colonial conceptions of landscape and settlement in the Iron Age Mediterranean and Spanish colonial Latin America. Hayes offers alternative perspectives on landscape with respect to Algonquian alliance and kinship and how that knowledge might translate into the categories of indigenous and diasporic peoples that contemporary scholars perhaps use uncritically. Categories that at their face appear to be easily definable, like poverty, are embedded in the archaeological record in rather complex ways, reflecting our situated assumptions, as Mullins and Ylimaunu deftly demonstrate. Even the appearance of relative abundance or highly valued materials can actually indicate the existence of structural deficiencies, as the authors' comparative perspective reveals.

The contributions of alternative epistemological perspectives are amplified in narratives that result from engagement with contemporary stakeholders. In such cases, we can see not only the difference that standpoint makes but also most clearly the continued impacts of colonial categories and structures. Ferreira and Funari demonstrate that the multitude of disciplinary perspectives in Brazilian archaeology, including classical archaeologists with an interest in the issue of Roman slavery, combined with the political circumstances of independence created a scholarly focus on maroon communities (established by fugitives from slavery). Their focus has contributed greatly to a comparative perspective on slavery, but perhaps more importantly it has contributed to national discourse on the descendant maroon communities and to the embrace of diversity as a national heritage. As mentioned earlier, social and political recognition of Native American heritage highlights the ongoing impacts of colonialism; two chapters in this volume—by Hodge, Loren, and Capone and by Mrozowski, Gould, and Law Pezzarossi—address how descendant Algonquian peoples are actively engaged in the archaeology of their colonial ancestors by telling their own understandings of their forebears' roles in colonial society. These perspectives are critical; most white Americans have little experience living in two or more cultural worlds that are often in conflict, but Indian people today know this all too well and recognize how such a situation in the seventeenth or eighteenth century might have been negotiated.

But how are we to bring this perspective to bear in colonial circumstances of much deeper history? Can there be ongoing consequences even to ancient Greek and Roman colonialism? Even lacking a traceable social memory, such impacts may be comparable and informative to more recent colonial processes. As Wells illustrates, the spread of Greek material culture, despite the absence of Greek colonies in many areas, precipitated a long period of change in temperate Europe, creating a more globalized cultural and political world; today, moreover, this heritage of Greek material figures in discussions of European identity. The reception of the Roman past through heritage sites in Britain occupies a still more complex social place, as Hingley shows. While identification, valorization, and the concept of Romanization are commonly accepted by British visitors to Roman sites, the more recent role of Britain as an imperial power in its own right has brought attention by scholars to the detrimental aspects of Roman colonization. How can these alternative narratives be brought to a British descendant public that lacks a comparable politics of indigeneity and has been fed a rich diet of popular portrayals of the Roman past? The contributions of Wells and Hingley cause us to consider what the truly long-term consequences of colonialism could be—like greater cosmopolitanism or the inability to identify with subaltern positions—even as they draw upon more recent comparative cases to interpret the deeper past.

As our summarizing chapters by Silliman and Horning emphasize, the comparative archaeologies of colonialism acknowledge but cannot—perhaps should not—resolve the tensions in conflicting perspectives. Is it better for indigenous and other disenfranchised communities for our focus to lie in the shorter-term violence and upheaval of colonial entanglements or in the longer-term persistence of cultural practices and community identity? Likewise, is it better to focus on structures of violence or on the agency of creative responses? In a sense we are pondering the choice between the crisis mode of modernity's narratives and a longer view or even cyclical sense of history's unfolding. The colonial narratives presented in this volume demonstrate that these choices are false ones, as we need all of these perspectives—not in the form of some Cartesian, objective view of all history, but in the sense that we struggle with the multitude of standpoints informing political discourse, that we use our broadened view of colonialism to decolonize our language, practice, and scholarship.

Note

1. In the use of the term "critical geography" we are not explicitly referencing the frameworks of the geographer David Harvey, although our usage does share some of his broad aims.

References Cited

Atalay, Sonya
2012   *Community-Based Archaeology: Research with, by, and for Indigenous and Local Communities*. University of California Press, Berkeley.

Brooks, Joanna
2006   "This Indian World": An Introduction to the Writings of Samson Occom. In *The Collected Writings of Samson Occom: Literature and Leadership in Eighteenth-Century Native America*, edited by Joanna Brooks, pp. 1–43. Oxford University Press, Oxford.

Casella, Eleanor Conlin, and Barbara L. Voss
2012   Intimate Encounters: An Archaeology of Sexualities within Colonial Worlds. In *The Archaeology of Colonialism: Intimate Encounters and Sexual Effects*, edited by Barbara L. Voss and Eleanor Conlin Casella, pp. 1–10. Cambridge University Press, Cambridge.

Cave, Alfred A.
1996   *The Pequot War*. University of Massachusetts Press, Amherst.

Cipolla, Craig N.
2013   *Becoming Brothertown: Native American Ethnogenesis and Endurance in the Modern World*. University of Arizona Press, Tucson.

Colwell-Chanthaphonh, Chip
2010   *Living Histories: Native Americans and Southwest Archaeology*. AltaMira Press, Lanham, Maryland.

Colwell-Chanthaphonh, Chip, and T. J. Ferguson
2006   Memory Pieces and Footprints: Multivocality and the Meanings of Ancient Times and Ancestral Places among the Zuni and Hopi. *American Anthropologist* 108(1):148–162.

Gosden, Chris
2004   *Archaeology and Colonialism: Culture Contact from 5000 BC to Present*. Cambridge University Press, Cambridge, England.

Harrison, Rodney
2013   *Heritage: Critical Approaches*. Routledge, London.

Horning, Audrey J.
2006a   Archaeology, Conflict, and Contemporary Identity in the North of Ireland. Im-

plications for Theory and Practice in Comparative Archaeologies of Colonialism. *Archaeological Dialogues* 13(2):183–200.

2006b Focus Found. New Directions for Irish Historical Archaeology. *Archaeological Dialogues* 13(2):211–219.

2007   Cultures of Contact, Cultures of Conflict? Identity Construction, Colonialist Discourse, and the Ethics of Archaeological Practice in Northern Ireland. *Stanford Journal of Archaeology* 5:107–133.

Latour, Bruno

2005   *Reassembling the Social: An Introduction to Actor-Network-Theory*. Oxford University Press, Oxford.

Lightfoot, Kent G.

2005a *Indians, Missionaries, and Merchants: The Legacy of Colonial Encounters on the California Frontiers*. University of California Press, Berkeley.

2005b The Archaeology of Colonization: California in Cross-Cultural Perspective. In *The Archaeology of Colonial Encounters: Comparative Perspectives*, edited by G. Stein, pp. 207–235. School of American Research Press, Santa Fe, New Mexico.

Lightfoot, Kent G., Lee M. Panich, Tsim D. Schneider, Sara L. Gonzalez, Matthew A. Russell, Darren Modzelewski, Theresa Molino, and Elliot H. Blair

2013   The Study of Indigenous Political Economies and Colonialism in Native California: Implications for Contemporary Tribal Groups and Federal Recognition. *American Antiquity* 78(1):89–104.

Little, Barbara J. (editor)

2002   *Public Benefits of Archaeology*. University Press of Florida, Gainesville.

Lyons, Claire L., and John K. Papadopoulos

2002   Archaeology and Colonialism. In *The Archaeology of Colonialism*, edited by C. Lyons and J. K. Papadopoulos, pp. 1–26. Getty Research Institute, Los Angeles.

Lyons, Claire L., and John K. Papadopoulos (editors)

2002   *The Archaeology of Colonialism*. Getty Research Institute, Los Angeles.

Matthews, Christopher N.

2011   Lonely Islands: Culture, Community, and Poverty in Archaeological Perspective. *Historical Archaeology* 45(3):41–54.

Meskell, Lynn

2002   The Intersections of Identity and Politics in Archaeology. *Annual Review of Anthropology* 31:279–301.

Mrozowski, Stephen A., Holly Herbster, David Brown, and Katherine L. Priddy

2009   Magunkaquog Materiality, Federal Recognition, and the Search for a Deeper History. *International Journal of Historical Archaeology* 13:430–463.

Orser, Charles E. Jr.

2004   Archaeological Interpretation and the Irish Diasporic Community. In *Places in Mind: Public Archaeology as Applied Anthropology*, edited by P. A. Shackel and E. J. Chambers, pp. 171–191. Routledge, New York.

2011   The Archaeology of Poverty and the Poverty of Archaeology. *International Journal of Historical Archaeology* 15:533–543.

Panich, Lee M.
2013 Archaeologies of Persistence: Reconsidering the Legacies of Colonialism in Native North America. *American Antiquity* 78(1): 105–122.

Rothschild, Nan A.
2003 *Colonial Encounters in a Native American Landscape: the Spanish and Dutch in North America*. Smithsonian Books, Washington, D.C.

Schmidt, Peter R., and Thomas C. Patterson (editors)
1995 *Making Alternative Histories: The Practice of Archaeology and History in Non-Western Settings*. School of American Research Press, Santa Fe, New Mexico.

Scott, James C.
1985 *Weapons of the Weak: Everyday Forms of Peasant Resistance*. Yale University Press, New Haven.

Spector, Janet D.
1993 *What This Awl Means: Feminist Archaeology at a Wahpeton Dakota Village*. Minnesota Historical Society Press, St. Paul.

Stein, Gil J.
1999 *Rethinking World-Systems: Diasporas, Colonies, and Interaction in Uruk Mesopotamia*. University of Arizona Press, Tucson.
2002 From Passive Periphery to Active Agents: Emerging Perspectives in the Archaeology of Interregional Interaction. *American Anthropologist* 104(3):903–916.
2005 Introduction: The Comparative Archaeology of Colonial Encounters. In *The Archaeology of Colonial Encounters: Comparative Perspectives*, edited by Gil J. Stein, pp. 1–32. School of American Research Press, Santa Fe, New Mexico.

Stein, Gil J. (editor)
2005 *The Archaeology of Colonial Encounters: Comparative Perspectives*. School of American Research Press, Santa Fe, New Mexico.

Voss, Barbara L., and Eleanor Conlin Casella (editors)
2012 *The Archaeology of Colonialism: Intimate Encounters and Sexual Effects*. Cambridge University Press, Cambridge.

Part I

COLONIAL STRUCTURES PAST AND PRESENT

2

Colonial Consumption and Community Preservation

From Trade Beads to Taffeta Skirts

CRAIG N. CIPOLLA

Monday, April 30, 1917, was a fairly ordinary day for Belva Mosher (1917–1923:51). She began her diary entry with a short description of the cool, wet Wisconsin weather; an unfortunate spring rain kept her indoors for much of the day. She went on to mention several mundane events before concluding the day's entry: in the morning she visited with her friend Ella and, later that afternoon, sent away to Sears & Roebuck for a silk taffeta skirt. For me, this "everyday" example of consumption is of particular interest because Belva was indigenous. More specifically, she was a member of the Brothertown Indians (Cipolla 2013a; Jarvis 2010; Silverman 2010), a multitribal Christian community that formed on the U.S. east coast approximately 130 years before her diary entry. Belva's ancestors relocated to central New York state in the late eighteenth century and moved again during the second quarter of the nineteenth century to current-day Brothertown, Wisconsin, the place Belva called home (map 2.1).

This particular example of consumption fits well within the purview of archaeology, particularly recent studies that delve into the contemporary past. For some, the consumption of mass-marketed goods like Belva's skirt presents an intriguing challenge: How were ethnic, racial, class, and gender relations refracted and negotiated in such practices and materials? To rephrase using Latour's terminology (2005), how did local events of consumption reproduce, challenge, and transform the broader social categories listed above in concert with other local agencies? Recognizing the unique and valuable perspective offered through archaeology, Paul

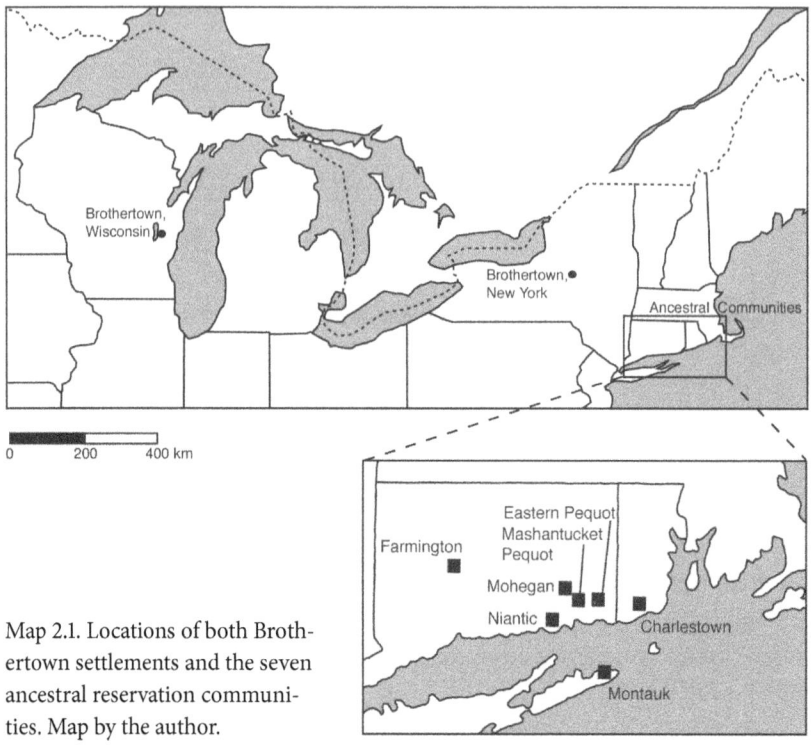

Map 2.1. Locations of both Brothertown settlements and the seven ancestral reservation communities. Map by the author.

Mullins (2011) argues for the untapped potential of archaeological consumption studies for addressing such questions. He first acknowledges the antiquated models of consumption that continue to inform certain archaeological approaches, referring to reductionist treatments that typically frame consumption as solely determined by broader forces of supply and demand. These approaches fall into the scalar trap, mentioned in chapter 1 of this volume, that frames "the local" as always subservient to "the global." Mullins prefers a more nuanced approach that recognizes the complexities and interconnections of various power structures and agencies involved in consumption. He defines consumption broadly as the socialization of material goods, noting its importance in self-determination and collective identification (Mullins 2004, 2011). Regarding the study of indigenous consumption practices in colonial contexts specifically, he highlights the limited importance placed on such goods by archaeologists.

Indeed, the history of archaeological studies of culture contact and colonialism in North America shows tendencies to value European-produced goods recovered from Native American contexts as either dating mechanisms or as indicators and barometers of cultural change (as critiqued in Rubertone 2000 and Silliman 2005, 2009). In decades past, archaeologists treated European-manufactured material culture found in Native American contexts as straightforward indicators of cultural loss. This general pattern also holds for studies of colonial consumption in the ancient world. In his study of Greek colonialism in ancient France, for example, Michael Dietler (2010:60) notes that archaeologists and historians tend to treat Greek consumption of indigenous goods as fundamentally different from indigenous consumption of Greek things. Similarly, in his 2011 study of Roman warfare and weaponry, Simon James points out that to truly understand Roman military history one must also understand those who opposed Roman conquest. The focus of his study, Roman weaponry, attests to frequent Roman adoptions of foreign military styles and materials. In each of these very different forms of colonialism, colonizers are often assumed to maintain their authenticity despite observed material changes, while indigenous populations are seen as fundamentally different (acculturated) because of observed material changes.

The deficiencies highlighted here stem largely from conflations of scale (and the a priori assumptions about different agencies that they mask, or at least obscure). In this sense, my approach parallels that of Latour's actor network theory in that I strive to flatten out these scales in hopes of exposing and challenging the assumptions they conceal. In Latour's words (2005:204), "No place dominates enough to be global and no place is self contained enough to be local." One must follow connections from local interactions to "the other places, times, and agencies through which a local site is made to do something" (173). The archaeological contexts discussed below have been traditionally dealt with in a lopsided manner, treating the local as subservient to broader forces such as European expansion, globalization, and capitalism. First, we must understand that these forces are produced locally through their various connections to the people and things that constituted them (often silently, as noted in Latour 2005:195). Second, we must recognize the other connections and agencies inside these local conditions, including non-European people, things, and practices. For these reasons, scrutiny is needed over our terminology and the conceptual baggage it cloaks, and various scalar terms often used haphazardly in archaeological interpretation—such as "indigenous," "foreign," "native," "local," and "nonlocal"—need to be challenged (Hayes, this volume; Hayes and Cipolla, this volume; Mullins and Ylimaunu, this volume).

Of course, archaeologists and historians are not the only ones with such rigid understandings of the "nonlocal" things that became socialized in indigenous societies. Dietler (2010:63) reminds us that through the ages, "foreign" goods were frequently seen by colonists and colonized alike as tools for controlling one another (also Wells, this volume). For instance, in colonial New England, this premise is supported by the work of seventeenth-century missionary John Eliot (Bross and Wyss 2008; Cogley 1999; O'Brien 1997; Salisbury 1974), who saw English goods and practices as vehicles of cultural and religious change in indigenous societies of the Massachusetts Bay Colony (Mrozowski, Gould, and Law Pezzarossi, this volume). The archaeology of Eliot's praying villages complicate and challenge his understanding of English goods and their purposes in Indian communities. Deterministic understandings of material culture such as Eliot's are still very much alive in contemporary American society, both in everyday understandings of Native American identities and in federal law (Cipolla 2013b).

In the spirit of consumption studies that move beyond economic determinism to consider consumer agency and choice (Douglas and Isherwood 1979; Miller 1987, 1995; Mullins 2004, 2011; Silliman and Witt 2010), I explore select indigenous consumption practices during the eighteenth, nineteenth, and twentieth centuries. An exhaustive treatment of this vast topic is well beyond the scope of this chapter. Yet, this cursory analysis highlights the promise of such a project by providing some general patterns along with a discussion of their implications for the past, present, and future of colonial North America. Contemporary archaeologies of colonialism reject the double standards introduced above. In the case of Native North America this means addressing the complexities of subaltern agency (always constrained), cultural appropriation, and cultural entanglement that are folded into practices of consumption and consumer choice (along with forces often typified as "global" in scope, such as capitalism). Archaeological considerations of Native American consumption are still few and far between. They are also dominated by the assumption that colonial politics color all facets of Native social life from moments of culture contact onward. While I do not deny the importance of colonial tensions, which certainly still exist, I argue that archaeologists must challenge such black-and-white portrayals of colonial history by approaching Native American consumption in terms of social dynamics within Native communities and by considering the impacts that certain forms of consumption had over the long term. This project goes beyond basic questions of acceptance or rejection of non-Indian-produced goods to consider how "foreign" things were socialized and to what effect (following Mullins 2011).

I place the observed patterns of consumption into their broader historical contexts, accepting arguments that cultural change and continuity are forever entangled (Ferris 2009; Silliman 2009; Scheiber and Mitchell 2010). Even in the most unexpected of places, archaeologists taking this approach have the potential to reveal connections between colonial practices and deeper traditions, spiritualities, and identities (for example, Crosby 1988). This point is nicely illustrated by the excavation of Magunkaquog, one of Eliot's praying villages in Ashland, Massachusetts (Mrozowski et al. 2009; Mrozowski, Gould, and Law Pezzarossi, this volume). Beneath three corners of the foundation of a structure interpreted as the communal meetinghouse of the village, Stephen Mrozowski and his colleagues found heat-treated crystals. Other researchers have documented the use and meaning of crystals in various Algonquian societies (Miller and Hamell 1986; White 1991:99; Williams 1973 [1643]). Miller and Hamell (1986:318) argue that crystals were "other worldly" for some indigenous groups, assuring "long life, physical and spiritual well-being, and success." Based on these findings, it seems plausible that at least some of the inhabitants of Magunkaquog saw Christianity as a complement to—rather than as a replacement of—long-standing Algonquian spiritual practices and symbols (Mrozowski et al. 2009:456). I argue that similar hints of ancient continuities are still evident in the archaeological remains of Native consumption in the eighteenth through twentieth centuries. Yet, the general patterns discussed below also shed light on colonialism as general process, including ancient, historical, and contemporary colonial contexts.

Background

I synthesize published data from four related contexts (map 2.1): the Eastern Pequot Reservation in North Stonington, Connecticut (Silliman 2005, 2009; Silliman and Witt 2010; also Hayden 2012 and Witt 2007), the neighboring Mashantucket Pequot Reservation in Ledyard, Connecticut

(McBride 1990; Kevin McBride, personal communication), Brothertown, New York, and Brothertown, Wisconsin (Cipolla 2013a, 2013b). The Eastern and Mashantucket Pequot are closely related since they were part of the same group until the mid-seventeenth century, at which time the English separated the Pequot onto two different reservations (Den Ouden 2005; McBride 1990). The Brothertown Indian community (Belva's group) incorporated Pequot peoples from each reservation along with Narragansetts, Eastern and Western Niantics, Mohegans, Tunxis, and Montauketts (Cipolla 2013a; Jarvis 2010; Silverman 2010). Factions of each of these northeastern reservation communities opted to leave their respective homelands for the opportunity to start anew in Brothertown, New York, subsequently moving to current-day Wisconsin.

Having recognized these connections, it is also important to point out the differences between the Eastern Pequot, Mashantucket Pequot, and Brothertown communities. For example, sites studied on the Mashantucket and Eastern Pequot reservations may have been created and used by individuals and families of comparatively lesser means than individuals and families living in the Brothertown settlements. This is partially because Brothertown Indians had more arable land than did reservation communities back east. The first generations of Brothertown Indians also made conscious choices to leave coastal reservations, rejecting traditional political structures and spiritualities while also leaving friends and family members behind (Cipolla 2013a).

I use data collected from each of these contexts to address two seemingly different forms of consumption: household items, such as ceramics, and grave markers. I see these two forms of consumption as distinct in terms of discursiveness, time scale, and social engagement. Many grave markers produced during the modern era were designed to explicitly say something about the deceased, while household tablewares functioned as part of a much more subtle form of social discourse (Mullins and Ylimaunu, this volume) that was perhaps unknown to—or resisted by—indigenous communities. Gravestones are also designed to last longer than ceramics. Finally, compared to household spaces, cemeteries were potentially visible to different types of people over time.

Notwithstanding these inferred distinctions, archaeologists must use caution when applying labels to past peoples and practices (Fowles 2013). It is highly plausible that Pequot and Brothertown peoples living in the eighteenth and nineteenth centuries regarded these practices differently than their descendants do today. The quotidian and the sacred may have been far less secularized than in contemporary perspectives. For instance, one of my indigenous colleagues once asked my field students to define "sacred" and pointed out that his ancestors likely applied the concept more liberally than he does today, perhaps not even distinguishing between the two categories. Due to these interpretive challenges, I treat these two types of consumption in terms of the contextual differences outlined above rather than assuming fundamental distinctions between household items and grave markers.

Building Homes and Setting Tables

With only a few exceptions, archaeologists have yet to pay much attention to the materiality of everyday life in eighteenth- and nineteenth-century Native contexts. To date, Stephen Silliman (2009) has reported the results of three household excavations from his ongoing work on the Eastern Pequot Reservation in North Stonington, Connecticut (also Hayden 2012; Witt 2007). These households provide a promising albeit tentative baseline with which to track Eastern Pequot consumption patterns between the mid-eighteenth century and early nineteenth century. Diagnostic material culture from the earliest household indicates an approximate date of occupation between 1740 and 1760 (Silliman 2009:219). However, these dates should be taken with a grain of salt since household contexts from the nearby Mashantucket Pequot Reservation often yield mean ceramic dates that predate the recorded period of occupation by five or more years, indicating the consumption of out-of-date or second-hand ceramics (Kevin McBride, personal communication). Silliman (2009:219–220) describes this mid-eighteenth-century dwelling as either a wigwam with "some nailed elements and at least one glass window pane or, alternatively, a small wooden framed structure with no foundation." He goes on to discuss the presence of nonindigenous-produced ceramics, both European and locally made, such as basic redware, Astbury-type ware, Staffordshire slipware, white salt-glazed stoneware, and Brown Reserve porcelain (Silliman 2009:220; Silliman and Witt 2010). In addition to ceramics, the dwelling contained a variety of European- or Euro-American-made items such as kettle fragments, straight pins, glass beads, and clay pipe fragments.

Kevin McBride has excavated similar types of dwellings on the neighboring Mashantucket Reservation. Like Silliman, McBride (1990:113) interprets these mid-eighteenth-century structures as a combination of wigwam and Euro-American-style framed houses. He and Sturtevant (1975) discuss observations recorded in the mid- to late eighteenth century by Ezra Stiles, an American academic who was keenly interested in Native American culture in New England. Stiles recorded the typical Pequot or Niantic dwelling structure in the 1760s as a "traditional" or unmodified wigwam. He noted the presence of "plates" in the wigwam (Sturtevant 1975:438); although he gave no further detail, these plates were likely of European manufacture. In summary, the mid-eighteenth-century structures studied by Silliman and McBride were distinct from the earlier structures described by Stiles, though the material culture might have been similar in the sense that it was possibly European- or Euro-American-produced.

The second structure described by Silliman was likely used during the last four decades of the eighteenth century. Distinct from the first, this structure included "significant surface and subsurface components as well as prominent alterations to the surrounding landscape" (Silliman 2009:220). Most notably, the site contained a comparatively large amount of fieldstone architectural debris, including two collapsed stone chimneys along with several other intact archaeological features, among them a full cellar. Silliman uncovered a wide variety of European-produced ceramics at this second structure, including white salt-glazed stoneware, slipware, agateware, creamware, early forms of pearlware, English brown stoneware, and Chinese porcelain (ibid.; also Silliman and Witt 2010). Compared to the older dwelling, this site contained an even wider variety of nonindigenous-produced material culture (Silliman 2009:220). Similar to the first, this structure roughly resembles contemporaneous structures studied by McBride (1990:113) on the Mashantucket Pequot Reservation. For instance, McBride notes an increase in fieldstone architectural elements at this time. Research on the types of material culture recovered from Mashantucket Pequot households dating to this period is still under way (Cipolla and McBride 2014).

The third dwelling reported by Silliman (2009:221) dates approximately to the first three or four decades of the nineteenth century. In form, this structure was a framed house with a large stone chimney, a small crawl space, and a rich trash deposit in a pit feature just outside the house.

Similar to the other dwellings discussed by Silliman, this last structure also contained redware, creamware, pearlware, English brown stoneware, and porcelain, along with pipe fragments, window and bottle glass, and a variety of other nonindigenous-produced items (ibid.). Of note, my own research on this site focused on the faunal remains (Cipolla 2005, 2008; Cipolla, Silliman, and Landon 2007) and offered insights into how European-produced materials such as metal knives and bottle glass may have been socialized in private reservation household contexts. Analysis of cut marks found on animal remains indicated that nearly half of the marks were made with metal cutting implements, while more than a quarter were made with nonmetal, chipped tools (possibly glass). This interpretation was strengthened with the excavation of the second structure discussed above, which contained a few stone flakes and chipped-glass artifacts (Silliman 2009:221).

This architectural pattern mirrors the general patterns observed archaeologically by McBride (1990:113) on the Mashantucket Pequot Reservation. Complementing the archaeology from this general period, in 1762 Ezra Stiles mentioned twenty-three Mashantucket Pequot dwellings, sixteen of which were described as wigwams and seven as framed houses (McBride 1990:113–114). Based on the archaeology and ethnohistory of the reservation, McBride interprets framed houses as the typical house form on the reservation by the mid-nineteenth century.

In summary, the two Pequot reservations provide important information on changes in household architecture and associated material culture during the eighteenth and early nineteenth centuries. There is no indication that the ceramic sherds studied on either reservation represent complete matching sets of tableware. This makes sense when considering the means by which Pequot peoples acquired such goods. Ledger books kept by Jonathan Wheeler, a white farmer and merchant living in the vicinity of the Pequot reservations, document Pequot men working as day laborers on the farm in exchange for cash and for credit that were often used to purchase seeds, vegetables, and goods from Wheeler or from local merchants through Wheeler (Silliman and Witt 2010:54–57; Witt 2007). Pequots also traded fish and wool to Wheeler in exchange for credit.

The presence of unexpected wares like porcelain in impoverished reservation contexts speaks to a theme discussed by Mullins and Ylimaunu (this volume). Like Mullins and Ylimaunu's silver items, the porcelain in these indigenous contexts demonstrates the need to move beyond the compilation of "laundry lists" of recovered ceramics to actually delving into the biographies of such items and asking how they were acquired, how they were used, and how their users' patterns of consumption compare to those among other contemporaneous sites. I would tentatively suggest that despite the similarities in the types of material culture present in these varied contexts, there were significant differences among households on each reservation and between Pequot and English households such as frequencies of European-produced ceramics, possible differences in use wear, and so forth. However, a detailed comparison of the various contexts has yet to be made.

Compared with the Pequot reservations, there has been little excavation conducted on Brothertown homes in New York and Wisconsin. Despite this lack of archaeological data, archival evidence does provide some initial clues into the structure of Brothertown dwellings and a few hints concerning Brothertown consumption of everyday household items. For example, on September 26, 1799, Timothy Dwight, president of Yale University, passed through Brothertown, New York, and recorded his observations (in Love 1899:304–305). Dwight held a strong interest in observing "civilized" Indian life and was impressed with the Brothertown Indians. He described an agricultural landscape: "Here forty families of these people have fixed themselves in the business of agriculture." He noted that only three families (among sixty documented as living in Brothertown at this time) lived in framed houses, with most other families living in log cabins similar to "those of whites." Dwight was particularly impressed with the household of Amos Hutton, writing, "He is probably the fairest example of industry, economy, and punctuality, which these people can boast" (304).

A collection of photographs of Brothertown homes in the next Brothertown settlement, in Wisconsin, affirms that most Brothertown Indians lived in either log cabins or framed structures like the house pictured on the top in figure 2.1. Built in 1842, this was the home of Benjamin Garret Fowler I, an important leader in the Brothertown community.

Brothertown record books (Brothertown Indians 1796) dating to the late eighteenth century provide indirect evidence of imported household goods. For instance, on November 15, 1796, the community received a large shipment of foodstuffs (a few barrels of pork), livestock (four yoke of oxen, six cows, fifty sheep) along with manufactured goods—"crockery,

Figure 2.1. Benjamin Garret Fowler I's house (*top*) and grave marker, Brothertown, Wisconsin (*bottom left*); shared grave marker of Benjamin Garret Fowler II and his wife, Hannah, Brothertown, Wisconsin (*bottom right*). The inscription on Benjamin Garret Fowler I's stone reads: "Benjamin G. Fowler died Dec. 12, 1848 AE 74 y's, He spoke the language of his Master, little children love one another." The epitaph likely refers to Benjamin's role as a minister and elder in the Freewill Baptist community at Brothertown (Love 1899:345). The stone of Benjamin's son and daughter-in-law reads, "AT REST, BENJAMIN G. FOWLER, D. APRIL 7 1887, Age 74 Yrs., HANNAH, WIFE of B. G. FOWLER, D. JUNE 10 1876, Age 44 Yrs." House photo from author's collection, courtesy of the Brothertown Indian Nation. Cemetery photos by the author.

pens needles & sundry small articles" (34). On December 17 of the same year, the community received another large shipment, which included two dozen bibles, three gross blue cups and saucers, and two dozen flowered tea pots (42). Limited excavations in Brothertown, Wisconsin, uncovered European-produced earthenwares and stonewares along with a variety of metal objects, including fragments of food-related cans and agricultural hardware.

Marking Sacred Spaces

During the Great Awakening of the early eighteenth century, Christianity spread through much of Native New England and many Native peoples began regularly marking the graves of their loved ones above the ground with unmodified fieldstones, stone piles, and stones modified into head- and footstones (Cipolla 2013a). Occasionally, Native communities marked burials from this period in ways similar to those of their Euro-American neighbors, with inscribed stones purchased from semiprofessional and professional carvers. This practice was rare, however. For instance, out of all of the cemeteries on the Mashantucket Pequot Reservation, only one text-bearing gravestone, dating to the late nineteenth century, was purchased from a professional carver during the entirety of the seventeenth, eighteenth, and nineteenth centuries (ibid.). This dearth of purchased stones certainly ties to economic limitations, but it also complied with traditional modes of commemoration in Native New England, discussed shortly.

There are many parallels between pre-twentieth-century cemeteries on the Mashantucket Pequot Reservation and those in Brothertown, New York. Between the late eighteenth and mid-nineteenth centuries, Brothertown Indians created no fewer than seven burial grounds in their first settlement (ibid.). Several Brothertown stones also sit in a multi-ethnic cemetery founded in the early nineteenth century by the increasing white population in the area. The first few generations of Brothertown Indians largely replicated the forms of commemoration practiced in their home communities at the time of the Brothertown exodus. Even the grave of Amos Hutton, whom Timothy Dwight mentioned as prosperous and well-off, was likely marked with a blank limestone grave marker, suggesting that this choice was not determined by the cost of store-bought markers. Rather than purchasing headstones from carvers, most Brothertown Indians marked the graves of their loved ones with locally made blank gravestones that ranged in form from unmodified fieldstones to stones roughly shaped to resemble those found in local white, Christian cemeteries.

The Brothertown Indians only began purchasing grave markers from professional carvers during the nineteenth century, and this practice became increasingly popular after 1830 (ibid.). The new store-bought markers often displayed inscribed names, death dates, and other biographical details of the deceased along with occasional décor and imagery such as the urn and willow motif. Just as they were beginning to radically transform their commemoration practices in the 1830s (by becoming consumers), the Brothertown Indians migrated once again. Ninety-nine percent of the markers in the Wisconsin settlement were store-bought. The assemblage includes headstones, obelisks, ledgers or flat slabs, and several other marker types catalogued in eight cemeteries. Figure 2.1 (bottom) shows a set of typical Brothertown grave markers. Compared to neighboring non-Brothertown Indian stones, the inscription details—combined with specific knowledge of Brothertown genealogy—and the general spatial distribution of the stones are the only means of distinguishing Brothertown grave markers from those of outsiders (Cipolla 2013a). As discussed next, I see the shift to these types of grave markers as partially related to Brothertown Indians' efforts to blur social distinctions between whites and Indians in Brothertown, Wisconsin.

Consuming the Quotidian and the Sacred

On the two Pequot reservations, European-produced ceramics and other household items largely replaced Native-made materials (specifically pottery) by the mid-eighteenth century, while there are no indications that Brothertown Indians in either New York or Wisconsin made their own ceramics. There is still much work to be done in terms of researching the ways in which Brothertown families socialized "foreign" things, but the archival record does suggest that Brothertown Indians had access to a plethora of European-produced goods, including ceramics. Overall, this brief synthesis of consumption on four closely related colonial contexts emphasizes the need for further comparison across reservation and other site boundaries. Further synthesis could shed more light on the shifting materialities of reservation households in terms of functionality, symbolism, and social relations, both intra- and intercommunally.

Changes in everyday material culture and cemetery material culture occurred in similar sequences across the different sites. Compared to the household contexts summarized, cemeteries changed much later. In Brothertown, New York, Brothertown Indians only purchased eight grave markers from professional stonemasons during the first three decades of the nineteenth century. The cemetery data from both Brothertown settlements show a sharp increase in purchased stones during the second quarter of the nineteenth century. This change is particularly evident in the cemeteries of Brothertown, Wisconsin, which house only four "homemade" (blank) grave markers, compared to 266 purchased stones. On the Mashantucket Pequot Reservation, there was at least a 150-year gap between changes in household consumption and changes in cemetery consumption. There was approximately an 80-year lag between shifts in Brothertown household consumption and changes in grave marker consumption. So, why was there such a delay between the consumption of nonindigenous-produced household items and nonindigenous-produced grave markers? With this question, I aim to explore much more than teleological arguments that employ purely technological or economic explanations as their central tenets.

To explain these patterns primarily in terms of financial issues oversimplifies colonial interaction and indigenous choice. Perhaps New England Indians simply did not have the money to purchase professionally made grave markers with inscriptions. This was certainly an important factor, but it was far from deterministic. As outlined in Silliman and Witt's (2010) important research, during the eighteenth century, some Pequot people had the financial means to purchase grave markers if they wished. Furthermore, the Brothertown Indians had productive farms, especially when compared to those of their families and friends who stayed behind on the home reservations. More specifically, there is evidence that Brothertown Indians paid two to three dollars for coffins in New York, while cheap gravestones likely sold for about four dollars and up during the early nineteenth century (Cipolla 2013a). Further demonstrating the independence of economic prosperity and the purchase of gravestones, Brothertown Indians only began purchasing stones en masse after 1830, precisely when the first settlement was becoming crowded, making farmland scarce and money tight (Jarvis 2010).

Others might explain this sequence in terms of literacy. Perhaps Indians did not purchase professionally made markers because most of them did not read. Given the prevalence of Indian schools and missionary efforts near each reservation during the eighteenth century (Fish 1983; Jarvis 2010; Love 1899; Silverman 2010), at least some individuals residing on reservations were familiar with the English language in some capacity. The Brothertown Indians, who were largely literate by the nineteenth century (Cipolla 2012a, 2012b), also avoided purchasing professionally made markers bearing text for several decades after gaining fluency in the English language. Also of note, five of the stones that they did purchase in the 1830s and 1840s were shaped by professional stonemasons but left completely blank (Cipolla 2013a).

I see the sequences of changing consumption patterns as related to a combination of these factors but also as driven by changing social relations and memory practices in Indian communities during the eighteenth and nineteenth centuries. Text-bearing grave markers took on new functions in communities like those of the Brothertown Indians, but the changes were far from straightforward replacements of indigenous practices and things ("the local") with European practices and things ("the nonlocal"). New forms of grave markers used in Brothertown cemeteries reconfigured enduring traditions of remembrance in coastal Algonquian societies, perhaps further segregating the quotidian from the sacred. New marker types in Brothertown, Wisconsin, also aided Brothertown Indians in their efforts to remain on their lands in a time when the federal government was pushing many Indian groups westward. Text-bearing stones literally allowed the deceased's loved ones to preserve their genealogical histories in stone, solidifying their rights to family-owned land. However, it is important to point out that by adopting "foreign" conceptions of landownership at this time, Brothertown Indians also held onto the rest of their community. Change and continuity went hand in hand.

The forms of commemoration practiced on eighteenth-century reservations and at both Brothertown settlements, which made use of blank handmade grave markers, represented a significant change from memory practices of the seventeenth century but not an abrupt replacement. These changes had pragmatic implications for the ways in which individuals and families remembered and related to one another (Cipolla 2013a). During the seventeenth century, indigenous communities of New England seemingly avoided using enduring forms of grave markers such as stones (Gibson 1980; Rubertone 2001; Simmons 1970). Outsiders observed Indians leaving garments belonging to the deceased above the graves, on the ground surface, or hung from nearby trees (DeForest 1964 [1851]; Williams 1973 [1643]). The garments were then left untouched and allowed to waste away, creating an iconic relationship between the mortal remains below the ground and the fabrics left out in the elements above it. This general pattern complements ethnohistoric accounts (Morgan 1962 [1851]; Williams 1973 [1643]) that noted that local Native American communities forbade the utterance of names of the deceased. Combined, these parallel practices encouraged a form of social forgetting over the long term. While the omission of purchased, inscribed grave markers in these cemeteries likely ties, in part, to the economic status of Native communities at the time, it should be noted that this pattern also relates to deeper traditions of spirituality and socially instituted forgetting in which emphasis was placed on a community of deceased ancestors who once lived in the deity Cauntantowitt's house (Simmons 1970). In this scenario, the quotidian and the sacred were perhaps much more closely melded (Rubertone 2001:127) than in modern, secular understandings of the world. (Fowles 2013 presents a postsecular approach to related problems.)

The case of Samson Occom's grave exemplifies the shift between seventeenth-century commemoration practices and those that emerged in the second quarter of the nineteenth century (Cipolla 2013a). Occom, a Presbyterian minister of Mohegan descent, was one of the Brothertown community's most famous leaders. At the time of his death in 1792, the Brothertown Indians were a community in transition; they still upheld forms of forgetting that tied back to the seventeenth-century practices just discussed. While Occom's grave likely sits in the largest communal cemetery in Brothertown, New York, its specific location within it is unknown because the community refrained from using an enduring form of text to mark the grave of its most prominent leader.

New forms of gravestone consumption in the coming decades transformed this tradition further by marking specific burial locations with names and basic biographical information of the deceased etched in stone (figure 2.1). Just as the Brothertown Indians began to embrace new memory practices, they also became U.S. citizens in 1839 with individual land rights (Cipolla 2013a). They petitioned the federal government arguing that they were a progressive group of Native peoples who embraced aspects of colonial change but yet had no means of protecting their lands as their Euro-American neighbors did. They were awarded citizenship, and their land was allotted to individuals and family groups within the community for the first time. The material changes I describe here supported the Brothertown Indians' general argument, aiding the community in its successful petition. Grave markers that emphasized the individuality of the dead solidified genealogical ties and familial land rights for the living. Benjamin Garret Fowler's land and house (figure 2.1) were passed down from generation to generation. Grave markers helped solidify these new connections but also served to further transform memory practices and conceptions of personhood and individuality within the community.

Consumption and Community

In Mullins's review article on the archaeology of consumption (2011:141), he notes that recent studies acknowledge "the complicated effects of commodity consumption across lines of difference." Such studies focus on the myriad ways in which different groups like overseas Chinese or African Americans accepted or resisted consumer culture. As a cursory analysis of consumption patterns in colonial New England, New York, and Wisconsin, in this chapter I have taken a similar tack. Rather than approaching these contexts in terms of acculturation or the preservation of untouched "Indianisms," I attempt to move beyond the dichotomizing tropes (essences of Indian and European) that still lurk in archaeologies of colonial North America. Brothertown consumption practices blurred boundaries between Indian and white and fostered new and likely unforeseen conceptions of personhood and individuality by way of shifts in long-term memory practices within the community. However, the changes also played a key role in maintaining intracommunal relations—in some ways portraying the boundary between insiders and outsiders as much more diffuse than in previous decades. These new representations aided the Brothertown community in its quest for citizenship and land rights.

The consumption of text-bearing gravestones also tied to Christianity, a central unifying force for the community since the eighteenth century. As evinced by Belva Mosher's diary entries, the Methodist church in Brothertown, Wisconsin, remained at the figurative center of the community in the early twentieth century. Perhaps Belva envisioned wearing her new silk taffeta skirt to communal events such as church meetings, dances, and other occasions at the Brothertown ballroom (figure 2.2), which she mentions frequently in her diary. She may have worn the skirt to the Brothertown Homecoming, an annual summer event for which

Figure 2.2. Brothertown ballroom, Brothertown, Wisconsin. Photo from the author's collection, courtesy of the Brothertown Indian Nation.

Brothertown Indians from far away come back to Brothertown, Wisconsin, to reconnect with family and friends. Of note, Belva's diary contains the earliest written mention of the event (Mosher 1917–1923), which still takes place today.

Consumption practices offer new slants on changing communal structures, including both continuities and changes in materiality, cultural traditions, and community relations. This brief summary of indigenous consumption speaks also to contemporary debates and struggles over indigenous sovereignty and identity (Hayes and Cipolla, this volume; Mrozowski, Gould, and Law Pezzarossi, this volume). Following recent calls in archaeology to address contemporary social issues in Native North America (Cipolla 2011, 2013a; Lightfoot et al. 2013; Mrozowski et al. 2009), I contend that the complexities of colonial interaction and endurance provide an important critique of the federal recognition process in the United States. As Kent Lightfoot and his colleagues (2013) point out, far too little attention has been paid to the ways in which indigenous societies shaped colonial developments in North America (how these broader processes were localized). Casting away simplistic narratives of cultural loss, Lightfoot and his colleagues (2013:99) argue that archaeologies of colonialism provide "ideal frameworks for evaluating what happened to specific tribal groups as they dealt with various colonial programs in a long-term perspective."

Rather than ending the colonial narrative with Pequot and Brothertown adoptions of foreign house styles, ceramics, and grave markers, I have attempted to extrapolate the reasons behind certain sequences of material change. Some of these practices related to deeper traditions of commemoration and symbolism despite their overtly "Europeanized" appearance in the eighteenth and nineteenth centuries. Tracking the changes in consumption from the eighteenth century to the present also sheds light on the long-term outcomes of certain cultural transformations. By linking consumer goods like Belva Mosher's skirt and Samson Occom's grave marker to internal social dynamics, new light is cast on the ways in which indigenous communities made their places in—and survived—the modern world. Yet, similar to the findings of Lightfoot et al. (2013), in this study I show the inequities of the federal recognition process. By asking tribal groups to demonstrate that they maintained communal ties, political structures, and identities in only one way and with only one result, the Bureau of Indian Affairs (BIA) has set many indigenous communities up for failure. This is evident in the BIA's recent negative ruling on the Brothertown Indians' petition for tribal sovereignty (Cipolla 2011, 2013a, 2013b). By bringing examples of colonial consumption into dialogue with more ancient cases, this chapter helps to demonstrate the complexities of colonial entanglement, highlighting the role that archaeology could play in reshaping the world in which we live.

References Cited

Bross, Kristina, and Hilary E. Wyss
2008   Introduction. In *Early Native Literacies in New England: A Documentary and Critical Anthology*, edited by Kristina Bross and Hilary E. Wyss, pp. 1–14. University of Massachusetts Press, Amherst.
Brothertown Indians
1788–1810, 1901   Brothertown Records. Manuscript on file, Wisconsin Historical Society, Madison.
Cipolla, Craig N.
2005   Negotiating Boundaries of Colonialism: Nineteenth-Century Lifeways on the

Eastern Pequot Reservation, North Stonington, Connecticut. Unpublished master's thesis, Department of Anthropology, University of Massachusetts Boston.
2008 Signs of Identity, Signs of Memory. *Archaeological Dialogues* 15(2):196–215.
2011 Commemoration, Community, and Colonial Politics at Brothertown. *Midcontinental Journal of Archaeology* 36(2):145–172.
2012a Peopling the Place, "Placing" the People: An Archaeology of Brothertown Discourse. *Ethnohistory* 59(1):51–78.
2012b Textual Artifacts, Artifactual Texts: An Historical Archaeology of Brothertown Writing. *Historical Archaeology* 46(2):91–109.
2013a *Becoming Brothertown: Native American Ethnogenesis and Endurance in the Modern World*. University of Arizona Press, Tucson.
2013b Native American Historical Archaeology and the Trope of Authenticity. *Historical Archaeology* 47(3):12–22.

Cipolla, Craig N., and Kevin A. McBride
2014 Globalizing the Local and Localizing the Global at Mashantucket. Paper presented at the 79th Annual Meeting of the Society for American Archaeology, Austin.

Cipolla, Craig N., Stephen W. Silliman, and David B. Landon
2007 'Making Do': Nineteenth-Century Subsistence Practices on the Eastern Pequot Reservation. *Northeast Anthropology* 74:41–64.

Cogley, Richard W.
1999 *John Eliot's Mission to the Indians before King Philip's War*. Harvard University Press, Cambridge.

Crosby, Constance A.
1988 From Myth to History, or Why King Philip's Ghost Walks Abroad. In *The Recovery of Meaning: Historical Archaeology in the Eastern United States*, edited by Mark P. Leone and Parker B. Potter, pp. 183–210. Smithsonian Institution Press, Washington, D.C.

DeForest, John W.
1964 [1851] *History of the Indians of Connecticut: From the Earliest Known Period to 1850*. Shoe String Press, Hamden, Connecticut.

Den Ouden, Amy
2005 *Beyond Conquest: Native Peoples, Reservation Land, and the Struggle for History*. University of Nebraska Press, Lincoln.

Dietler, Michael
2010 *Archaeologies of Colonialism: Consumption, Entanglement, and Violence in Ancient Mediterranean France*. University of California Press, Berkeley.

Douglas, Mary, and Baron Isherwood
1979 *The World of Goods: Toward an Anthropology of Consumption*. Norton, New York.

Ferris, Neal
2009 *The Archaeology of Native-Lived Colonialism: Challenging History in the Great Lakes*. University of Arizona Press, Tucson.

Fish, Joseph
1983   *Old Light on Separate Ways: The Narragansett Diary of Joseph Fish 1765–1776*, edited by William S. Simmons and Cheryl L. Simmons. University Press of New England, Providence, Rhode Island.

Fowles, Severin M.
2013   *An Archaeology of Doings: Secularism and the Study of Pueblo Religion*. School for Advanced Research, Santa Fe.

Gibson, Susan G. (editor)
1980   *Burr's Hill, a 17th Century Wampanoag Burial Ground in Warren, Rhode Island*. Brown University Press, Providence.

Hayden, Anna K.
2012   Household Spaces: 18th- and 19th-Century Spatial Practices on the Eastern Pequot Reservation. Unpublished master's thesis, Department of Anthropology, University of Massachusetts Boston.

James, Simon
2011   *Rome and the Sword: How Warriors and Weapons Shaped Roman History*. Thames and Hudson, New York.

Jarvis, Brad
2010   *The Brothertown Nation of Indians: Land Ownership and Nationalism in Early America, 1740–1840*. University of Nebraska Press, Lincoln.

Latour, Bruno
2005   *Reassembling the Social: An Introduction to Actor-Network-Theory*. Oxford University Press, Oxford, England.

Lightfoot, Kent G., Lee M. Panich, Tsim D. Schneider, Sara L. Gonzalez, Mathew A. Russell, Darren Modzelewski, Theresa Molino, and Elliot H. Blair
2013   The Study of Indigenous Political Economies and Colonialism: Implications for Contemporary Tribal Groups and Federal Recognition. *American Antiquity* 78(1):89–103.

Love, William D.
1899   *Samson Occom and the Christian Indians of New England*. Syracuse University Press, Syracuse, New York.

McBride, Kevin
1990   The Historical Archaeology of the Mashantucket Pequot. In *The Pequots: The Fall and Rise of an American Indian Nation*, edited by Laurence M. Hauptman and James D. Wherry, pp. 96–116. University of Oklahoma Press, Norman.

Miller, Christopher L., and George R. Hamell
1986   A New Perspective on Indian-White Contact: Cultural Symbols and Colonial Trade. *Journal of American History* 73(2):311–328.

Miller, Daniel
1987   *Material Culture and Mass Consumption*. Blackwell, New York.

Miller, Daniel (editor)
1995   *Acknowledging Consumption: A Review of New Studies*. Routledge, New York.

Morgan, Lewis H.
1962 [1851]   *League of the Iroquois*. Citadel Press, Secaucus, New Jersey.
Mosher, Belva
1917–1923   Diary. Manuscript on file, Brothertown Indian Nation Archive, Fond du Lac, Wisconsin.
Mrozowski, Stephen A., Holly Herbster, David Brown, and Katherine L. Priddy
2009   Magunkaquog Materiality, Federal Recognition, and the Search for a Deeper History. *International Journal of Historical Archaeology* 13(4):430–463.
Mullins, Paul
2004   Ideology, Power, and Capitalism: The Historical Archaeology of Consumption. In *A Companion to Social Archaeology*, edited by Lynn Meskell and Robert W. Preucel, pp. 195–211. Blackwell, Malden, Massachusetts.
2011   The Archaeology of Consumption. *Annual Review of Anthropology* 40:133–144.
O'Brien, Jean M.
1997   *Dispossession by Degrees: Indian Land and Identity in Natick, Massachusetts, 1650–1790*. Cambridge University Press, Cambridge.
Rubertone, Patricia E.
2000   The Historical Archaeology of Native Americans. *Annual Review of Anthropology* 29:425–446.
2001   *Grave Undertakings: An Archaeology of Roger Williams and the Narragansett Indians*. Smithsonian Institution Press, Washington, D.C.
Salisbury, Neal
1974   Red Puritans: The "Praying Indians" of Massachusetts Bay and John Eliot. *William and Mary Quarterly* 31(1):27–54.
Scheiber, Laura L., and Mark D. Mitchell (editors)
2010   *Across a Great Divide: Continuity and Change in Native North American Societies, 1400–1900*. University of Arizona Press, Tucson.
Silliman, Stephen W.
2005   Culture Contact or Colonialism? Challenges in the Archaeology of Native North America. *American Antiquity* 70 (1):55–74.
2009   Change and Continuity, Practice and Memory: Native American Persistence in Colonial New England. *American Antiquity*, 74(2):211–230.
Silliman, Stephen W., and Thomas A. Witt
2010   The Complexities of Consumption: Eastern Pequot Cultural Economics in 18th-Century Colonial New England. *Historical Archaeology* 44(4):46–68.
Silverman, David J.
2010   *Red Brethren: The Brothertown and Stockbridge Indians and the Problem of Race in Early America*. Cornell University Press, Ithaca, New York.
Simmons, William S.
1970   *Cautantowwit's House: An Indian Burial Ground on the Island of Conanicut in Narragansett Bay*. Brown University Press, Providence, Rhode Island.
Sturtevant, William C.
1975   Two 1761 Wigwams at Niantic. *American Antiquity* 40(4):437–444.

White, Richard
1991   *The Middle Ground: Indians, Empires, and Republics in the Great Lakes Region, 1650–1815*. University of Cambridge Press, Cambridge, England.

Williams, Rodger
1973 [1643]   *A Key into the Language of America*, edited by J. J. Teunissen and E. J. Hinz. Wayne State University Press, Detroit, Michigan.

Witt, Thomas A.
2007   Negotiating Colonial Markets: The Navigation of 18th-Century Colonial Economies by the Eastern Pequot. Unpublished master's thesis, Department of Anthropology, University of Massachusetts Boston.

3

Globalizing Poverty

The Materiality of Colonial Inequality and Marginalization

PAUL R. MULLINS AND TIMO YLIMAUNU

In a late-eighteenth-century tour of Finland, Joseph Acerbi (1802:218–219) remarked, "You must not be surprised in Finland, if in a small wooden house, where you can get nothing but herrings and milk, they should bring you water in a silver vessel of the value of fifty or sixty dollars." Acerbi was puzzled by such contradictions in the midst of what he considered to be materially spare conditions if not poverty. In 1913 Mrs. Alec Tweedie's Finnish travelogue *Through Finland in Carts* recounted a comparable visit to a rural Finnish home. Like Acerbi more than a century earlier, Tweedie echoed his sense of contradiction when she indicated that she and her companion "were indeed amazed when we were each handed a real silver spoon—not tin or electro—but real silver, and very quaint they were too, for the bowls were much bigger than the short handles themselves . . . They had not those things because they were rich; for, on the contrary, they were poor. Such are the ordinary Finnish farmers' possessions; however small the homestead, linen and window curtains are generally to be found. So many comforts, coupled with the bare simplicity of the boards, the long benches for seats, and hard wooden chairs" (Tweedie 1913:398).

For much of the past half millennium, observers have routinely been vexed over how to define poverty across various lines of class, cultural, color, and colonial difference. Acerbi and Tweedie share with contemporary historical archaeologists an aspiration to explain impoverishment, but they betrayed little interest in its connection to Finland's distinctively liminal colonial status; that is, while Finland is rarely conceived of as a colonial territory, Acerbi toured Finland when it was a part of Sweden, and in Tweedie's case it was a Grand Duchy of Russia. Acerbi's and Tweedie's attention was initially drawn to Finnish poverty because seemingly opulent silver artifacts or fine linen provided a stark visual contrast to material paucity. Simultaneously, though, Acerbi struggled to define the social meanings of poverty and affluence. On one hand, Acerbi (1802:218–219) clumsily suggests that Finnish material distinctions reflected incomparable standards of living: "In comparison to those who travel among them, they are poor, but in relation to themselves they are rich; since they are supplied with everything that constitutes, in their opinion, good living." On the other hand, though, Acerbi interpreted the material scarcity of the Finnish countryside as a statement on Western standards of affluence. When a Finnish peasant refused payment for assisting Acerbi (1802:235–236), the traveler suggested,

> [O]ur narrow minds, that are filled with notions of what is called refinement, are at a loss to conceive how those people, who appear so poor and low in our eyes, merely because they have not a coat cut after the model of our's [sic], should refuse money . . . Such examples, but too rare and too little known in the polished circles of great towns, are not so in those places which are far removed from a metropolis, where morals have become the victim of selfish and corrupt passions. It is the traveller, who, constantly carrying about with him his ideas of civilization (which is often only a different name for a system of refined selfishness), introduces his degraded notions into the bosom of a simple people, obliging from instinct, and generous and beneficent from nature.

Acerbi's lament over the corrupting sway of affluence repeated a paternalistic critique of wealth that has been sounded by a half millennium of consumer ideologues. The Finnish peasantry was painted by Acerbi as a model of an ethical life untouched by "degrading" material affluence, a rhetorical maneuver that ignored the systematic marginalization of the Finnish countryside by the Swedish crown (map 3.1), the symbolic meanings of silver in Fennoscandia (Scandinavia and Finland) across more than a millennium, and the complications of interpreting materiality across colonial divides. Poverty was an aesthetically visible contradiction for Acerbi, a familiar narrative that illuminated Western consumption more than it revealed northern European colonial marginalization. Rather than providing a stark contrast to paucity, though, silver invoked

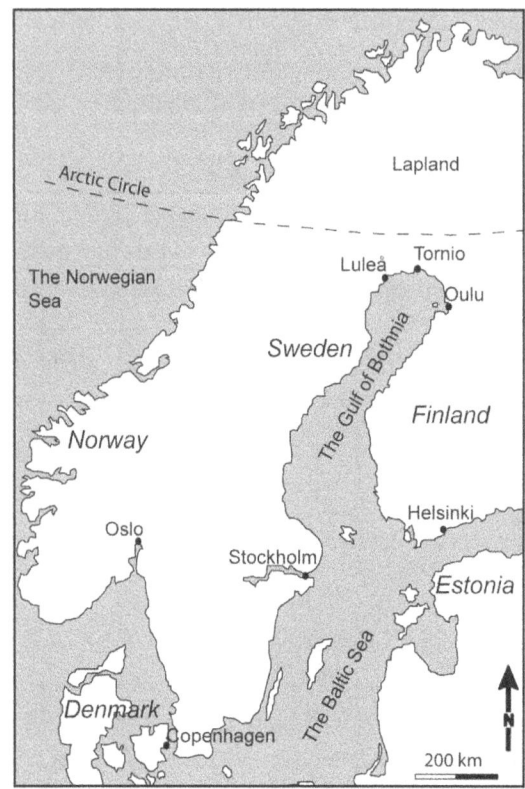

Map 3.1. Fennoscandia. Map created by Timo Ylimaunu.

a deep-seated heritage of Swedish state power, centuries of indigenous and regional silver trade, and the roots for colonial marketing that existed long before the Swedes joined Europeans colonizing the globe.

We could dismiss Acerbi's or Tweedie's commentaries as idiosyncratic historical observations, but they and many more Western scribes used poverty as a narrative device for bourgeois readers who constantly struggled to define what it meant to be poor but did not root such marginalization in colonization's heritage. North American historical archaeology has long focused on poverty and consumer marginalization and undermined many of the ideological pictures of impoverishment painted in Western narratives since the eighteenth century (Orser 2011; Spencer-Wood and Matthews 2011); nevertheless, models of impoverishment and inequality constructed to address a specific set of urban U.S. contexts are not always useful in international settings, and travelers' accounts and archaeological studies of the colonized subject have rarely contemplated the Nordic world.

Poverty has complicated social meanings and archaeological manifestations, and ambiguous pictures of paucity, identity, and marginality are not especially useful interpretive frameworks to examine either experiences of poverty or of dominant structural conditions. A global picture provides a rigorous analysis of impoverishment that places poverty at the heart of life in the past five hundred years yet recognizes it has been experienced in many different forms. In this chapter we examine the constitution of poverty in Finland, focusing on silver consumption and its rich historical meanings to outline how scarcity, inequality, and material consumption are constructed in distinctive ways across global lines of difference. The American discussion of poverty has often intentionally linked impoverishment to communities of color and ethnicity, particularly in urban places. Finns have a comparably long heritage of rural paucity, but that historical experience has been largely masked by the emergence of a relatively wealthy contemporary Finnish society. We are particularly interested in the ways an exceptionally broad range of impoverished experiences are at the heart of colonial experience, and we are focused on how metaphors of marginalization, affluence, and globalization inflect archaeological interpretation.

Poverty and "Mainstream" Society

Impoverishment is an utterly material experience, yet much of the North American archaeology of poverty tends to focus on how poor consumers defied the deterministic limits of impoverishment; that is, archaeologies often celebrate the lives of the impoverished and use everyday materiality to show that dominant representations of poverty and the poor were ideological distortions. This scholarship has focused on disciplinary discourses like etiquette guides and advertising, which crafted an idealized social and material "mainstream" against which consumers (and subsequent scholars) measured themselves and their neighbors. Archaeology tends to contrast such transparent ideologies to genuine consumer patterns that demonstrate the triumph of human spirit in its capacity to resist ideological expectations (Hayes and Cipolla, this volume). The dilemma with this position is that it assesses materiality as a negotiation of a contrived ideological mainstream; that is, we are interpreting concrete material culture in relation to the terms posed by bourgeois social and marketing ideologues. This risks minimizing the structural processes that produce poverty, and it hazards awkwardly ignoring our contemporary social aspiration to invest the past with creative consumer agents.

Perhaps the most distinctive structural and ideological dimension of American poverty has been its persistent link to anti-black racism in particular and ethnic xenophobia in general. The ethnically xenophobic threads of poverty discourses were shared by British ideologues as well, and in both America and Britain dissections of poverty devoted considerable energy to reducing poverty and tenement life to an aesthetic experience. In 1899, for instance, traveler William Archer (1899:27) concluded that New York's "slums have a Southern air about them, a variety of contour and colour—in some aspects one might almost say a gaiety . . . in the clear, sparkling atmosphere characteristic of New York, the most squalid slum puts on a many-coloured Southern aspect." Five years later Ray Stannard Baker (1904:61) noted that in Southern cities, "The temperament of the Negro is irrepressibly cheerful, he overflows from his small home . . . and his squalour is not unpicturesque."

Poverty is a powerful sensory experience, so much of the commentary of privileged visitors through the nineteenth and twentieth centuries revolved around their emotionally cathartic response to the visual and sensory landscape of poverty. This is actually an interesting entry point for archaeologists: an archaeology of poverty might productively illuminate the material and aesthetic dimensions of paucity that tug at our senses and impose themselves on our collective imagination. Travelers' aesthetic descriptions of slums and far-flung places like Finland dissected much of this visual landscape, but they strategically avoided the structural footing for impoverishment and often rationalized its brutal ugliness: for Western observers, the aesthetics of impoverished neighborhoods were implicitly rooted in various essential distinctions like race and ethnicity.

Silver and Poverty in Finland

Today a bastion of affluence and cutting-edge technology, Finland was among the most impoverished countries on the face of the planet throughout much of the nineteenth century. Some Finnish communities profited from trade and marketing relationships, and as Joseph Acerbi recognized after his 1799 trip, costly things could be found in many of the most remote rural settings. Yet Finnish rural life in particular was excep-

Figure 3.1. A seventeenth-century silver spoon from the town of Oulu. Photo by Titta Kallio-Seppä.

tionally unpredictable, and famine was a persistent backdrop to Finnish agriculture.

American historical archaeology often gravitates toward pricy material things as indicators of position along a continuum of wealth, but Acerbi's confusion over silver consumption in modest Finnish homes reflects the complications of such logic in Finland (Cipolla, this volume, offers a similar example). Acerbi was struck by the presence of silver (figure 3.1)—a good he viewed as a sign of affluence—in the most apparently marginalized Finnish households, but he did not recognize the historically complicated meanings of silver in northern Fennoscandia. Rather than being simply an expression of affluence, silver had been a common means of exchange, a material of luxury, and a medium expressing power long before the arrival of western European visitors (Nordin 2010, 2012; Spangen 2009).

The area now known as Finland was a Swedish colony until 1809, with trade through the colony strictly controlled by the Crown. In the eighteenth century the Bothnian Gulf town of Tornio (figure 3.2) controlled trade into and out of Lapland, so it and many surrounding rural settings became home to some wealthy residents. Tornio was one of many small towns in eighteenth-century Sweden; it had just six hundred to seven hundred residents during the second half of the century (Mäntylä 1971:422). Probate inventories provide one mechanism to examine emergent wealth disparities and material consumption in Tornio. The first probate inventory was completed in Tornio in 1666, when the list of Anders Persson's property was compiled. In 1734, the Swedish Parlia-

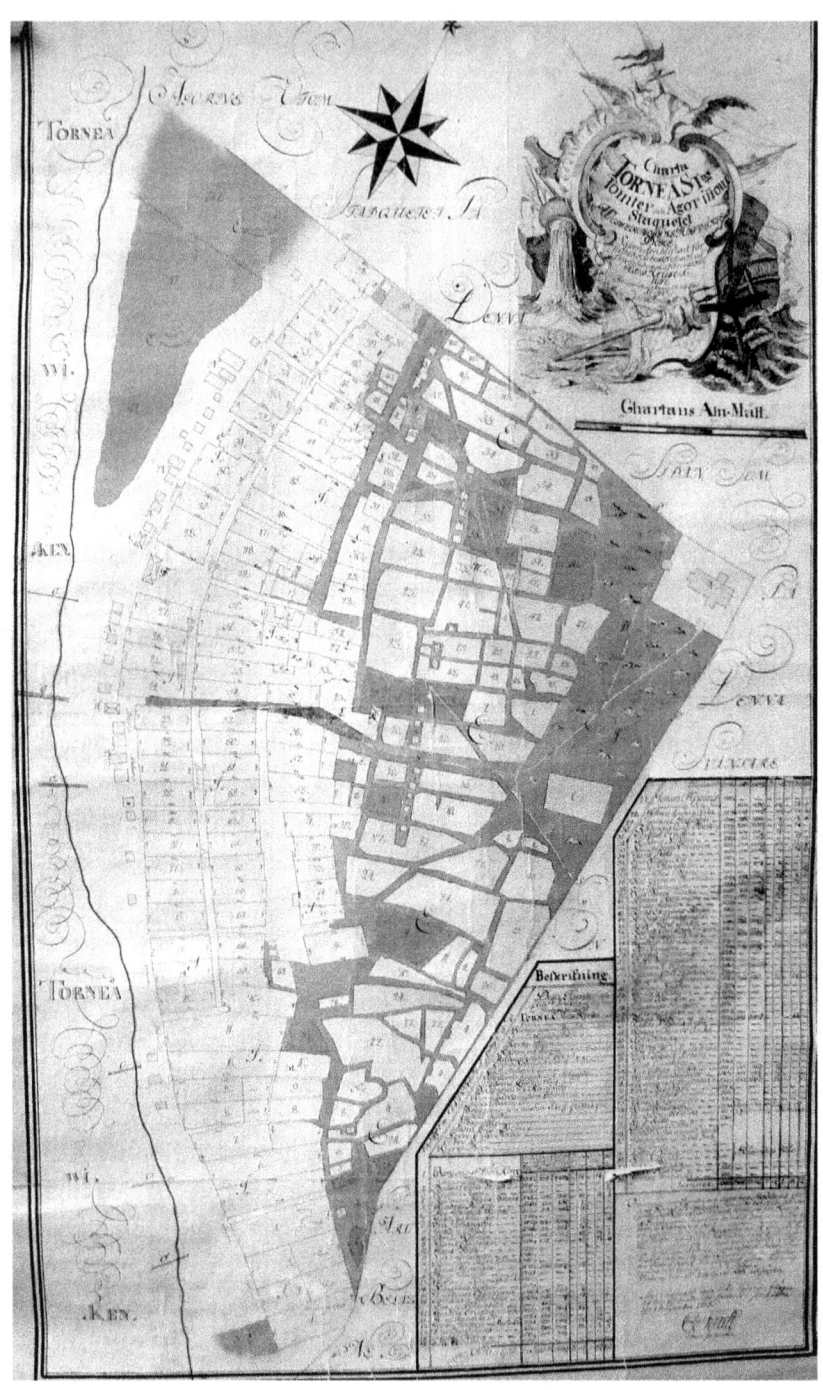

Figure 3.2. The town of Tornio at the end of seventeenth century. Photo by Timo Ylimaunu.

ment decreed that probate inventories had to be compiled of all deceased persons' property, and all items had to be listed in inventories, though goods like ceramics and wooden items were sometimes missing from inventories (Markkanen 1988; Helistö 1992). Ultimately, inventories were compiled for roughly every second deceased person in Tornio during the eighteenth century (Nordberg 1996), and inventories of poor residents are less common. Nevertheless, inventories were compiled for servants as well as wealthy burghers.

Probate inventories from the third quarter of the eighteenth century reflect increasing wealth disparities in Tornio. In the third quarter of the eighteenth century, about 86 percent of the wealth of Tornio residents was owned by 17 percent of its residents who collectively owned more than 15,518 copper dalers. The daler was the Swedish coin minted in silver since 1534. The name was changed to riksdaler in 1604, and the riksdaler was the official Swedish currency until 1873. The dalers were also minted in copper beginning in 1624 (Lagerqvist and Nathorst-Böös 1997, 10–16). The inequities in wealth distribution are much like those found in the American colonies, but the goods used to mark wealth were somewhat distinctive. Almost 80 percent of wealthy Tornio merchants owned several reindeer, which were essential to transport goods through Lapland in the winter. Merchants typically owned cabins in the winter marketplaces in which they stayed overnight and stocked up on Lapland goods (Mäntylä 1971:105; Symonds et al. 2015).

The common American stereotype of distinctive rural paucity and urban affluence does not hold up especially well in Finland. A comparison between Tornio residents and peasants living in Lautiosaari hamlet, for instance, indicates that the rural population had some genuine wealth. No peasants rivaled the holdings of the wealthiest Tornio burghers, but their median property value was higher than Tornio residents' because the peasants in the Kemijoki River area profited from control of salmon fishing. This meant that the rural population in the Kemijoki River area was actually wealthier than the average rural population in contemporary northern Finland (Satokangas 1997:186, 204–207).

As Joseph Acerbi noted in his late eighteenth-century tour of Finland, silver was among the most important Finnish status goods, but it was meaningful not simply as a shallow display of wealth. Two-thirds of Tornio residents had silver holdings from 1666 to 1776, including every resident whose property value was more than 2,000 copper dalers. Three-quarters of the poorer residents whose property was valued between 800 to 1,999 copper dalers had silver holdings, and 49 percent of Tornio residents whose property was valued at less than 800 copper dalers had silver holdings, even if it was only some buttons. In 1772, for instance, cooper Johan Remahl had property valued at 663 copper dalers, and he owned some silver mugs and rings valued at 72 copper dalers.

Tornio was a Crown-sanctioned marketplace on the Tornio River estuary island during the medieval period (ca. 1200–1550) and into the later sixteenth century. Several medieval marketplaces were situated in the estuaries of other main rivers, including the Kemi, Ii, and Oulu along the eastern coastal area of the Bothnian Gulf. Swedish, Norwegian, Finnish, Karelian, and Russian traders and indigenous Sámi people gathered to trade in these Crown market harbors during the summer months. Furs and dried fish were two of the main trade goods, and Karelian traders bought huge amounts of furs, using hemp, linen, salt, and other goods as payment. However, the furs that Karelians bought were much more valuable than the Karelians' own goods, so the remainder of their payment was made in coins and other items made of silver (Friberg 1983:221–224).

Several medieval or sixteenth-century hoards with silver coins as well as archaeological excavations have yielded silver finds in northern Finland attesting to the historical depth of the silver trade. Older ones (fourteenth to sixteenth century) predominately contain Scandinavian and Finnish coins, but the sixteenth-century hoards in particular include Novgorod and Russian coins (Jylkkä-Karppinen 2011; Koivunen 1991:142). Swedish historian Kjell Lundholm (1991:298) has argued that one consequence of the Karelian and Russian trade was that silver accumulated into the hands of Sámi peoples and ordinary peasants in the north beginning in the late medieval period (Friberg 1983:221–224). However, that process may have begun far earlier: late-prehistoric and early medieval hoards and Sámi sacrifices contain silver artifacts with Scandinavian, Finnish, Baltic, and northern Russian origins. The Sámi might have favored silver artifacts in the fur trade with Novgorod, making silver artifacts "socially and ritually valuable objects instead of purely economic returns of their products" (Spangen 2009:102). Consequently, it seems, silver may have had cultural and religious meanings and values in addition to narrow economic ones, especially for the indigenous Sámi, and these meanings were formed since the first millennium.

Sweden launched its own colonial projects during the seventeenth and eighteenth centuries, developing colonies in the U.S. Delaware River valley as well as in Fennoscandia north of the Arctic Circle (Lindmark 2012:131; Naum and Nordin 2012). The rich natural resources of the north in the Arctic Circle drove the Swedish and Danish Crowns and the city-state of Novgorod to all attempt to colonize, control, and exploit those regions and the indigenous Sámi people as soon as the early medieval period (that is, after the first millennium; Fur 2012:25–27; Lappalainen 2007:87–92; Ylimaunu et al. 2014). Perhaps the most intensive early effort to exploit silver ores and to start mining took place in 1634 in Northern Sweden along the border with Norway. However, this silver project did not last long, and the mine in Nasafjäll was destroyed by the Danish-Norwegian troops in 1659, only twenty-five years after the mine's opening (Nordin 2010, 2012).

The Swedes' unsuccessful silver exploitation elevated the symbolic and economic value of copper in the Swedish court, and copper became the main material for Swedish coinage. However, the overproduction of copper led to a fall in its price during the seventeenth century (Lappalainen 2007:86–102), and the Nordic War (1700–1721) contributed to the state's rapid decline in the eighteenth century. This was one reason for the continued importance of silver among early modern Finns; they did not have much gold at all, but silver retained its value.

One fundamental attraction of silver was that it could be pawned in difficult moments (Helistö 1994:169). For instance, Anna Tornström's probate inventory from 1772 indicated that some articles of gold and silver were pawned to burghers of Tornio. This was the case in the rural Lautiosaari hamlet, too. Nearly two-thirds (63 percent) of peasants had some gold and silver holdings during the years 1697 to 1810 (Helistö 1992:169). The silver rings, goblets, and small spirit mugs were the most common silver items that peasants had in Lautiosaari. Martti Helistö (1992:169) has noted that almost every household, rich or poor, had some silver items in Lautiosaari hamlet.

This pattern changed somewhat during the nineteenth century. In 1809 Finland ceased being a Swedish colony and became a Russian Grand Duchy until its independence in 1917; the vast majority of residents were very slow to move to towns like Tornio. More than 80 percent of the population at the outset of the nineteenth century was involved in manual agriculture, but the bleak environment required Finland to import half of its grains. Nevertheless, in 1910 only 10 percent of the nation lived in a city, and only 12 percent worked in industry, so for the whole of the nineteenth century Finland had a large rural population practicing subsistence agriculture with marginal land and few resources. Finns had high mortality rates, low literacy rates, little social mobility, and they exported only raw materials, mostly timber and tar. When Mrs. Tweedie commented on the seemingly sparse material appointments of Finnish homes and the apparently contradictory items marking some affluence, she was witnessing the forms taken by impoverishment in much of rural Finland.

The unpredictability of food and labor made rural Finnish life exceptionally challenging. The culmination of that poverty came in a famine in 1866–1868 in which roughly 9 percent of the population died, a fivefold increase in mortality rates; but starvation was a constant structural reality of agrarian life. From 1899 to 1910, just over 148,000 Finns migrated to the United States, with a single-year high of 18,776 in 1903 (U.S. Immigration Commission 1911:338).

Finnish impoverishment was not clearly centered in a discrete space, although Finnish cities had pockets of impoverishment that rivaled American and British tenements. Poverty became a structural reality of life in a country that was overwhelmingly rural and agricultural long after transitions to urbanization and industrialization had been made in much of the Western world. An aesthetically distinct poverty centered in high-density cities, and the vicious status hierarchies of competitive consumption detailed in late-nineteenth-century Chicago by Thorstein Veblen (1899) do not have especially clear parallels in the Finnish experience of poverty. Consequently, archaeological metaphors focused on "cost-status" (that is, social status marked by expensive material culture) and a striking aesthetics of impoverishment—like those seemingly illuminated by silver—are not particularly good fits in Finland.

Conclusion

Poverty offers a powerful archaeological metaphor rooted in a concrete material reality and an aesthetic and corporeal experience. Therefore, it is one of the few dimensions of colonial life over the past half millennium that may offer a truly global interpretive framework. Nevertheless, how poverty and affluence are viewed in various historical moments and places differs quite dramatically despite colonizers' efforts to eliminate significant local distinctions. Material things like silver carried rich and often contradictory meanings across space and time, and in Finland silver's meanings had historical roots lost on later observers like Joseph Acerbi. Rather than reduce silver to a shallow mask for poverty, Finnish silver consumption instead underscores how colonization brought together quite distinctive material things and meanings with histories that began long before intensive colonization.

Acknowledgements

We would like to thank Titta Kallio-Seppä, Sami Lakomäki, Vesa-Pekka Herva, Eero Jarva, Riita Leinonen, and Risto Nurmi for their help, comments, and discussion during the preparation of this paper. Paul R. Mullins's travels to Oulu were funded by the Research Council of University of Oulu. Paul Mullins's research was supported by an IUPUI Arts and Humanities Internal Grant and a Fulbright Scholar grant. Timo Ylimaunu's research and travel to Leicester was supported and funded by the Academy of Finland and the Emil Aaltonen foundation.

References Cited

Acerbi, Joseph
1802 *Travels through Sweden, Finland, and Lapland, to the North Cape: In the Years 1798 and 1799*. Vol. 1. Joseph Mawman, London.
Archer, William
1899 *America To-Day: Observations and Reflections*. Charles Scribner's Sons, New York.
Baker, Ray Stannard
1904 *Following the Color Line: An Account of Negro Citizenship in the American Democracy*. S. S. McClure, New York.
Friberg, Nils
1983 *Stockholm i bottniska farvatten. Stockholms bottniska handelsfält under senmedeltiden och Gustav Vasa*. Stockholms kommun, Stockholm.
Fur, Gunlög
2012 Colonialism and Swedish History: Unthinkable Connections? In *Scandinavian Colonialism and the Rise of Modernity. Small Time Agents in a Global Arena*, edited by Magdalena Naum and Jonas M. Nordin, pp. 17–36. Springer, New York.
Helistö, Martti
1992 Lautiosaaren kylän pesäluetteloja 1697–1810. *Jatuli* XXII:328–385.

1994 Lautiosaarta vuosisatain takaa. *Jatuli* XXIII:120–84.

Jylkkä-Karppinen, Kirsi
2011 Rahalöydöt—varhaisia jälkiä monetarisoituvasta pohjoisesta. In *Iin vanhan Haminan kirkko ja hautausmaa*, edited by Titta Kallio-Seppä, Janne Ikäheimo and Kirsti Paavola, pp. 77–87. Oulun yliopisto, Oulu, Finland.

Koivunen, Pentti
1991 Suomen Tornionlaalson esihistoriaa. In *Tornionlaakson historia 1: Jääkaudelta 1600-luvulle*, edited by Olof Hederyd, Yrjo Alamäki, Matti Kenttä, and Hannele Huuva, pp. 101–159. Tornionlaakson kuntien historiakirjatoimikunta, Haaparanta, Sweden.

Lappalainen, Mirkka
2007 *Maailman painavin raha. Kirjoituksia 1600-luvun pohjolasta.* Werner Söderström Osakeyhtiö, Helsinki.

Lagerqvist, Lars O. and Nathorst-Böös, Ernst
1997 *Vad kostade det? Priser och löner från medeltid till våra dagar.* LTs förlag, Stockholm.

Lindmark, Daniel
2012 Colonial Encounter in Early Modern Sápmi. In *Scandinavian Colonialism and the Rise of Modernity. Small Time Agents in a Global Arena*, edited by Magdalena Naum and Jonas M. Nordin, pp. 131–146. Springer, New York.

Lundholm, Kjell
1991 Elinkeinojen kehitys. In *Tornionlaakson Historia I. Jääkaudelta 1600-luvulle*, edited by Olof Hederyd, Yrjö Alamäki and Matti Kenttä, pp. 266–301. Tornionlaakson kuntien historiatoimikunta, Haaparanta, Sweden.

Mäntylä, Ilkka
1971 *Tornion kaupungin historia 1. Osa, 1621–1809.* Tornion kaupunki, Tornio, Finland.

Markkanen, Erkki
1988 *Perukirja tutkimuslähteenä.* Jyväskylän yliopisto, Jyväskylä, Finland.

Naum, Magdalena, and Jonas M. Nordin
2012 Introduction: Situating Scandinavian Colonialism. In *Scandinavian Colonialism and the Rise of Modernity. Small Time Agents in a Global Arena*, edited by Magdalena Naum and Jonas M. Nordin, pp. 3–16. Springer, New York.

Nordberg, Henri
1996 Pesäluetteloiden kirjamaininnat 1700-luvun Torniossa. *Tornionlaakson vuosikirja* 1996:149–167.

Nordin, Jonas M.
2010 Det Emblematiska Silvret. Sverige i det Atlantiska världen vid 1600-talets mitt. In *Modernitetens Materialitet. Arkeologisak perspektiv på det moderna samhällets framväxt*, edited by Anna Lihammar and Jonas M. Nordin, pp. 47–70. Museum of National Antiquities Studies 17, Stockholm.

2012 Embodied Colonialism: The Cultural Meaning of Silver in a Swedish Colonial Context in the 17th Century. *Post-Medieval Archaeology* 46(1):143–165.

Orser, Charles E. Jr.
2011   The Archaeology of Poverty and the Poverty of Archaeology. *International Journal of Historical Archaeology* 15:533–543.

Satokangas, Reija
1997   Nousun aika (1721–1859). In *Keminmaan historia*, edited by R. Satokangas, pp. 178–248. Keminmaan kunta, Keminmaan seurakunta, Keminmaa, Finland.

Spangen, Marte
2009   Silver Hoards in Sámi Areas. *Iskos 17*: 94–106.

Spencer-Wood, Suzanne, and Christopher N. Matthews (editors)
2011   Archaeologies of Poverty. Special issue, *Historical Archaeology* 45(3).

Symonds, James, Timo Ylimaunu, Anna-Kaisa Salmi, Risto Nurmi, Titta Kallio-Seppä, Tiina Kuokkanen, Markku Kuorilehto, and Annemari Tranberg
2015   Time, Seasonality, and Trade: Swedish/Finnish-Sami Interactions in Early Modern Lapland. *Historical Archaeology* 49(3).

Tweedie, Mrs. Alec
1913   *Through Finland in Carts*. Thomas Nelson and Sons, New York.

U.S. Immigration Commission
1911   *Emigration Conditions in Europe*. U.S. Government Printing Office, Washington, D.C.

Veblen, Thorstein
1899   *The Theory of the Leisure Class*. Dover, New York.

Ylimaunu, Timo, Sami Lakomäki, Titta Kallio-Seppä, Paul R. Mullins, Risto Nurmi, and Markku Kuorilehto
2014   Borderlands as Spaces: Creating Third Spaces and Fractured Landscapes in Medieval Northern Finland. *Journal of Social Archaeology* 14(2): 244–267.

4

Indigeneity and Diaspora

Colonialism and the Classification of Displacement

KATHERINE H. HAYES

It is difficult to avoid using some kind of label when we attempt to interpret the experience of colonial subjects of the past despite our understanding that contemporary subject positions are the product, not precursor, of historical processes. In the United States, very often those labels are racialized; all the more so when we assume that racial tensions have their roots in the earliest colonial days of slavery. Certainly in the rhetoric of the colonists who wrote of enslaved Africans and Native Americans, the differences—in social status, physical appearance, and cultural practice—were stark. But in circumstances in which Native people and Africans, whom colonists saw as so clearly different, had the common role of laborer, must we assume that the differences the colonists saw (their emergent categories of race) were shared by all? In certain plantation contexts it is indeed exceedingly difficult to archaeologically distinguish enslaved African spaces and practices from those of Native Americans, precisely because they were doing much the same things in the same places. Yet Africans and Indians were also not the same. Each arrived at plantations via rather different routes and histories, and those differences might be best captured in the alternative frameworks of "diaspora" and "indigeneity." What are the implications of using these terms in historical contexts?

Both of these terms have multiple valences. Though they may be thought of as essentially geographic referents, their emergences in archaeology derive also from politically specific conditions. Archaeologies of African America have been well established since the 1980s, arising from the era of civil rights movements, while the study of colonial-period

Native Americans through archaeology took off from the historical consciousness of the Columbian quincentenary and the political consciousness of NAGPRA in the 1990s. In general, each is treated as a distinct subject of study, although many historians and archaeologists have acknowledged that their social spheres were not mutually exclusive. This distinction may be a product of the way we approach colonialism in our research. Colonialism is a process in which colonizing or settling populations exploit local resources, especially land and labor, but critically also impose new systems of social and economic order. In the United States it might be said that the former exploitation is largely yet not entirely in the past, but the latter—the imposition of social and economic orders—are sites of ongoing colonialism. In historical archaeology we have tended to focus our attention on the former process. Native Americans and African Americans are treated as separately oppressed groups, polarizing their experiences along lines like land removal versus labor exploitation; forcible transport to the Americas versus forcible displacement from American homelands; decreasing population versus increasing; and the contemporary categorization of descendant communities as diasporic versus indigenous. Although we recognize the inescapable contemporary political and social environment in which we interpret historical experiences (the environment in which indigenous and diasporic identity is most meaningful), still it is the historical experience that our evidence is taken to derive from—and we should strive to recognize how we have read those historical circumstances through the lenses of their longer-term outcomes (Leone 1982) rather than their immediate uncertainty.

Without dismissing the quite different historical points of entry and contemporary political priorities for Native and black communities, I question why we do not see more research in the intersection of the two in the study of colonialism. In this chapter I explore two main lines of speculation on this question: first, to think through current definitions of "indigeneity" and "diaspora"; and second, to argue that a comparative perspective highlights a significant distinction between the manner in which diasporic and indigenous communities imagined their political locations and futures. These geographic and political imaginaries are reduced and ignored when the terms are simply used as glosses for racialized or otherwise essentialized groups, something that occurs when we assume a kind of historical inevitability (Kenrick 2011). I compare two archaeological case studies throughout to speculate not just on how the past and memory informed the colonial encounter but also on how historical agents imagined and acted on ideas of what the future would bring.

From Opposite Sides of the Algonquian World

A comparison of two rather different sites of colonial entanglement from the eastern and western margins of the Algonquian world demonstrates how shared concepts of social inclusion yet radically different experiences of colonization play into colonial outcomes (map 4.1). In the east, European colonization proceeded at a fairly rapid pace where British colonies sought land for long-term settlement and the Dutch colony of New Netherland, though more interested in engaging in trade, was ultimately taken over by the British by 1674 (Siminoff 2004). In the west, the French colonizers struggled in their efforts to establish long-term settlement and were most successful in accessing the interior only through local trade partners, many of whom were Anishinaabe people migrating in that direction due to pressure from the eastern British colonies (White 1991).

For the northeast colonies, there is a popular narrative of the colonial era that has suppressed the consideration of indigeneity and diaspora: that due to the disappearance of Indian people and the lack of slavery, the colonies were quite socially homogeneous (Melish 1998; O'Brien 2010). Neither of these conditions was the case, and the site of Sylvester Manor is a prime counter example. This estate on Shelter Island, at the east end of Long Island in New York, was a provisioning plantation operated, per documentary evidence, by the labor of enslaved Africans. In initially approaching the interpretation of the site, the expectation was that difference according to black/white racialized identity would be evident, an approach that was confounded on two fronts. First, the plantation at Sylvester Manor was established in 1652, prior to the legal codification of slavery in racial categories (1674 at the earliest in New York). This is not to say that those categories were not already part of the colonists' discourse, but they were inchoate. Second, the plantation laborers included not only the enslaved Africans as identified in wills and other documents but also Native Americans, based on the archaeological evidence of their technological traditions, skills, and iconographic representations. One such technological tradition identified was wampum production (figure 4.1), the manufacture of shell beads that served as a mainstay of coastal Algonquian tribute payments and as a standardized currency in both Dutch

Map 4.1. Eastern U.S. site areas: 1, Shelter Island, New York; 2, central Minnesota; Algonquian precolonial language areas, shaded in light gray. Map adapted by the author from "Algonquian langs." Licensed under Creative Commons Attribution 2.0 via Wikimedia Commons, http://commons.wikimedia.org/wiki/File:Algonquian_langs.png#mediaviewer/File:Algonquian_langs.png.

and English colonies. The structure of the plantation remains shows an intimately spaced core working and residential area and no evidence of separate spaces for laborers apart from the colonists or of one group of laborers from another (Hayes 2013; Mrozowski et al. 2007; Mrozowski, Hayes, and Hancock 2007).

Thus a shared heritage of enslavement—or at least plantation labor, as documentary remains do not record the status of the Indian laborers and only rarely acknowledge their presence in any capacity—appears to cut across the lines of race that our eyes have inherited. As some of the descendant communities in the region acknowledge, this shared heritage

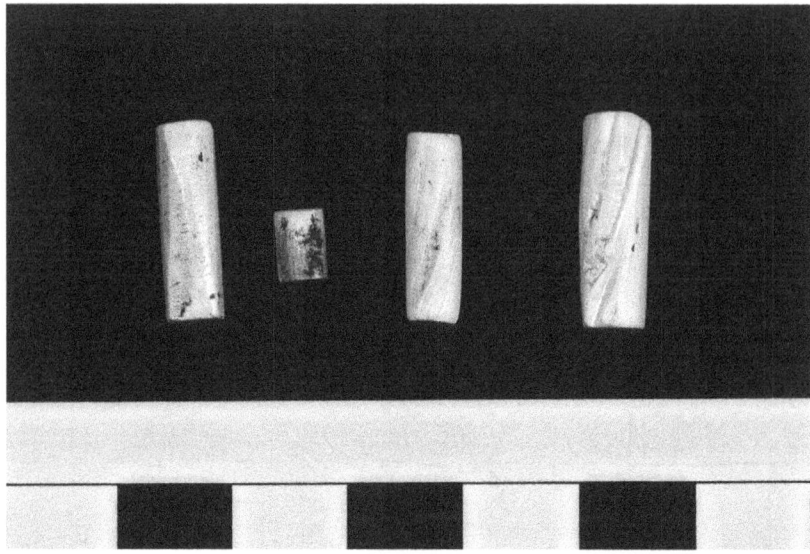

Figure 4.1. Wampum (shell beads) produced at Sylvester Manor plantation. Photo by Melody Henkel.

accompanies a history of intermarriage (for example, Boissevain 1956 on the Narragansetts' refusal to reject tribal members with African ancestry), though given the implicit expectations for racial identity in federal recognition cases, such an admission is dangerous for tribes currently seeking recognition (McKinney 2006). Given this context, we need instead an approach that "decolonizes" our expectations for the kinds of affiliations and distinctions that arose on the plantation.

A contrasting colonial trajectory on the other side of the Algonquian world was first brought to my attention when engaging with the work of historian Michael Witgen (2012). A student of Richard White, Witgen recognized the contribution of White's "middle ground" (1991) as a concept of creative misunderstanding in colonial contexts of mutual dependence in the Upper and Western Great Lakes (the *pays d'en haut*). In redescribing the early colonial encounters between French colonial authorities and the populous Native communities, however, Witgen insists that from the Native Anishinaabe perspective, the alliances with the vastly outnumbered French were only a small part of their own major reimagination of the political landscape. Reading through accounts of a 1660 Feast of the Dead written by Pierre Radisson, who claimed to have arranged the event as a means of declaring French authority through alliance, Witgen argues that instead the French presence was somewhat incidental to the efforts of the Anishinaabeg, who sought alliance with other Native political entities, the Cree and the Dakota, to construct a powerful network of trade and expand the territory of their hunting. Unlike in White's historical reading, where the Anishinaabeg were viewed as refugees (a diaspora) pushed west by European settlement, Witgen posits that their alliance and kin network assured their access to place; in the Anishinaabe political world, rights are assured not in territory but in relations of either kin or enemy, categories that could and did shift over time (Bohaker 2006 offers a critique based in the role of kin groups). A refugee is a type of person who does not fit these categories. Neither, for that matter, do identifications like diasporic or indigenous. So what do these terms do analytically or politically today that we think to assign them to the past?

Defining Diaspora

If one were asked to provide the most immediate association of diaspora, likely the response would be of a dispersed population retaining cultural associations with and memories of a homeland to which they cannot return due to traumatic dislocation. Clifford (1997), in his oft-cited discussions of diaspora, notes that this forms the basis of Safran's foundational contribution (1991). But Clifford urges us to introduce flexibility to this definition because of the boundary conditions the term implies. He notes, for example, that diaspora is often problematically defined in opposition to both nation-states and indigeneity (1997:250); to this I would add that diaspora, in the polarization of homeland and dispersal, draws attention to the originary rupture, precluding a more emergent or temporally fluid sense of diasporic identity.

The concept of diaspora has been a very productive framework for addressing enslaved Africans and African Americans. The nature of their dislocation and ongoing experience was certainly traumatic, their numbers were dispersed widely, and subsequent generations were barred from return. As neither essentialized identity nor an absolute rupture from culture and history, the diaspora concept allows us to explore the self-conscious reference and reproduction of a distinctive identity among the enslaved and their descendants. Archaeologists have well demonstrated the retention of certain cultural ties or memories through material and ritual practices, even as these retentions were reshaped under the conditions of enslavement (among them Fennell 2007; Franklin 2001; Heath and Bennett 2000; Wilkie and Farnsworth 2005). Historians of American slavery also have written eloquently about the self-conscious associations to Africa that enslaved and later free African American communities evoked as a form of survivance (Gomez 1998; Hall 2005; Horton and Horton 1979; Wilder 2005).

But Paul Gilroy (1991, 1993) and other cultural critics have pointed out that the location of diasporic African identity for many descendant communities has shifted away from Africa and more to the shared histories of enslavement and marginalization (prompting his use of the term "Black Atlantic"). How can a diasporic community remain so without reference to a homeland? Indeed, such a reference retains a form of opposition to nation-states—not purely American, but distinguished as African or black Americans. Gilroy argues emphatically against the static national or racial locations of diaspora and instead for transnationalism, culture located in transition and travel. Homeland is, to some extent, turned inward by a creative response to dislocation; as Barbara Bender (2001:78) has noted, "Dislocation is always also relocation." Creative relocation is a theme that has been explored by archaeologists, for example in situating the experience of slavery in broader landscapes rather than singular sites (McKee 1992). This was likely the case at Sylvester Manor. We need not only consider the relocation of enslaved Africans into the core plantation, tightly controlled by the Sylvester family, for livestock, field, and orchard work would have brought them to landscapes little seen or controlled (Trigg and Landon 2010), perhaps even seen as an Indian landscape.

Clifford further explored the implied opposition of diaspora to indigeneity. Citing historical American Indian displacements and removals as well as contemporary migrations to and from reservation lands, he has noted that it seemed reasonable to speak of diasporic identity for "tribal peoples" (1997:253). In fact, these communities may most strongly identify with the original definitions of diaspora. Ironically, in making these distinctions Clifford also notes the specific legal contexts prompting his use of the term "tribal" rather than "indigenous" in which Indian land claims came to be judged based on historical continuity. "Tribe" is a term, like "continuity," that he felt connoted rootedness rather than movement, which is implied in both "diaspora" and the anthropological term "band." We see an ambiguous conflation of social structure (tribes and bands) with place in the context of Indian claims occurring in the aftermath of countless historical removals.

Finally we might think of diaspora's location in experience and history rather than in place. Lilley (2006) has suggested viewing both indigenous and settler Australians as diasporic to draw attention to how each descendant group has located its identity to some extent in colonial oppression. Arguably such an approach carries a desire to avoid questions of origin, equating very different kinds of claims with one another and undercutting the position of indigenous polities in particular. On the other hand, from the perspective of vindicationist scholars, diasporan subjectivity directly challenges the essentialism of racial identity while still retaining shared history and heritage as a basis for defining community (Mullins 2008). Thus while diaspora might in a very basic way be defined by dislocation and movement, it must be more to set it apart from the dislocations and movements that occur on a common and massive scale today (Bender 2001; Connerton 2009). The "more" becomes apparent when comparing diaspora to concepts of indigeneity.

Defining Indigeneity

If the concept of diaspora is a moving target (so to speak), "indigenous" is no simpler despite its metaphors of rootedness. The term is most often taken as simply a marker of local descent or origins, as with "autochthonous." In this sense, often heard in Europe, "indigenous" might be defined in opposition to "immigrant" (Holtorf 2009); viewed in this fashion, indigenous identity has been regarded with the suspicion for claims to essentialism (Kuper 2003; also Gausset, Kenrick, and Gibb 2011; Kenrick and Lewis 2004). But when related to issues of heritage, colonialism, and sovereignty, indigeneity quickly becomes complex. In his 2005 broad review of indigenous perspectives on archaeology, Watkins notes the construction of indigeneity in relation to colonization, either historical or contemporary. The term may refer to a history of structural disenfranchisement or marginalization and the maintenance of political and cultural distinction within a surrounding nation. These definitions indicate that indigeneity is a political identity; American Indians, for example, are not minorities (another term often mapped onto "diaspora") because they occupy a categorically different relationship with the federal government

(Wilkins and Stark 2011). Thus indigeneity in the initial sense may be applied to historical communities as a way of distinguishing local from nonlocal; but in the latter sense it is best understood in contemporary Native communities, encompassing a deep historical relationship with settler states. Within this framework, indigeneity also carries connotations of vulnerability, imminent risk, or threat to survival (Harrison 2013:30–31). While such an approach does characterize many contemporary Native nations' experience, it also carries the double bind in equating indigeneity with poverty or disadvantage. Does indigeneity disappear when economic stability is achieved (Cattelino 2010), or does history not play a continuing role in defining community as it does through diaspora?

Though these issues figure heavily in settler societies, they may be less laden in Africa. Writing about how to conceptualize indigenous archaeologies in Africa, Lane (2011) notes that indigeneity there has parallels to ethnicity in its boundary construction. For many contemporary African societies, Kenrick and Lewis note (2004:6), indigeneity is relative: "Africans view themselves as indigenous relative to colonial and post-colonial powers. Additionally, Africans who live in the same regions as African hunter-gatherers and former hunter-gatherers recognize these groups as being indigenous relative to themselves." In this sense, indigenous identity is an act of critical geography, a situated assertion of what is native or foreign. It is by such acts that communities project the imagined political landscape, much in the same way that Witgen (2012) describes in the *pays d'en haut* of the Western Great Lakes. This, I would argue, is a valuable approach if we want to employ the concept of indigeneity in a way that is neither analytically oversimplified nor politically overdetermined. It also presses us to consider boundaries beyond those of nation-states that were still historically significant (Chang 2011).

This framework for indigeneity shares other parallels with the discourse of diaspora. For Clifford, in his "flexible" construction, "the term 'diaspora' is a signifier not simply of transnationality and movement but of political struggles to define the local, as distinctive community, in historical contexts of displacement" (1997:252). In the contemporary political moment, those struggles may be defined by recourse to the capitalized "Indigenous" identification given the international movements and legal structures that are emergent. But to address the local and distinctive communities in the past and their imagined futures, we have to situate them within the historically contingent conditions of colonialism as well as their shifting grounds over time. Colonialism in the United States (and other places) has become reliant upon a racialized episteme, one that consistently separates diaspora and indigeneity and brings them into conflict with one another. Were we to attend to imagined futures instead, we might be exploring the historical struggles over the concepts of citizenship and sovereignty and highlighting how those comprise, in large part, the shifting grounds of colonial discourse (Byrd 2011; Camp 2013).

Here I want to reiterate that I am not suggesting there is no substantive difference between diaspora and indigeneity or even that these concepts are only meaningful in contemporary political discourse. Often, however, these critical nuances are overlooked in scholars' appropriation of the terms. For example, one of the characteristics of diaspora included in Safran's foundational definition (1991:83–84) is that members are dispersed to two or more locations; in other words, community itself is dispersed as perhaps family units or individuals in the case of African enslavement. Indigenous communities, on the other hand, often have been displaced as communities. This difference parlays into routes to defining the local and the distinctive nature of the community as well as the recourse to structures of governance that may be maintained by communities but not by families or individuals. We might also think about ethnogenesis and community formation, which perhaps have their roots in diasporic peoples but occur in conditions that allow for the development of indigenous (local) governance and identity, as in the Brothertown Indian Nation (Cipolla 2013, this volume). Here we see a clear connection to discourse of citizenship and sovereignty.

Comparing Cases

Is there any way to mobilize these nuanced concepts of political and geographic imagination, however, in archaeological interpretations? It might be enough that the concepts remind us of the ongoing impacts of colonialism in the very categories we might otherwise uncritically apply to past communities. In that sense, we should avoid the use of these two terms as simple glosses for race or ethnicity. Of greater significance to the historic contexts themselves, indigenous and diasporic identities trace different ideas about the reproduction of communities within larger societies rather than reflecting static attachments to origin and tradition. As such we should see these ideas as evolving through time, in part because the conditions and structures of colonial society that manage alterity have also evolved constantly. These colonial structures include discourses of race, governance, human rights, manifest destiny, social contracts, and the idea of free market economy. Thus in identifying groups as indigenous and/or diasporic, we could look to what options might have been open to a community at the time that would enable it to exist within or separate from those colonial structures.

As noted earlier, the context of the French in the Western Great Lakes provides a tantalizing comparative perspective. To take the case which Witgen (2012) wrote of in the *pays d'en haut*, we would stop thinking about the fur trade in the western interior, far from the large colonial posts, as either directed by Euro-American traders or an equal "middle ground" between traders and the Native communities they traveled with. Instead, we would view the traders as subject to the conditions and political landscape of the Anishinaabeg, who were themselves engaged in expanding their territory and in effect staking a claim to local sovereignty. Fur-trade-related sites in Minnesota, along the western edge of the eastern woodlands, are quite ephemeral because of the short-term occupation by Anishinaabe hunters and their families as they moved through the territories they claimed either through alliance or warfare with Eastern Dakota people. This is true also of the traders who either lived as their local partners did or who established rare winter-only fortified posts that they dismantled or destroyed upon leaving (Birk 1991, 1999; Hayes 2011, 2014). Rather than take this ephemerality as a marker of the precarious balance of indigenous lifeways under colonial conditions, it may be seen as the precarious nature of Euro-American lifeways under indigenous conditions.

Life in this region was dictated by the political landscape of negotiation, the terms of which were not set by white traders. In other words, their success in this landscape was dependent upon being incorporated into the local; incorporation has recently been explored as a process of indigenous autonomy among seventeenth- and eighteenth-century Haudenosaunee (Jordan 2013). Two late-eighteenth-century fur-trade sites in central Minnesota, Little Round Hill (Hayes 2014) and the Réaume Post site, demonstrate the radical difference that such incorporation makes.[1]

Both sites are located within the greater Mississippi River watershed within ten miles of each other, dating to a period when the rivers were a major highway system facilitating the fur trade in this ecologically rich transition between woodland and plains. The region was periodically contested by Anishinaabe and Dakota peoples (Warren 1984 [1885]), each staking claims to the rich hunting grounds. Both sites were temporary (winter-only) base camps, archaeologically and in historical records identified as places of engagement between Anishinaabe hunters and trappers and Euro-Canadian traders exchanging food and furs for a variety of trade goods. The two sites were, however, captured in very different kinds of archival records, hinting at their positions within the political landscape.

While the trader Joseph Réaume was employed variously by established companies and referred to by his fellow traders in their journals and memoirs (Allard 2013), the trader at Little Round Hill is nowhere to be found in the same archive. Instead he is referred to in William Warren's 1885 *History of the Ojibway People*, a compilation of oral histories collected by Warren, who was partly of Ojibway ancestry, spoke the language fluently, and made it his mission to record what must be considered indigenous historiography (MacLeod 1992; Warren 1984 [1885]). In Warren's account, the trader at Little Round Hill was named in English only "a Blacksmith," a translation of Ah-wish-to-yah, though he was identified as French and at one point as white. Likely an independent trader and possibly of mixed ancestry, Ah-wish-to-yah's camp was also occupied by a few of his *coureurs-du-bois* and ten Pillager band hunters and their families (Warren 1984 [1885]:275–278). While Réaume does make an appearance in Warren's account, traveling with the well-known trader Jean Baptiste Cadotte (280), his engagement warrants no further mention.

Caught in two different archives, from the perspective of the large fur-trade companies on the one hand and the perspective of Warren's indigenous historians on the other, these two sites illustrate two quite different modes of dwelling on the landscape. Ah-wish-to-yah's camp at Little Round Hill, though in a dangerous area and supposedly attacked by a band of Dakota warriors, resembles contemporaneous or earlier Anishinaabe or Dakota camps, with several semisubterranean structures, likely covered by light-framed superstructures, and central hearths. While the structures resembled one another, slight variations in associated artifacts suggest different occupants; for example, locally produced pottery was not found in all dwellings, and iron items were found only in one dwelling. Glass seed beads for embroidery were found in most dwellings, but many more were recovered in the activity areas between structures.

The activity area was well-used; both lithic debris (including obsidian, a rare import from far west of Minnesota) and firearm fragments were found, along with fragments of reworked brass sheet fragments (figure 4.2). These items index participation in a multitude of trade networks. Faunal remains, evidence of past meals and of the business of the fur trade, were found across the site. Perhaps most telling, the camp was not protected by a stockade wall; its occupants likely regarded the features of the landscape, including the riverbanks themselves, as reliable defense. The occupants of this site appear, in their general lack of defensiveness,

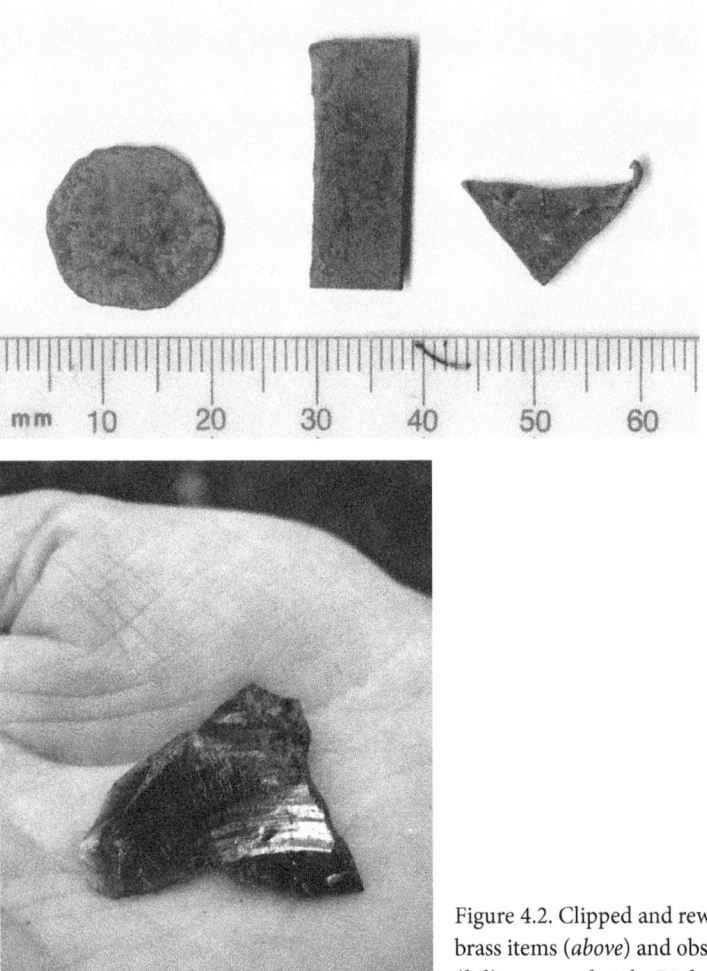

Figure 4.2. Clipped and reworked brass items (*above*) and obsidian flake (*left*) recovered at the Little Round Hill site. Photos by the author.

Figure 4.3. Interpretive sign, including artist's renditions, at the Little Round Hill site. The man depicted is Esh-ke-bug-e-coshe, also known as Flatmouth, the chief of the Pillager Leech Lake Ojibwe who related the site's story. The stockade wall shown did not exist. The site is now on the National Register of Historic Places and located within Wadena County parkland. Photo by the author.

to have belonged there, perhaps assured by their place within a broader network of kin and allies despite the ethnic diversity we tend to assume was significant. It is an occupation at odds with the interpretive signage at the Little Round Hill site, depicting a somewhat idealized fur-trade post structure as a bastion in the wilderness (figure 4.3). In fact, the structures located in excavation most closely resemble the round dwellings meant to indicate Anishinaabe housing in the depiction.

The Réaume Post site, on the other hand, appeared as a heavily fortified camp, carefully maintaining isolation behind sturdy stockade walls, timber structures, and substantial stone and daub chimneys, and more closely resembling the squared structures in the interpretive sign at Little Round Hill. Although a rather similar range of faunal remains and trade materials (particularly beads, copper or other metal adornments, iron implements, and firearms) were found within Réaume Post's fortlike walls, no lithic debris or local pottery was found, suggesting that while Native trade partners may have come inside its walls, they likely were not living there. Faunal remains, though similar in species represented, appear to have been discarded in restricted areas, perhaps in an attempt to create a particular appearance for the post area. All of the wooden structures at the Réaume site were completely burned, though it may have occurred after the winter occupation was left behind. While Réaume may have been engaged in the trade, his post suggests that he was less engaged in the Native political landscape. I would suggest that he knew he was not in control of the arena in which he was operating; and though neither he nor other company traders had any interest in permanent settlement there, Réaume's post indicates an insistence on separation that is not in evidence at Ah-wish-to-yah's camp. In other words, each trader operated within a rather different construction of the local, Ah-wish-to-yah's turned outward to the indigenous landscape and Réaume's turned inward.

In the *pays d'en haut* we see an indigeneity negotiated not strictly in terms relative to colonists in a model of domination and resistance; the local was made by long-standing structures of kinship and alliance, not in reaction to colonists per se. Because the Native place was so created and European-descended traders were apparently willing to participate under these conditions (Sleeper-Smith 2001; White 1991), the future was anticipated through the ongoing negotiation of an alliance network. This perspective suggests a somewhat different way of looking at plantation contexts like Sylvester Manor and others where eastern Algonquian people were caught up in colonial enterprises.

Rather than viewing the rapid colonization and displacement of Native peoples in the Atlantic Northeast as a terminal narrative, we can focus on an ongoing renegotiation of their place in a much more complex network of belonging to secure a future. The Manhanset of Shelter Island in New York brought their complaints to the colonial court system when the Sylvesters and their financial partners began to build on the island in 1652. Though the details of the settlement are ambiguous, the case was resolved through what colonial authorities (and contemporary legal scholars) would regard as a quit claim, relinquishing control of the land to the Sylvesters. Archaeological excavations of the plantation subsequently built there show that the Manhanset did not leave the island, however, but rather were entangled in the plantation labor and production of wampum. Such a choice to stay might be regarded as acquiescence to the new colonial system. Instead I would suggest that the Manhanset saw the political landscape as still offering an indigenous system within which to work. They may have chosen to place themselves under the protection of the Sylvesters, *yet* still viewed their future as one of a sovereign community, in an understanding of political structure consistent with their earlier experiences with the Pequot or the Mohawk as tribute holders. A sovereign future is similarly acted upon by tribes today that petition for recognition and claim the right of historical self-representation (as described in Mrozowski, Gould, and Law Pezzarossi, this volume; and Hodge, Loren, and Capone, this volume).

By the same token, enslaved Africans may have regarded the Manhanset on the plantation as a potentially supportive network and possibly a means to create or maintain their own community. As noted earlier, the wider plantation landscape may have offered the opportunity to engage, to "relocate" as an emergent diaspora, or even to be incorporated into an Indian sovereign landscape. Such possibilities are difficult to imagine today because they require thinking past centuries of racial discourse. From the perspective of enslaved Africans in the seventeenth century, however, there was no reason to believe that one day their descendant generations would be pressed into mutually exclusive categories with quite different recourses to sovereignty (in-depth coverage of Sylvester Manor archaeology and history is presented in Hayes 2013 and in Hayes and Mrozowski 2007).

Conclusion

Diaspora and indigeneity are identifications that operate most apparently today but do indeed have significance for the way we approach the past. They are also subjectivities grounded in tracing a connection in past, present, and future. The African diaspora, as distinctive and local but simultaneously within a larger social structure, draws upon the past to push back against racialized structures in important ways. Diaspora today emphasizes the common historical background the community shares in defining itself in defiance of a neoliberal, "color-blind" rhetoric, while in the colonial past, we can imagine, it created the grounds for autonomy despite the system of racial slavery in which it existed. The African Burial Ground site in New York exemplifies both. The expression of diaspora in the past can be seen in the use of symbols of African origin on bodies or on coffins and in the apparent care taken by a community in committing the dead to their burials and maintaining the space itself for continued use (Perry, Howson, and Bianco 2006). In the recent past and present, the New York African diaspora community has pointed to a shared heritage of slavery to identify its right to be involved in the future of the rediscovered burial ground (Blakey 1998; LaRoche and Blakey 1997). In Brazil, maroon sites like Palmares have become places to locate a diverse heritage of diasporic cultural exchanges as well as slavery, a challenge to simple narratives of race and class as Ferreira and Funari (this volume) demonstrate. As Baker (1998) has described in his overview of anthropology's evolving constructions of race, the Boasian contribution of culture as both not hierarchically comparable and historically particular has not been adopted in social policy in a balanced fashion, and references to diaspora can help to reappropriate the historically particular end of the formula.

I suppose, in a sense, the conclusion I draw from this extended musing over the terms "diaspora" and "indigeneity" is not so much that we should stop or radically reconsider our use of them. Indeed, in the examples just explored, a more nuanced consideration of how the terms intersect leads us potentially to new avenues and questions to pose of the archaeological contexts. Rather, it is that they incite us to introduce another level of temporality to the way we or other stakeholders portray past communities in the advent of colonization. We are accustomed to thinking about how the past (or tradition) has shaped our historical subjects' way of living in the world and how colonialism was disruptive of that past. But I suggest we think also how their imagined political futures shaped their dwelling as well, even under conditions that were quite changed.

Note

1. Both sites were excavated by University of Minnesota archaeologists under the direction of the author from 2009 to 2013. This discussion is based on results reported in Hayes 2014 on Little Round Hill and preliminary analyses by Amélie Allard, whose dissertation on the Réaume site is in preparation as of this writing.

References Cited

Allard, Amélie
2013 "Feeding the Crew: Foodways and Faunal Remains at Réaume's Trading Post Site, Central Minnesota." Paper presented at the Society for Historical Archaeology Annual Meeting, January 9–12, Leicester, England.

Baker, Lee D.
1998 *From Savage to Negro: Anthropology and the Construction of Race, 1896–1954.* University of California Press, Berkeley.

Bender, Barbara
2001 Landscapes on-the-Move. *Journal of Social Archaeology* 1(1):75–89.

Birk, Douglas
1991 French Presence in Minnesota: The View from Site Mo20 near Little Falls. In *French Colonial Archaeology: The Illinois Country and the Western Great Lakes*, edited by John A. Walthall, pp. 237–266. University of Illinois Press, Urbana.
1999 The Archaeology of Sayer's Fort: An 1804–1805 North West Company Wintering Quarters Site in East-Central Minnesota. Unpublished master's thesis, Department of Anthropology, University of Minnesota Twin Cities.

Blakey, Michael L.
1998 The New York African Burial Ground Project: An Examination of Enslaved Lives, A Construction of Ancestral Ties. *Transforming Anthropology* 7(1):53–58.

Bohaker, Heidi
2006 "Nindoodemag": The Significance of Algonquian Kinship Networks in the Eastern Great Lakes Region, 1600–1701. *William and Mary Quarterly*, 3rd Series, 63(1):23–52.

Boissevain, Ethel
1956 The Detribalization of the Narragansett Indians: A Case Study. *Ethnohistory* 3(3):225–245.

Byrd, Jodi A.
2011 *The Transit of Empire: Indigenous Critiques of Colonialism.* University of Minnesota Press, Minneapolis.

Camp, Stacey Lynn
2013 *The Archaeology of Citizenship.* University Press of Florida, Gainesville.

Cattelino, Jessica R.
2010 The Double Bind of American Indian Need-Based Sovereignty. *Cultural Anthropology* 25(2):235–262.

Chang, David
2011 Borderlands in a World at Sea: Concow Indians, Native Hawaiians, and South Chinese in Indigenous, Global, and National Spaces. *Journal of American History* 98:384–403.

Cipolla, Craig N.
2013 *Becoming Brothertown: Native American Ethnogenesis and Endurance in the Modern World.* University of Arizona Press, Tucson.

Clifford, James
1997   *Routes: Travel and Translation in the Late Twentieth Century.* Harvard University Press, Cambridge.
Connerton, Paul
2009   *How Modernity Forgets.* Cambridge University Press, Cambridge, England.
Fennell, Christopher C.
2007   *Crossroads and Cosmologies: Diasporas and Ethnogenesis in the New World.* University Press of Florida, Gainesville.
Franklin, Maria
2001   The Archaeological Dimensions of Soul Food: Interpreting Race, Culture, and Afro-Virginian Identity. In *Race and the Archaeology of Identity*, edited by Charles E. Orser Jr., 88–107. University of Utah Press, Salt Lake City.
Gausset, Quentin, Justin Kenrick, and Robert Gibb
2011   Indigeneity and Autochthony: A Couple of False Twins? *Social Anthropology* 19(2):135–142.
Gilroy, Paul
1991   *"There Ain't No Black in the Union Jack": The Cultural Politics of Race and Nation.* University of Chicago Press, Chicago.
1993   *The Black Atlantic: Modernity and Double Consciousness.* Harvard University Press, Cambridge.
Gomez, Michael A.
1998   *Exchanging Our Country Marks: The Transformation of African Identities in the Colonial and Antebellum South.* University of North Carolina Press, Chapel Hill.
Hall, Gwendolyn Midlo
2005   *Slavery and African Ethnicities in the Americas: Restoring the Links.* University of North Carolina Press, Chapel Hill.
Harrison, Rodney
2013   *Heritage: Critical Approaches.* Routledge, London.
Hayes, Katherine
2011   "Being Located in a Dangerous Neighborhood": Investigating the Fur Trade in the Colonial Borderlands of Minnesota. Paper presented at the 2011 Annual Meeting of the Society for Historical Archaeology, Austin, Texas, January 5–9.
2013   *Slavery Before Race: Europeans, Africans and Indians at Long Island's Sylvester Manor Plantation, 1651–1884.* New York University Press, New York.
2014   Results of Survey and Excavation of the Little Round Hill (21WD16) and Cadotte Post (21WD17) Sites in Wadena County, Minnesota: A View of the Fur Trade in the Late Eighteenth Century. Report prepared for the Wadena County Historical Society and the Minnesota State Historic Preservation Office.
Hayes, Katherine, and Stephen Mrozowski (editors)
2007   The Historical Archaeology of Sylvester Manor. Special issue, *Northeast Historical Archaeology* 36.
Heath, Barbara J., and Amber Bennett
2000   "The Little Spots Allow'd Them": The Archaeological Study of African-American Yards. *Historical Archaeology* 34(2):38–55.

Holtorf, Cornelius
2009   A European Perspective on Indigenous and Immigrant Archaeologies. *World Archaeology* 41(4):672–681.

Horton, James Oliver, and Lois E. Horton
1979   *Black Bostonians: Family Life and Community Struggle in the Antebellum North.* Holmes and Meier, New York.

Jordan, Kurt A.
2013   Incorporation and Colonization: Post Columbian Iroquois Satellite Communities and Processes of Indigenous Autonomy. *American Anthropologist* 115(1):29–43.

Kenrick, Justin
2011   Scottish Land Reform and Indigenous Peoples' Rights: Self Determination and Historical Reversibility. *Social Anthropology* 19(2):189–203.

Kenrick, Justin, and Jerome Lewis
2004   Indigenous Peoples' Rights and the Politics of the Term "Indigenous." *Anthropology Today* 20(2):4–9.

Kuper, Adam
2003   The Return of the Native. *Current Anthropology* 44(3):389–402.

Lane, Paul
2011   Possibilities for a Postcolonial Archaeology in Sub-Saharan Africa: Indigenous and Usable Pasts. *World Archaeology* 43(1):7–25.

LaRoche, Cheryl J., and Michael L. Blakey
1997   Seizing Intellectual Power: The Dialogue at the New York African Burial Ground. *Historical Archaeology* 31(3):84–106.

Leone, Mark P.
1982   Some Opinions about Recovering Mind. *American Antiquity* 47(4):742–760.

Lilley, Ian
2006   Archaeology, Diaspora, and Decolonization. *Journal of Social Archaeology* 6(1):28–47.

MacLeod, D. Peter
1992   The Anishinabeg Point of View: The History of the Great Lakes Region to 1800 in Nineteenth-Century Mississauga, Odawa, and Ojibwa Historiography. *Canadian Historical Review* 72(2):194–210.

McKee, Larry
1992   The Ideals and Realities behind the Design and Use of 19th Century Virginia Slave Cabins. In *The Art and Mystery of Historical Archaeology: Essays in Honor of James Deetz*, edited by Anne Elizabeth Yentsch and Mary C. Beaudry, 195–213. CRC Press, Boca Raton, Florida.

McKinney, Tiffany M.
2006   Race and Federal Recognition in Native New England. In *Crossing Waters, Crossing Worlds: The African Diaspora in Indian Country,* edited by Tiya Miles and Sharon P. Holland, 57–79. Duke University Press, Durham, North Carolina.

Melish, Joanne Pope
1998 *Disowning Slavery: Gradual Emancipation and "Race" in New England, 1780–1860.* Cornell University Press, Ithaca, New York.

Mrozowski, Stephen A., Katherine Hayes, and Anne P. Hancock
2007 The Archaeology of Sylvester Manor. *Northeast Historical Archaeology* 36:1–15.

Mrozowski, Stephen A., Katherine Hayes, Heather Trigg, Jack Gary, David Landon, and Dennis Piechota
2007 Conclusion: Meditations on the Archaeology of a Northern Plantation. Special issue, *Northeast Historical Archaeology* 36:143–156.

Mullins, Paul R.
2008 Excavating America's Metaphor: Race, Diaspora, and Vindicationist Archaeologies. *Historical Archaeology* 42(2):104–122.

O'Brien, Jean
2010 *Firsting and Lasting: Writing Indians Out of Existence in New England.* University of Minnesota Press, Minneapolis.

Perry, Warren R., Jean Howson, and Barbara A. Bianco (editors)
2006 *New York African Burial Ground Archaeology Final Report.* Vol. I. Report prepared by Howard University, Washington, D.C., for the U.S. General Services Administration Northeastern and Caribbean Region.

Safran, William
1991 Diasporas in Modern Societies: Myths of Homeland and Return. *Diaspora* 1(1):83–99.

Siminoff, Faren R.
2004 *Crossing the Sound: The Rise of Atlantic American Communities in Seventeenth-Century Eastern Long Island.* New York University Press, New York.

Sleeper-Smith, Susan
2001 *Indian Women and French Men: Rethinking Cultural Encounter in the Western Great Lakes.* University of Massachusetts Press, Amherst.

Trigg, Heather B., and David B. Landon
2010 Labor and Agricultural Production at Sylvester Manor Plantation, Shelter Island, New York. *Historical Archaeology* 44(3):36–53.

Warren, William W.
1984 [1885] *History of the Ojibway People.* Minnesota Historical Society Press, St. Paul.

Watkins, Joe
2005 Through Wary Eyes: Indigenous Perspectives on Archaeology. *Annual Review of Anthropology* 34:429–449.

White, Richard
1991 *The Middle Ground: Indians, Empires, and Republics in the Great Lakes Region, 1650–1815.* Cambridge University Press, Cambridge, England.

Wilder, Craig Steven
2005 Black Life in Freedom: Creating a Civic Culture. In *Slavery in New York,* edited by Ira Berlin and Leslie M. Harris, 215–237. New Press, New York.

Wilkie, Laurie A., and Paul Farnsworth
2005   *Sampling Many Pots: An Archaeology of Memory and Tradition at a Bahamian Plantation.* University Press of Florida, Gainesville.

Wilkins, David E., and Heidi Kiiwetinepinesiik Stark
2011   *American Indian Politics and the American Political System.* 3rd edition. Rowman and Littlefield, Lanham, Maryland.

Witgen, Michael
2012   *An Infinity of Nations: How the Native New World Shaped Early North America.* University of Pennsylvania Press, Philadelphia.

5

Cultural Colonization without Colonial Settlements

A Case Study in Early Iron Age Temperate Europe

PETER S. WELLS

The terms "colonization" and "colonialism" most often refer to the establishment of physical places—outposts of a society—within the territory of another society. The phenomenon can be identified throughout much of the world over the past six thousand years, since the city of Uruk established the colony of Hacinebi in what is now Syria early in the fourth millennium BC, apparently to acquire metals needed by the growing urban centers of southern Mesopotamia (Stein 2002).

The case presented here is different from that of most colonial entanglements. In this case, representatives of commercial interests in the Greek world of the sixth and fifth centuries BC used the presentation to elites of specially crafted objects associated with feasting practices to establish favorable relations for political and economic interactions. At the same time, they introduced new forms of architecture and sculpture into temperate Europe. Immediate effects for the Greek world were favorable political relations and access to needed goods. For the societies of interior Europe, the immediate effect was to encourage elites to begin to identify with and to become more actively engaged with the larger world, especially that of the cosmopolitan societies of the Mediterranean basin.

Yet as recent discoveries make clear, access to Mediterranean imports and participation in the changes set in motion were by no means restricted to elites. Long-term effects were transformational for all parties involved.

Cultural Colonization

What I call "cultural colonization" here is the deliberate introduction of extraordinary goods and associated practices, together with new technologies of architecture and sculpture, by the colonizing society into another society for the purposes of gaining political and economic goodwill and advantage. The deliberate transmission of goods, practices, and to some extent even attitudes and values is critical. The process is more deeply embedded in cultural values than the terms "trade" and "gift giving" imply, in that the colonizing society purposely "colonizes" the aspirations of the elites of the colonized society. The impact of this variety of colonization can be as strong as that of the establishment of colonial settlements in a landscape, though its material signatures are more subtle. A situation similar in significant ways to the one explored here is presented by Domínguez (2002) in his analysis of Greek activity in Iberia.

A well-documented (because supported by texts) example from a half millennium later is the Roman policy of cultivating "client kings" (Braund 1984). Client kings typically were rulers of indigenous societies who inhabited lands beyond the imperial frontiers. Roman officials established friendly diplomatic relations with them, sometimes extending the privilege of Roman citizenship and even equestrian status, making them in effect elite members of Roman society. They were invited into the Roman lands, even to Rome itself, and during their visits acquired a taste for and a knowledge of cultural practices of elite Romans, such as the customs surrounding banqueting and other ceremonies of social and political significance. Some sent their sons to Rome to learn Roman customs and values. Along with special status and knowledge, client kings received material goods that represented their political connections with Rome. These included sets of feasting equipment and special personal ornaments. In the earlier Roman Period, the grave at Mušov in Moravia, with its rich assemblage of lavish feasting vessels (Peška and Tejral 2002), and in the later Roman Period, the grave of Childeric in Tournai in Belgium, with its gold onion-head fibula (Halsall 2001), illustrate the material manifestations of these policies and transactions. The case presented next has no directly associated texts and thus relies exclusively on archaeological evidence.

Early Iron Age Temperate Europe and the Mediterranean Imports

Already in the later decades of the nineteenth century, archaeological investigations yielded objects that were recognized as luxury imports from the Mediterranean world, such as Attic painted pottery (from Athens) and fine bronze vessels from workshops in Etruscan Italy. When settlement excavations at the Heuneburg in southwest Germany began in the early 1950s, the recovery of Attic pottery sherds in a settlement context generated great scholarly and public interest. Also in the 1950s, Greek and Etruscan imports were recovered in the rich burial at Vix and on the neighboring hilltop settlement of Mont Lassois, at Châtillon-sur-Seine in eastern France. Since that time, Greek and Etruscan luxury imports of the sixth and fifth centuries BC have been recovered at many settlements and in many graves throughout temperate Europe (overviews are presented in Beilharz et al. 2012 and Hansen and Böhr 2011).

Recent discoveries make it clear that access to such imports was not restricted to elites at the major centers; they were available to members of many small communities throughout temperate Europe (Bouzek and Smrž 1994; Cicolani 2012:181; Krause 2012:151; Michálek 1992). Imported raw materials from the Mediterranean world such as coral and items from farther afield including ivory are well represented at sites in the countryside away from centers (Schussmann 2012:155; Wells 1987:147, fig. 6.3).

The Greek and Etruscan objects recovered in central regions of the continent have generated a vast literature. In the 1950s and 1960s, most studies focused on the issue of trade, often asking what was traded in exchange. In the 1970s and 1980s, much of the interest shifted to cultural dynamics, striving to understand the role that the imports played in social and political changes in the societies of temperate Europe (comparable concerns in the context of colonial North America are discussed in Cipolla, this volume). In the 1990s and 2000s, a number of studies addressed what the imports can tell us about cultural practices that were transmitted and about their reception and integration into local societies (Krausse 1996). Now that it is apparent that Mediterranean goods were available to and consumed by a broader spectrum of society than was hitherto thought, larger questions about the interactions and their impact are being posed (Wells 2012, chapter 11).

The Model

The great majority of the Greek imports date to the sixth and early fifth centuries BC and include Attic pottery, Greek transport amphorae (for wine), bronze vessels, and other luxuries, Etruscan imports and some from the Near East, and more modest items from the Mediterranean world. It must be emphasized that I am using the names "Greeks" and "Etruscans" only as modern designations for diverse peoples of the Aegean and central Italian regions. The identities of the different Mediterranean-based societies of this time are complex and problematic and far beyond the scope of this paper. Between 800 and 500 BC, many Greek cities established colonies along the shores of the Mediterranean and Black Seas (Boardman 1999). Like many other colonies, these were towns founded and inhabited by persons from the Greek homelands who identified with their places of origin. Architecture similar to that of the home cities was erected, and religious, governmental, and cultural practices of the homeland dominated in the colonial settings (Dietler 2010). Examples of Greek colonies established during this period include Emporion in Spain, Massalia in France, Tarentum in Italy, Syracuse in Sicily, and Olbia on the west coast of the Black Sea (also Cornell, this volume).

Despite all of the Greek imports recovered north of the Mediterranean shores in France, Germany, Austria, the Czech Republic, and elsewhere (Hansen and Böhr 2011:291, fig. 6), there is no evidence, either archaeological or textual, for the establishment of Greek colonies within temperate Europe; all Greek colonies remained on the coasts. The pattern is similar elsewhere in the greater Mediterranean region, as Greek colonies were established on the coasts, not in the interiors, though their merchants traded with indigenous communities that inhabited the interior regions (Cornell, this volume). But through developing contacts and relations with elites in the interior of temperate Europe, representatives of Greek political and commercial interests were able to achieve their goals through colonizing the culture of elites in Early Iron Age Europe without the need to build colonial settlements in the unfamiliar landscapes of the continental interior.

My argument is based primarily on the presence in temperate Europe of a series of unique objects manufactured in Greek workshops and on architectural features displaying the application of technical expertise from the Mediterranean world.

Centers of Early Iron Age West-Central Europe

During the sixth and fifth centuries BC, a number of major settlement centers emerged in west-central Europe, in eastern France, northern Switzerland, and southwestern Germany (map 5.1). They are distinguished from the majority of settlements in being situated on hilltops defended with substantial walls, in having abundant evidence of on-site manufacturing in a variety of materials, and for interaction with societies of the Mediterranean world. Around them are burial mounds much larger than the average size containing chamber burials unusually richly outfitted with grave goods. The most fully investigated of these centers are the Heuneburg on the upper Danube River in southwest Germany, Mont Lassois on the upper Seine River in eastern France, and the Hohenasperg on the plain of the Neckar River north of Stuttgart. Recent excavations at the Heuneburg have revealed extensive suburbs around the fortified hilltop, and demographic analyses have suggested populations as high as five thousand for this early urban complex (Krausse and Fernández-Götz 2012:120). While the settlements on Mont Lassois and on the Heuneburg have been extensively excavated, at the Hohenasperg, the hilltop was destroyed by medieval construction; it is the burial mounds surrounding this settlement that inform us about its character.

The Objects

Hochdorf cauldron

The Hochdorf tomb is part of the Hohenasperg complex. The grave, dating to around 530 BC (Beilharz and Krausse 2012:194), contained the remains of an adult man and a rich assemblage of grave goods (Biel 1985). The bronze cauldron (Biel 1985:117–130, and plates 33–37) is an enormous, almost spherical object that visually dominated the burial assemblage (reconstruction in Biel and Balzer 2012:140, fig. 160). It stands 80 centimeters high and has a maximum diameter of 104 centimeters and a capacity of

Map 5.1. Principal sites discussed in the chapter. Under "Hohenasperg," the top dot represents the plateau settlement site, the dot to the left represents the Hochdorf tumulus, that to the right Grafenbühl, and the bottom dot the Römerhügel tumulus. The right-hand dot next to "Heuneburg" represents the settlement, that to the left the Giessübel-Talhau group of four tumuli. Map by the author with help from Kristina Golubiewski-Davis.

around 500 liters. It is thought to have been made in a Greek colonial workshop in southern Italy. It is decorated on the rim with three bronze figurines of lions. Herodotus, writing in Greek around the middle of the fifth century BC, describes a vessel that must have been somewhat similar to the Hochdorf cauldron (1946:I, 69). He writes that the Greek people known as the Lacedaemonians, in order to repay favors from Croesus, king of Lydia in Asia Minor from 560 to 547 BC, had made for him a bronze vessel decorated with figurines and with an unusually large capacity. From this assertion by Herodotus we can reasonably hypothesize that the Hochdorf cauldron, a unique object much larger than any other vessel in prehistoric Europe except the Vix krater, was made to serve as a political gift between a community of Greeks and a potentate of some kind in the middle of the continent.

The grave did not contain any other Greek imports, but it did include an entire set of feasting vessels and associated paraphernalia. These included a gold bowl with the cauldron, probably to serve as a ladle; nine drinking horns, the largest of iron, the other eight of cattle horn, all decorated with gold bands; nine bronze bowls; three bronze basins; and an iron axe, thought to have been intended for slaughtering an animal for a feast.

Among the other unusual objects in the grave was a couch 2.75 meters long made of sheet bronze with an iron frame supported by eight ornate bronze figurines of women whose feet were on axles attached to wheels. The back of the couch was ornamented with scenes in repoussé showing pairs of men fighting with swords and others riding wagons and holding swords and shields. The couch, upon which the deceased man was laid, had been placed between the cauldron at the north end of the chamber and the drinking horns, which hung on the chamber wall at the south end.

Dirk Krausse (1996; Beilharz and Krausse 2012:194–197) has analyzed the arrangement of the feasting equipment in the Hochdorf grave and has argued convincingly that the assemblage reflects the transformation of the Greek *symposion* into the milieu of Early Iron Age Europe. The *symposion* was a ritual feast in the Greek world of this period at which a host provided his guests (as far as we know, hosts and guests were all male) with fine wine and other delicacies as well as with entertainment. This ritual played a significant role in competition for and display of social status among elites in Greek society (Murray 1990; Wehgartner 1995). We have accounts of specific *symposia* in the writings of Plato and Xenophon and representations of them painted in scenes on Attic pottery. The material culture of the Greek *symposion* included large vessels that contained wine mixed with water, drinking vessels for guests to hold, and couches on which they reclined as they feasted. Especially important in linking the Hochdorf burial assemblage with the Greek *symposion* is the complete assemblage of objects and the way they were arranged in the tomb chamber (Boardman 1990).

Grafenbühl Couch

In another mound that is also part of the Hohenasperg complex, archaeologists recovered a lavish assemblage of imported luxury materials from a grave that had been looted in antiquity (Zürn 1970). From what the looters left behind, we can only imagine the wealth that the grave must have contained originally. Most significant for our purposes are numerous carved pieces of ivory, amber, and bone that belonged to a couch made in a Greek workshop (Fischer 1990). Other feasting equipment included remains of an ornate bronze and iron tripod, two bronze basins, and an iron drinking horn (Baitinger 1996). An ivory lion's foot may have been part of the couch, or it may have belonged to another piece of furniture. An unusual iron object may have been a castanet, an instrument represented in scenes of feasting in the Greek world (Krausse 1996:328). The Grafenbühl grave is believed to date to about 500 BC (Biel and Balzer 2012:141).

Objects very similar to the couch parts in the Grafenbühl grave were also recovered in two other rich burials, one at Römerhügel, also part of the Hohenasperg complex, and another in one of the Giessübel-Talhau mounds at the Heuneburg, 120 kilometers to the south (Krausse 1996:327).

Vix Krater

The Vix grave is part of the Mont Lassois complex; it was excavated in 1953 (Rolley 2003). The Vix krater is the largest bronze vessel known from the ancient world, and it was found not where one might expect, in Rome, Athens, or any other city of the Classical world, but in this burial of a woman at Châtillon-sur-Seine. The krater is 1.64 meter tall and weighs 208 kilograms. Around the neck are mounted cast-bronze figures of Greek warriors. The burial, dating to about 500 BC (Chaume, Nieszery, and Reinhard 2012:135), contained a range of other special objects, including two Attic drinking cups, an Etruscan bronze jug, a silver bowl with gold *omphalos,* and three bronze bowls—a complete and import-based drinking set. The woman was ornamented with bronze brooches decorated with gold and with coral imported from the Mediterranean, and she was buried with an ornate four-wheeled wagon.

The krater was manufactured in a Greek city, probably a colony in southern Italy, around 530 BC. In the Greek world, kraters were used for mixing wine and water; the standard custom was to mix one part wine and three parts water. The comment by Herodotus cited above applies to the Vix krater as well as to the Hochdorf cauldron.

The Architecture

Heuneburg clay brick wall

Around 600 BC a wall built of clay bricks set on a foundation of stone blocks was constructed around the perimeter of the 3.5-hectare plateau of the Heuneburg (Burkhardt 2010). The wall, with at least eleven bastions, or towers, projecting along the west side of the site faced the suburban settlements below the fortress (Steffen 2012:94 fig. 93). Clay brick architecture is foreign to Europe north of the Mediterranean. It was a common building technique in the Near East and in the Mediterranean basin (Burkhardt 2010) but is unsuited to the damp climate of the continental interior. The clay bricks of the Heuneburg wall match in size and shape bricks in walls around Greek settlements. Stratigraphic analyses suggest that the clay brick wall was destroyed around 525 BC and replaced by a wall constructed using typical local materials and techniques.

Mont Lassois Apsidal Buildings

Recent excavations at Mont Lassois, a plateau site similar to the Heuneburg and situated above the Vix burial mound, have revealed the foundations of two buildings that may indicate borrowing of architectural themes from the Greek world (Chaume, Nieszery, and Reinhard 2012:134, fig. 152). Each is rectangular and has a rounded apse at its west end, an unusual shape for an Early Iron Age building in temperate Europe (Grübel et al. 2011). Associated material provides an approximate date of 540–465 BC for the structures. The larger one measures 35 by 22 meters; the smaller is slightly more than half that size. Around the perimeter are three rows of postholes, and three internal walls divided the space into four rooms.

Much discussion (such as in Chaume, Nieszery, and Reinhard 2011 and Mötsch, Haffner, and Müller 2011) revolves around whether these structures indicate direct connections to Greek architectural traditions of the period, but the matter has not yet been resolved.

Effects of Greek Cultural Colonization on Early Iron Age Elites

The three principal burials discussed above—Hochdorf, Grafenbühl, and Vix—provide important evidence for cultural colonization by Greek interests. Supporting evidence is also available from many other graves, but these three are the richest in information. The character and combinations of the vessels for drinking and eating and their arrangement in the burials strongly suggest that the elites represented were practicing a version of the Greek *symposion*. Key components of that ritual were a large mixing vessel, a serving vessel, drinking vessels for individual participants, bowls for foods, and couches on which participants reclined while enjoying the festivities. All of these components were present in Hochdorf; all but the couch were in Vix (the woman's body had been laid on the rectangular box of the wagon, from which the wheels had been removed—perhaps a substitute for a couch); in Grafenbühl, even though the grave had been looted, the mixing vessel and couch were still represented by distinctive fragments, as was a musical instrument—the castanet. The fact that the contents of the Vix burial reference the practice of a version of the *symposion* is particularly significant as regards the matter of transformation of the Greek ritual into something different in temperate Europe. In Greece at this time, it is believed that the participants in the *symposion* were all elite men. In contrast, elite women participated in the ritual along with men in Etruscan Italy and apparently in temperate Europe (Bonfante 2011:239, 257).

The way objects were arranged in the Hochdorf burial is especially informative for what it can tell us about the meanings that those who conducted the funerary ceremony were communicating to the community members who witnessed it. (Ways in which spaces in burial chambers were used to communicate information are presented in Wells 2012:131–154). It is apparent that the performers of the ceremony wanted to emphasize that the man buried had, while living, hosted this important ritual and that the funerary event was socially and politically significant to the community. The deceased man was laid out on the couch. At his feet was the great cauldron along with the little gold bowl. At his head were the nine drinking horns. The enormous horn, of iron—90 centimeters long and weighing almost 3 kilograms—was hung above his head; the other eight of more modest size were hung in a row along the chamber wall. The arrangement at Vix, a generation or two later, was different. Here all of the feasting vessels were arranged between the woman's body and the west wall to her right. In Hochdorf, the monumental cauldron was the only Mediterranean import; at Vix, the entire feasting assemblage consisted of Mediterranean imports.

The key question here is how the receiving of the spectacular imports—the Hochdorf cauldron, the Grafenbühl couch, and the Vix krater, together with the other feasting gear—affected the identities of the individuals buried in these graves (and presumably to some extent of the social groups of which they were members). These individuals were not just receiving imported objects; they were receiving imports that they integrated into a practice that closely resembled the Greek ritual of the *symposion*. We do not possess textual information about Iron Age Europeans visiting Greek and Italian towns until a couple of centuries later, but it is highly likely that some of these individuals had witnessed and participated in the Greek rituals, perhaps at the colonial city of Massalia near the mouth of the Rhône River.

I propose that the receiving of these special imports and their use in feasting rituals in temperate Europe enabled the individuals to feel that they were adopting aspects of the identity of the Greek and Etruscan elites with whom they interacted. But their aspirations probably went much further than just to those northern Mediterranean elites. This was a time when connections between communities in temperate Europe and those in other parts of the world were expanding rapidly and widely. Performing the new rituals using the imported objects to conduct them were actions that the elites could undertake in order to represent their increasingly close connections with the outside world. As Cipolla (this volume) emphasizes, consumption, especially of exotic foreign products, involves not simply trade but a complex array of interconnections between the individuals of the different societies participating in the interchanges. In this case, it is difficult to determine whether either party in the interactions can be regarded as more powerful, possessing more agency, than the other. The Greeks wanted raw materials and were prepared to furnish unique, costly, and difficult-to-transport items to the elites who could provide the materials. From all of the archaeological evidence, those elites eagerly accepted the proffered special goods and quickly integrated them into their existing systems of ritual practice. Ritual feasting can be traced back to the Early Bronze Age (2000 BC) in temperate Europe (Needham, Lawson, and Woodward 2010) and probably further. New in the sixth century BC was the integration of the unique imported objects into the practice and elaboration of the scale of feasting.

The burial contents and their arrangements are strong evidence for the elites having fashioned new identities as members of an interregional community that spanned much of Europe, the Mediterranean, and beyond to other parts of Eurasia. The architectural evidence of the clay brick wall at the Heuneburg and perhaps that of the apsidal buildings at Mont Lassois supports my argument that the elites were displaying their growing feeling of association with the elites of societies elsewhere. The northern elites wanted to create material representations of the societies to the south with whom they were identifying, as well as practicing their rituals. They were fashioning new, more complex ideas about who they were or who they were becoming—both as elites within their own communities and in relation to the societies with which they were interacting in the Mediterranean world. The analogy with the client kings of Rome is apt here.

It is important to emphasize that the elites in temperate Europe were not practicing a Greek ritual exactly as it was practiced in Greece. The Vix grave, for example, makes it apparent that elite women were participants in the feasts along with men. Feasting rituals were important social and political events in temperate Europe as well as in Greece and in many other societies around the world, and the participation of women as well as men underscores how aspects of the Greek version of the ritual were transformed to integrate into the local society. There is nothing like the Hochdorf cauldron or the Vix krater in the Greek world, and it is likely that both were made specifically for non-Greek potentates. The other feasting vessels represented in these three graves were drawn from different sources, some Greek, such as the Attic pottery in the Vix grave and the tripod and ivory lion's foot at Grafenbühl; some Etruscan, such as the bronze jug and basins in the Vix grave; and some local, such as the nine drinking horns and nine bronze plates in Hochdorf. The Greek ritual was not simply transplanted into the center of the continent. Aspects of it were borrowed, transformed, and adapted to local practices and local needs among the elites there.

The elites who participated in these cultural borrowings and transformations were a small minority in European Iron Age societies, perhaps 1 or 2 percent of the population. The interactions that resulted in the exotic imports in the graves discussed above also had impacts on the rest of

Iron Age society. The clearest direct evidence is in goods imported from the Mediterranean world that have been recovered in graves throughout the region of west-central Europe (Wells 1987). At the same time that the lavish Greek products were arriving at the Hohenasperg, the Heuneburg, and Mont Lassois, quantities of coral from the Mediterranean Sea, multicolored glass beads, and carved amber ornaments (with amber mostly from the Baltic region but carved in the Mediterranean lands) were arriving as well and were distributed among small communities throughout the region. As we learn from their arrangements in burials, these objects were worn as personal ornaments and played important roles in representing status and identity (Wells 2008:64–84).

Exactly how the systems of goods circulation operated is not well understood. But it is most likely that the outlying communities supplied the centers with the materials—metals, textiles, leather, furs, pitch, tar—that the Greek and Etruscan trade partners sought. The Mediterranean imports in the graves belonging to these communities represent their participation in the transactions. It is likely that members of these communities occasionally witnessed at least part of the ritual feasts that the elites conducted at the centers.

As other burials are discovered and excavated, more evidence will be collected relating to this topic. Results of recent research at Bragny and Bourges in eastern France, as well as at the Ipf in southern Germany (Krause 2012), suggest that these sites may have played roles similar to those of Mont Lassois, the Hohenasperg, and the Heuneburg. Especially with the ever-greater attention being paid to organic remains, we are likely to obtain much richer documentation in the near future. For example, traces of imported wine and of dyes for textiles have been identified (Kreuz 2012), and it is likely that traces of other imported foodstuffs will be noted in the course of future analysis.

Effects on Iron Age Europe as a Whole

At least two major purposes drove the Greeks to provide European potentates with elaborate luxury vessels as well as with more usual imports such as Attic pottery, wine, and Etruscan bronze jugs and bowls. One was to gain access to trade goods. During these centuries, the growing Greek cities were increasingly in need of foodstuffs and a variety of raw materials that included metals and supplies for their expanding shipping activity, including timber, pitch, and tar (Boardman 1999). None of these materials is likely to survive archaeologically. Tin from Cornwall has been much discussed as a likely trade item during this period, and it is mentioned in later texts; overland routes via the Seine (past Mont Lassois and Vix) and Rhône Rivers have been proposed for the transmission of tin to the shores of the Mediterranean (Ellmers 2010). Slaves were a probable trade item from temperate Europe to the Greek world (Briggs 2003; Egg 2012:177), but again, archaeological evidence is sparse. Though trade goods from temperate Europe to the Mediterranean are very difficult to recognize archaeologically, goods transported the other way are abundant, with significant new discoveries made often. They include large quantities of Attic pottery and other kinds of ceramics, Greek transport amphorae, coral, Etruscan bronze vessels, and a wide variety of ornaments (a recent summary is presented in Egg 2012).

The second purpose may well have been political connections for recruiting mercenaries to fight in Greek wars. For the fourth and third centuries BC, we have abundant textual evidence for "Celtic" mercenaries fighting with armies in Greece and in other locations in the eastern Mediterranean region (Szabó 1995). We have no direct evidence for such mercenary service in the sixth and fifth centuries BC, but there is every reason to think that it took place before it came to be mentioned in texts.

Effects on the Greek World

Very little consideration has been given to the effects that the Iron Age peoples of temperate Europe had on the Greek "colonizers," a similar issue to the one addressed by Cipolla in this volume. Traditionally it has been assumed that the prehistoric Europeans were eager to borrow from the more complex civilization, but no serious efforts have been made to examine the other side of the interaction. Yet in every cross-cultural interaction, all parties are affected. A major impediment to investigating this issue is the dearth of objects from temperate Europe that have been recovered in Greek contexts. But I suspect that a thorough search of materials recovered archaeologically at the Greek colony of Massalia and the surrounding settlements would yield such evidence. Also, a full examination of Greek architecture, foodstuffs, and material culture in the colonial settings could provide information about effects of the interactions on the colonists. Such investigations could yield exciting results, but the subject is beyond the scope of this paper.

The Larger Context

The appearance during the sixth and early fifth centuries BC of the special vessels from Greek workshops and of the architectural features noted above happened in the context of two important and interrelated larger-scale processes. One was Greek colonization—the establishment of colonial centers in many coastal regions throughout the Mediterranean basin between 800 and 500 BC (Boardman 1999). Closest to the west-central European centers was the colony of Massalia, on the site of the modern city of Marseille, founded about 600 BC by Greeks from the city of Phocaea on the Aegean coast of Asia Minor (Dietler 2010:104–111). The chronological congruence of the founding and growth of Massalia on the coast and the arrival of Greek imports, including both the special objects highlighted above and the more mundane luxury imports, and the architectural features, together with the distribution of Greek objects up the Rhône valley, makes it highly probable that the majority of these objects arrived through the port of Massalia. Thus, the cultural colonization for which I am arguing here was part of a much larger expansion of Greek activity throughout the greater Mediterranean region, most of it aimed at acquiring resources.

The other was a change on an even larger scale. Christopher Ehret (2002) and W. V. Harris (2007) argue that fundamental political and economic changes took place during the final millennium BC in the greater Mediterranean world, including the coastal regions of the Near East and North Africa. A result of these changes was a shift in the principal driver of trade from potentates to merchants. Rather than carrying out commercial ventures at the behest of and for the benefit of kings, queens, and other rulers, merchants were increasingly working for their own gain (Fletcher 2012; Hodos 2009). The cultural colonization for which I argue needs to be considered in the context of the large-scale social, political, and economic changes that were taking place throughout much of Eurasia and the greater Mediterranean region.

An important effect of the opening of temperate Europe to the larger world beyond was political and social change on the continent. The centers of Early Iron Age Europe, including Mont Lassois, the Heuneburg, and the Hohenasperg, declined in importance during the fifth century BC. The very rich burials declined in number and in richness. There was an overall decrease in the numbers of imported objects from the Greek world to enter into central regions of temperate Europe.

But at the same time, the adoption of a new style of design and ornament indicates that the communities in Europe were becoming more integrated into the larger world of Eurasia (a full discussion is found in Wells 2012, chapters 11 and 12). Men from central Europe became involved as mercenaries in armies of Greece and other regions of the east Mediterranean, a phenomenon well documented for the fourth and third centuries BC. This growing interaction with the societies of the Mediterranean world soon resulted in other fundamental changes, including the introduction of coinage in the late fourth and third centuries BC (Allen and Nash 1980).

The cultural colonization by Greek mercantile interests of west-central Europe in the sixth and early fifth centuries BC thus had immediate effects in changing the cultural behavior of elites and other groups in that region and long-term effects in contributing to the expansion of European contacts, commerce, and outlook in the much larger world. The expansion of activity involving trade, mercenary service, and other kinds of movement, stimulated at least in part by the Greek cultural colonization of European elites in the late sixth and early fifth centuries BC, resulted in much closer connections among communities in temperate Europe and those of the Mediterranean region and even farther afield in the Near East and Eurasia during the subsequent centuries of the Iron Age. Although no direct reference to this Greek colonial activity of the sixth and fifth centuries BC is known from Roman written sources, Rome's expansion northward into western and central Europe was greatly aided by the interactions that had become a regular part of life during the second half of the final millennium BC.

Afterlife in Renaissance and Modern Europe and America

Since the Renaissance of the fifteenth century and even more so since the Enlightenment of the eighteenth, educated Europeans have been fascinated with the culture of ancient Greece (Dietler 2005; Wilton-Ely 2013). Classical archaeology emerged as a field of study in Germany in the 1760s, and from 1875, German archaeological teams undertook major excavations at Olympia, Pergamon, and other ancient Greek sites (Dyson 2006:1, 115).

For English aristocrats, the Grand Tour of the eighteenth and nineteenth centuries brought travelers into direct contact with Greek material remains—both architecture and portable objects such as pottery and bronze vessels—in the Greek colonial cities of southern Italy. Byron wrote poetry about Greece, and Keats evoked the glories of ancient Greece as reflected through its material culture in the British Museum—Attic pottery ("Ode on a Grecian Urn") and the Parthenon sculptures ("On Seeing the Elgin Marbles") (discussion in Beard 2002:16).

Scholars in England (Jenkins 2003) and Germany (Marchand 1996) felt that Greek objects provided models of aesthetic beauty. The passion for things Greek is plainly evident in modern Europe and America, particularly in the architecture of governmental buildings, museums, educational institutions, and banks (Galinsky 1992).

Effects Today

The effects of cultural colonization can be recognized in responses on the part of scholars and the public to the ongoing revelation of the intensive interactions between Early Iron Age centers of west-central Europe and Greek and Etruscan communities of the Mediterranean region. Since the 1950s, when Attic pottery and Greek amphorae were found in the settlement layers at the Heuneburg and the enormous ornate krater and other imports were recovered in the Vix grave, a transformation has taken place in thinking about the character of the Iron Age in Europe and thus about the identity of modern Europeans with respect to their ancestral past.

This change is well reflected in major syntheses about the Iron Age. In three fundamental works of the 1920s, Moritz Hoernes's *Urgeschichte der bildenden Kunst in Europa von den Anfängen bis um 500 vor Christi* (1925), Joseph Déchelette's *Manuel d'archéologie préhistorique, celtique et gallo-romaine III: Premier age du Fer ou époque de Hallstatt* (1927), and V. Gordon Childe's *The Danube in Prehistory* (1929), Greek and Etruscan imports found in Early Iron Age temperate Europe are mentioned but without systematic consideration of how their arrival might have affected economic, social, and ideological developments. In more recent treatments like *The Celts,* edited by Sabatino Moscati et al. (1991), and *Die Welt der Kelten: Zentren der Macht—Kostbarkeiten der Kunst,* edited by Denise Beilharz et al. (2012), numerous articles focus on the imports and on the dynamics of interaction between members of the different societies. The works situate these phenomena in the context of Europe rapidly becoming a much more active participant in the configurations of the wider world from the fifth century BC onward (Bowersock 2013).

The long-term consequences of (cultural) colonialism referred to by Hayes and Cipolla (this volume) are clear in the case of temperate Europe. The colonial experience of the elites of the sixth and early fifth centuries BC was followed by an opening up of the interior of the continent to contacts and interactions with peoples elsewhere—in the Mediterranean basin, the Near East, and beyond—to an extent much greater than at any time previously. From the fifth century BC on, the societies of temperate Europe became intensively involved in the economic and political affairs of the rest of Eurasia, and this situation has persisted to the present day.

Richard Hingley (this volume) raises the interesting question of whether modern populations of Britain regard the Roman occupation of Britain as a good thing or a bad thing. For the case I explore in this chapter, we as archaeologists do not know enough yet to judge whether the cultural colonization of the Early Iron Age societies by Greek interests was on balance good or bad. It will be interesting to see what results Hingley obtains from his study about modern British attitudes to the Roman conquest and occupation and, in the more distant future, to see what future generations make of the Greek cultural colonization of Early Iron Age Europe.

References Cited

Allen, Derek F., and Daphne Nash
1980   *The Coins of the Ancient Celts.* Edinburgh University Press, Edinburgh.
Baitinger, Holger
1996   Ein Trinkhorn aus dem späthallstattzeitlichen Prunkgrab Asperg "Grafenbühl," Kr. Ludwigsburg? *Archäologisches Korrespondenzblatt* 26:173–177.
Beard, Mary
2002   *The Parthenon.* Profile Books, London.
Beilharz, Denise, and Dirk Krausse
2012   Symbole der Macht: Repräsentation in frühkeltischer Zeit. In *Die Welt der Kelten: Zentren der Macht—Kostbarkeiten der Kunst,* edited by Denise Beilharz, Thomas Hoppe, Dirk Krausse, Felix Müller, and Caroline von Nicolai, pp. 187–199. Jan Thorbecke Verlag, Ostfildern, Germany.

Beilharz, Denise, Thomas Hoppe, Dirk Krausse, Felix Müller, and Caroline von Nicolai (editors)
2012 *Die Welt der Kelten: Zentren der Macht—Kostbarkeiten der Kunst.* Jan Thorbecke Verlag, Ostfildern, Germany.

Biel, Jörg
1985 *Der Keltenfürst von Hochdorf.* Konrad Theiss Verlag, Stuttgart.

Biel, Jörg, and Ines Balzer
2012 Fürstensitz und mehr: Der Hohenasperg. In *Die Welt der Kelten: Zentren der Macht—Kostbarkeiten der Kunst,* edited by Denise Beilharz, Thomas Hoppe, Dirk Krausse, Felix Müller, and Caroline von Nicolai, pp. 139–144. Jan Thorbecke Verlag, Ostfildern, Germany.

Boardman, John
1990 Symposium Furniture. In *Sympotica: A Symposium of the Symposium,* edited by Oswyn Murray, pp. 122–131. Clarendon Press, Oxford, England.
1999 *The Greeks Overseas: Their Early Colonies and Trade.* Thames and Hudson, New York.

Bonfante, Larissa
2011 The Etruscans: Mediators between Northern Barbarians and Classical Civilization. In *The Barbarians of Ancient Europe: Realities and Interactions,* edited by Larissa Bonfante, pp. 233–281. Cambridge University Press, New York.

Bouzek, Jan, and Zdenek Smrž
1994 Drei Fragmente attischer Keramik aus Droužkovice in Nordwestböhmen. *Germania* 72:581–86.

Bowersock, Glen W.
2013 Review of *The Axial Age and Its Consequences,* edited by Robert N. Bellah and Hans Joas. *New York Review of Books,* May 9, 2013, pp. 56–58.

Braund, David
1984 *Rome and the Friendly King: The Character of the Client Kingship.* St. Martin's Press, New York.

Briggs, Daphne
2003 Metals, Salt, and Slaves: Economic Links between Gaul and Italy from the Eighth to the Late Sixth Centuries BC. *Oxford Journal of Archaeology* 22(3):243–59.

Burkhardt, Nadin
2010 Die Lehmziegelmauer der Heuneburg im mediterranen Vergleich. In *"Fürstensitze" und Zentralorte der frühen Kelten,* part II, edited by Dirk Krausse and Denise Beilharz, pp. 29–50. Konrad Theiss Verlag, Stuttgart.

Chaume, Bruno, Norbert Nieszery, and Walter Reinhard
2011 Le bâtiment palatial du mont Saint-Marcel: The House of the Rising Sun. In *Le complexe aristocratique de Vix: Nouvelles recherches sur l'habitat, le système de fortification et l'environnement du mont Lassois,* edited by Bruno Chaume and Claude Mordant, 2:795–838. Éditions Universitaires de Dijon, Dijon, France.
2012 Ein frühkeltischer Fürstensitz im Burgund: Der Mont Lassois. In *Die Welt der Kelten: Zentren der Macht—Kostbarkeiten der Kunst,* edited by Denise Beilharz,

Thomas Hoppe, Dirk Krausse, Felix Müller, and Caroline von Nicolai, pp. 132–138. Jan Thorbecke Verlag, Ostfildern, Germany.

Childe, Vere Gordon
1929 *The Danube in Prehistory.* Clarendon Press, Oxford, England.

Cicolani, Veronica
2012 Offene Handelsplätze, offener Warenaustausch: Weite Wege für Waren. In *Die Welt der Kelten: Zentren der Macht—Kostbarkeiten der Kunst,* edited by Denise Beilharz, Thomas Hoppe, Dirk Krausse, Felix Müller, and Caroline von Nicolai, pp. 180–182. Jan Thorbecke Verlag, Ostfildern, Germany.

Déchelette, Joseph
1927 *Manuel d'archéologie préhistorique, celtique et gallo-romaine* III: *Premier age du Fer ou époque de Hallstatt.* Editions Auguste Picard, Paris.

Dietler, Michael
2005 The Archaeology of Colonization and the Colonization of Archaeology: Theoretical Challenges from an Ancient Mediterranean Colonial Encounter. In *The Archaeology of Colonial Encounters: Comparative Perspectives,* edited by Gil Stein, pp. 33–68. School of American Research Press, Santa Fe, New Mexico.
2010 *Archaeologies of Colonialism: Consumption, Entanglement, and Violence in Ancient Mediterranean France.* University of California Press, Berkeley.

Domínguez, Adolfo J.
2002 Greeks in Iberia: Colonialism without Colonization. In *The Archaeology of Colonialism,* edited by Claire L. Lyons and John K. Papadopoulos, pp. 65–95. Getty Research Institute, Los Angeles.

Dyson, Stephen L.
2006 *In Pursuit of Ancient Pasts: A History of Classical Archaeology in the Nineteenth and Twentieth Centuries.* Yale University Press, New Haven, Connecticut.

Egg, Marcus
2012 Kontaktzone: Transalpine Beziehungen und benachbarte Hochkulturen. In *Die Welt der Kelten: Zentren der Macht—Kostbarkeiten der Kunst,* edited by Denise Beilharz, Thomas Hoppe, Dirk Krausse, Felix Müller, and Caroline von Nicolai, pp. 171–177. Jan Thorbecke Verlag, Ostfildern, Germany.

Ehret, Christopher
2002 *The Civilizations of Africa: A History to 1800.* University of Virginia Press, Charlottesville.

Ellmers, Detlev
2010 Der Krater von Vix und der Reisebericht des Pytheas von Massalia—Reisen griechischer Kaufleute über die Rhône nach Britannien im 6.-4. Jahrhundert v. Chr. *Archäologisches Korrespondenzblatt* 40:363–381.

Fischer, Jutta
1990 Zu einer griechischen Kline und weiteren Südimporten aus dem Fürstengrabhügel Grafenbühl, Asperg, Kr. Ludwigsburg. *Germania* 68:115–127.

Fletcher, Richard Nathan
2012 Opening the Mediterranean: Assyria, the Levant, and the Transformation of Early Iron Age Trade. *Antiquity* 86:211–220.

Galinsky, Karl
1992   *Classical and Modern Interactions: Postmodern Architecture, Multiculturalism, Decline, and Other Issues.* University of Texas Press, Austin.

Grübel, Tamara, Alfred Haffer, Angela Mötsch, and Ulrich Müller
2011   Étude des structures du grand bâtiment absidial. In *Le complexe aristocratique de Vix: Nouvelles recherches sur l'habitat, le système de fortification et l'environnement du mont Lassois,* edited by Bruno Chaume and Claude Mordant, 2:385–428. Éditions Universitaires de Dijon, Dijon, France.

Halsall, Guy
2001   Childeric's Grave, Clovis' Succession, and the Origins of the Merovingian Kingdom. In *Society and Culture in Late Antique Gaul,* edited by Ralph W. Mathisen and Danuta Shanzer, pp. 116–133. Ashgate, Aldershot, England.

Hansen, Leif, and Elke Böhr
2011   Ein seltener Fund aus Westhofen (Lkr. Alzey-Worms): Fragment einer attischen Trinkschale. *Archäologisches Korrespondenzblatt* 41:213–230.

Harris, William V.
2007   The Late Republic. In *The Cambridge Economic History of the Greco-Roman World,* edited by Walter Scheidel, Ian Morris, and Richard Saller, pp. 511–539. Cambridge University Press, Cambridge, England.

Herodotus
1946   Translated by A. D. Godley. Harvard University Press, Cambridge.

Hodos, Tamar
2009   Colonial Engagements in the Global Mediterranean Iron Age. *Cambridge Archaeological Journal* 19:221–241.

Hoernes, Moritz
1925   *Urgeschichte der bildenden Kunst in Europa von den Anfängen bis um 500 vor Christi.* 3rd edition. Kunstverlag Anton Schroll, Vienna.

Jenkins, Ian
2003   Ideas of Antiquity: Classical and Other Civilizations in the Age of Enlightenment. In *Enlightenment: Discovering the World in the Eighteenth Century,* edited by Kim Sloan, pp. 168–177. British Museum Press, London.

Krause, Rüdiger
2012   Zentralort und Machtzentrum: Der Ipf im Nördlinger Ries. In *Die Welt der Kelten: Zentren der Macht—Kostbarkeiten der Kunst,* edited by Denise Beilharz, Thomas Hoppe, Dirk Krausse, Felix Müller, and Caroline von Nicolai, pp. 146–153. Jan Thorbecke Verlag, Ostfildern, Germany.

Krausse, Dirk
1996   *Hochdorf III: Das Trink- und Speiseservice aus dem späthallstattzeitlichen Fürstengrab von Eberdingen-Hochdorf (Kr. Ludwigsburg).* Konrad Theiss Verlag, Stuttgart.

Krausse, Dirk, and Manuel Fernández-Götz
2012   Die Heuneburg: Neue Forschungen zur Entwicklung einer späthallstattzeitlichen Stadt. In *Die Welt der Kelten: Zentren der Macht—Kostbarkeiten der Kunst,*

edited by Denise Beilharz, Thomas Hoppe, Dirk Krausse, Felix Müller, and Caroline von Nicolai, pp. 116–123. Jan Thorbecke Verlag, Ostfildern, Germany.

Kreuz, A.
2012 Von Ackerbau und Viehzucht: Landwirtschaft und Ernährung. In *Die Welt der Kelten: Zentren der Macht—Kostbarkeiten der Kunst*, edited by Denise Beilharz, Thomas Hoppe, Dirk Krausse, Felix Müller, and Caroline von Nicolai, pp. 78–82. Jan Thorbecke Verlag, Ostfildern, Germany.

Marchand, Suzanne L.
1996 *Down from Olympus: Archaeology and Philhellenism in Germany, 1750–1970*. Princeton University Press, Princeton, New Jersey.

Michálek, Jan
1992 Eine mediterrane Glasscherbe aus Südböhmen-ČSFR. *Germania* 70:123–126.

Moscati, Sabatino, Otto-Herman Frey, Venceslas Kruta, Barry Raftery, and Miklós Szabó (editors)
1991 *The Celts*. Rizzoli, New York.

Mötsch, Angela, Alfred Haffner, and Ulrich Müller
2011 Le grand bâtiment à abside—Réflexions sur sa genèse et sa fonction. In *Le complexe aristocratique de Vix: Nouvelles recherches sur l'habitat, le système de fortification et l'environnement du mont Lassois*. 2 vols., edited by Bruno Chaume and Claude Mordant, pp. 773–794. Éditions Universitaires de Dijon, Dijon, France.

Murray, Oswyn (editor)
1990 *Sympotica: A Symposium on the Symposion*. Oxford University Press, New York.

Needham, Stuart, Andrew J. Lawson, and Ann Woodward
2010 "A Noble Group of Barrows": Bush Barrow and the Normanton Down Early Bronze Age Cemetery Two Centuries On. *Antiquaries Journal* 90:1–39.

Peška, Jaroslav, and Jaroslav Tejral
2002 *Das germanische Königsgrab von Mušov in Mähren*. 3 vols. Verlag des Römisch-Germanischen Zentralmuseums, Mainz.

Rolley, Claude (editor)
2003 *La tombe princière de Vix*. 2 vols. Picard, Paris.

Schussmann, Markus
2012 Die armen Vettern im Osten: Bayern und Franken. In *Die Welt der Kelten: Zentren der Macht—Kostbarkeiten der Kunst*, edited by Denise Beilharz, Thomas Hoppe, Dirk Krausse, Felix Müller, and Caroline von Nicolai, pp. 155–156. Jan Thorbecke Verlag, Ostfildern, Germany.

Steffen, Markus
2012 Komplexe Zentren nördlich der Alpen: Die Entstehung der Fürstensitze. In *Die Welt der Kelten: Zentren der Macht—Kostbarkeiten der Kunst*, edited by Denise Beilharz, Thomas Hoppe, Dirk Krausse, Felix Müller, and Caroline von Nicolai, pp. 94–97. Jan Thorbecke Verlag, Ostfildern, Germany.

Stein, Gil
2002 Colonies without Colonialism: A Trade Diaspora Model of Fourth Millennium BC Mesopotamian Enclaves in Anatolia. In *The Archaeology of Colonialism*, ed-

ited by Claire L. Lyons and John K. Papadopoulos, pp. 27–64. Getty Research Institute, Los Angeles.

Szabó, Miklós

1995   Guerriers celtiques avant et après Delphes: Contribution à une période critique de monde celtique. In *L'Europe celtique du Ve au IIIe siècle avant J.-C.: Contacts, echanges et mouvements de populations*, edited by Jean-Jacques Charpy, pp. 49–67. Kronos B. Y. Editions, Sceaux, France.

Wehgartner, Irma

1995   Das Symposion. In *Luxusgeschirr keltischer Fürsten—Griechische Keramik nördlich der Alpen*, edited by Irma Wehgartner and Helge Zöller, pp. 25–31. Mainfränkisches Museum, Würzburg, Germany.

Wells, Peter S.

1987   Sociopolitical Change and Core-Periphery Interactions: An Example from Early Iron Age Europe. In *Polities and Partitions: Human Boundaries and the Growth of Complex Societies*, edited by Kathryn M. Trinkaus, pp. 141–155. Arizona State University, Tempe.

2008   *Image and Response in Early Europe*. Duckworth, London.

2012   *How Ancient Europeans Saw the World: Vision, Patterns, and the Shaping of the Mind in Prehistoric Times*. Princeton University Press, Princeton, New Jersey.

Wilton-Ely, John

2013   Paestum and the Greek Revival. In *Piranesi, Paestum and Soane*. Prestel, Munich.

Zürn, Hartwig

1970   Der "Grafenbühl" bei Asperg, Kr. Ludwigsburg. In *Hallstattforschungen in Nordwürttemberg: Die Grabhügel von Asperg (Kr. Ludwigsburg), Hirschlanden (Kr. Leonberg) und Mühlacker (Kr. Vaihingen)*, edited by Hartwig Zürn, pp. 7–51. Verlag Müller and Gräff, Stuttgart.

6

Colonial Encounters, Time, and Social Innovation

PER CORNELL

In a wider colonial setting, there are often certain settlements outside the area of direct colonial control or where the colonial control is weak. This kind of settlement ought to be of particular interest, but there are surprisingly few in-depth studies of this phenomenon. This kind of settlement has been difficult to handle in scholarly research for many reasons but in part because they are often, it seems, difficult to find. Several tricky questions arise that concern archaeologists' abilities to argue about and characterize such sites. It will thus be of necessity to dwell on intricate and complex theoretical issues, which are, in the end, related to very palpable questions about social life. How should these kinds of "indigenous" contexts be addressed? Are they simply "backward" and rather irrelevant in a wider social process, or do they have wider implications? This chapter consists of some theoretical and methodological discussion, illustrated by a brief consideration of an Iron Age Mediterranean case and a more extensive examination of a case from the Americas.

Thinking History and the Colonial Project

In addressing the colonial context, it is important to look at and compare different kinds of colonial projects. The basic premise is that we have at least two separate "formations," which enter into some kind of encounter. When we talk about a colonial situation, this encounter is never symmetrical, and in most cases it will involve a substantial amount of conflict, abuse, and exploitation. In certain cases, it will even be a question of complete or almost complete annihilation of people in one of the formations involved. However, in most cases there will remain a substantial population in the colonized area. In the following, this latter kind of colonial context is under discussion. Even if there is a high degree of variability prior to the moment of colonization, the asymmetrical relations established in colonial encounters will tend to create two separate entities, of which one is the conquered and one is the conqueror. In the case of the European colonization of the Americas, just to take one important example, the concept of the Indian was created (Bonfil Batalla 1992; Cabrera Vargas 1995), which gave a certain minimal common denominator to all those conquered, who previously, in many cases, had no or little contact which each other. Within this generality, however, there remains a lot of variability, and the colonial process at the same time introduces new categories that correspond to palpable realities of the colonial world (Mrozowski, Hayes, and Hancock 2007).

The Argentine historian Chiaramonte, in discussing historical concepts and the history of Latin America in 1983, saw major problems in the available theories of social forms and colonial projects. Much of the perspective he criticized is still in use in addressing problems like the expansion of the Roman Empire or European states, slavery, feudalism, or capitalism. One line of research has tended to stress the feudal character of many colonies, such as those in Latin America. Carmagnani's study from 1976 is a good example, in which the dualism between the feudal form and "communitarian" models is in focus. In certain ways his discussion resembles a certain type of "Asiatic mode of production" (Sofri 1969; Spivak 1999).

Fernand Braudel (1967), on the other hand, discussed the relation between capitalism and basic structures in varied areas in his global studies. This idea of a division between certain basic structures related to natural environments and demographics on one hand and the spheres of exchange and politics on the other is still frequently quoted. The basic structures were fairly stable and changed slowly, while exchange and politics had the potential for an accelerated rhythm. Braudel was certainly correct in insisting on the importance of the "basic structures," but his perspective is somewhat difficult to relate to these different levels of social structures, and his definitions of the basic structures are at times hard to follow. One example is his discussion of Andean pre-Hispanic farmers as hoe cultivators. Braudel based his characterization on one singular artifact, the *taccla* or "foot-plough," not considering their advanced hydraulic technology and terracing (Braudel 1967:121–128; Cornell 1988:18).

Scholars like Wallerstein (1974–1980) and Frank (1979) stressed the capitalist nature of the Latin American colonies. Undoubtedly these thinkers have demonstrated the relevance of important global processes and exploitation affecting social and daily life in depth. But their analyses tend to look at the expansion of Europe as a one-sided affair in which indigenous people of the colonies did not contribute anything significant in terms of social structure. Further, their use of the term "capitalism" is all too general and actually of little operative value.

Robert Brenner (1993) criticizes the views of scholars like Wallerstein, insisting on the importance of looking at particular histories of European countries in order to explain the historical development in "the center." Brenner's discussion on London and merchants in the sixteenth century is very stimulating despite its limitations, since he does link colonial developments to those of the center. Another main type of critique comes from historians in Latin America insisting on the importance of decolonizing the continent, largely by looking closer at its pre-Hispanic past (Colombres 1977). In the more extreme versions of such a perspective, the writing of the history of the colonial period is, by definition, a colonial act.

In this chapter, I argue that there may be, in certain cases, quite active indigenous projects, perhaps even a kind of process of social innovation among the colonized. This is not to deny the horrors of conquest or the destructive effects of exploitation. Traditional discussions of colonialism have only addressed the power of the colonizer. When the colonized are addressed, they are mainly framed as victims of a history to which they contributed little or nothing. It is necessary to look at the colonized as having a history that is almost never reduced to being exploited by the colonizer. Thus, in this chapter I largely follow the line of research discussed in Ferreira and Funari (this volume). I also agree with Mrozowski, Gould, and Law Pezzarossi (this volume) that prehistory has become a destructive concept. While "prehistory" had a kind of liberating force in the nineteenth century by identifying new parts of the past, it has become a problematic term, establishing a dividing line between the truly civilized and those less civilized.

Subaltern Life and the Question of History

Hayes (this volume) interestingly problematizes concepts like "diaspora" and "indigeneity." There are varied positions on these complex issues within the field of postcolonial debate. To briefly summarize, scholars like Gayatri Chakravorty Spivak (1999) stress the difficulty of communicating between the colonized and the colonizer, as she summarizes in her famous words, "the subaltern cannot speak." Homi Bhabha (1994) has a somewhat different position, in which there may be a kind of "third space of enunciation" with room for communication between the colonized and the colonizer, albeit through indirect means; it is not necessarily based on an actual understanding but rather on observations about sociocultural effects.

The evident question arising from the postcolonial debate is certainly one concerning the question of what history could be. If there were no communication, as Spivak asserts, it would be difficult or at least not easy and straightforward to write a unified history for the colonial period. If there can be a general history—and I am inclined to think there is—it must include conflict, difference, and variability as parts of the historical process. However, the logistics of such a history should not be limited to one set of actors or social settings, but rather it should focus on the results of interactions or lack of interactions among different social settings.

I do believe concepts like feudalism and capitalism may have a value in understanding certain kinds of colonial settings such as those of the Americas in the sixteenth and seventeenth centuries. I even think these concepts may correspond to particular processual tendencies (Bois 1976; Godelier 1972; Roskams 2006; Wickham 2007). But these tendencies operate on a complex range of settings that cannot be reduced to these processes and instead correspond to aspects of these settings. I am referring to something similar to the idea of critical temporalities, discussed by Hayes and Cipolla (this volume).

Thus, we must be prepared to find other kinds of social realities that may constitute entities that escape most of the present theoretical concepts that archaeologists typically draw upon. The French philosopher Jacques Derrida, who developed interesting discussions on the concept of time and the Other, has urged us to remember that it is not sufficient to make a repository of catalogued examples. There is in his discussion a difference between the other as defined as something of a potential enemy and the Other as the unknown, what we do not know (Derrida 1967, 2000). What he addresses is the unexpected—*l'objet trouvé*—and the continued relevance of such unexpected encounters and their importance for any historical development (Marder 2009).

Archaeology and the Trace

In *Chora L Works,* Derrida, speaking with architects, states, "When I speak of writing or texts usually I insist that I don't just refer to writing words on the page, for me building is the writing of a text. I call this writing, and I call this text" (Derrida and Eisenman 1997:112). Derrida argues at length about traces in relation to communication and of the importance of a broad concept of communication based on the idea of effect rather than deep understanding. These traces are not about absolute origin but rather a condition for communication. Derrida's insistence about time is relevant for archaeologists, and the question of "spatialized time" (1965–1966; also Cornell and Nilsson 2011) offers fascinating perspectives.

Inspired by the archaeologist Leroi-Gourhan, Derrida discusses cave art in terms of advanced communication across time (Derrida 1965–1966, 2000), almost at the limit of deconstruction, in the Derridean way. Similarly, I suggest that we must be prepared to find evidence of an unknown Other in relation to the colonial setting, inside or outside the immediate realm of the power of the empire. It is in the encounter with these "mute" objects, lacking an evident signature, that the Other human social setting and the Thing (in Derrida's terms) is closest to us, and it is a true moment in which an impossible event of the Other can occur. When it comes to history, there is the rest, the cinder, and it is the officially vomited (but not at all irrelevant) part of history. It is what comes close to the "Thing," to the "real thing" (Marder 2009). But what we may encounter are merely traces, never the authentic past preserved in a bottle, a point of utmost importance.

Spanish Colonial Settlements in the Americas

In order to discuss indigenous settlements in colonial America, it will help to briefly discuss Spanish settlements. Here, I am dealing with the Spanish conquest of the "New World," which was a very violent historical process, with the eventual establishment of a complex stratification and distinct elite with particular social forms (Mörner 1983; Zúñiga 1999). It involved warfare, general brutality, and exploitation as well as the introduction of a set of diseases, all of which resulted in massive mortality. However, the results of the Spanish conquest varied considerably among regions in America. In a sense, looking from the perspective of the Spanish Crown, the conquest of the *altiplano* of Mexico was one of the most productive. In this area, several of the pre-Hispanic urban settlements were transformed into Spanish cities. Thus, Tenochtitlán became what is today the center of Mexico City, and parts of the structure of the old settlements are still present in the modern city (Calnek 1972; González Aragón 1993; also Sanders 1971). The Spanish conquest of this area was followed by a sharp decline in population. Cattle, nonexistent prior to the Spanish conquest, were imported, and by 1560 there were more head of cattle than indigenous people. This region became a center of the Spanish colonies. There were also special experiments such as the utopian settlements for indigenous populations created by Vasco de Quiroga in Michoacan (McAndrew 1965:621–649; Zavala 1941).

In contrast, the conquest of the Maya area was considerably more difficult for the colonizer (overviews of colonial Maya are presented in Andrews 1984, Farris 1984, and García Targa 1995). Certain areas of Yucatan became relatively prosperous with some commercial centers, and several large indigenous sites even increased in population by the end of the sixteenth century (Quezada 1993:430). In other areas, the conquest was difficult; the last Maya stronghold was taken only by the end of the seventeenth century.

The region of what is Quintana Roo today, in Caribbean Mexico, was densely inhabited and urbanized prior to the conquest; there, the Spaniards failed to construct a stable occupation. The population of this region declined quickly, and only small enclaves were inhabited by 1600. At least part of the explanation for this quick decline is related to intentional migration of the local population out of the area dominated by Spaniards. The region remained almost empty for several centuries (Velázquez 2011). The reasons are many for these differences in outcome of the Spanish conquest in different areas. In part they are related to differences in natural environment. It can also be argued that they are partially related to different kinds of pre-Hispanic urban forms. The urban character in Tenochtitlán resembled a dense urban setting in Spain to some extent, while the urban pattern in the Maya area was less dense and more like an urban region than an urban center (Nalda 1998, 2010).

In the South American Andes, there were a number of urban settlements in the pre-Hispanic period, but the more general scenario was a widely dispersed settlement pattern of a large number of small entities. The Spanish administration sought systematically to create larger settlement units and urban centers, but this political agenda largely failed. Even when the population was brought to an urban context by force, people tended to leave the new settlements at the first opportunity. It was not until the eighteenth century that the populations of the new settlements grew and prospered (Spalding 1984; Stern 1984). A very special kind of large settlement site resulted from the entry of Jesuits in the La Plata region, which had its own, very particular history (Mörner 1953).

The towns first established by the Spanish Crown in the New World were mainly fortifications or missionary stations. Established in hastily chosen areas, the first cities were rather fortified campsites that did not survive for long. Their internal structures were probably more similar to the Spanish medieval winding streets than to the regularly planned ones that came to be the norm (Watters 2001). During the 1530s and 1540s, the Spanish Crown expanded rapidly, resulting in more than one hundred cities established before the 1550s (Hardoy 1978; Socolow and Johnson 1981). It was also during the 1530s that the model of the Spanish American colonial city reached a format, a physical form, that in the majority of cases was repeated until long after the colonial period with no major modification (Kubler 1978; Rose-Redwood 2008). This Spanish-American grid-plan pattern in some ways represents a new type of urban form.

While planned elements and parts of towns are visible in earlier cities—for example, camps and cities in the Roman Empire and European Renaissance cities, at times with a grid pattern—the Spanish-American colonial town is the first fully systematic application of the grid in planning a large number of towns. Renaissance ideas and practices—but also other experience from European towns, which had a wide variety of layouts—were certainly brought to Latin America. But equally important in this context is the influence from pre-Spanish traditions in the Americas. It seems the Spanish Crown often established cities on top of existing Indian settlements and cities, and these pre-Spanish urban formations had an influence on the general outlines and street grids of the Spanish towns (Markman 1978; Socolow and Johnson 1981; Stanislawski 1947). Both the colonizers' own ideas and conceptions of what a city should be and the kinds of pre-Spanish urban forms the conquistadors met had effects on the structural outcomes of the cities. A well-known case is Tenochtitlán, a city based on rectangular units, almost a grid plan (González Aragón 1993), which also exhibited an enormous central plaza. The Nürnberg-born artist and thinker Albrecht Dürer, for example, used it as an inspiration in his ideal city plan. This is actually the case of an idea from indigenous settlement planning, a particular innovation, that exercised a certain influence over Europe and European practices. In part based on the impact of Tenochtitlán, the Spanish early modern town project in Latin America created a new standard that had effects on town planning in Europe.

Some rules about ordered cities seem to have been applied from the beginning, like the 1513 "instructions" from which Pedrarias Dávila built the gridded Panama City in 1519 (Gasparini 1991). Nevertheless, the rules and instructions about the grid, the royal ordinances, the "decrees on population" did not show up officially documented until signed by Philip II in 1573. The Laws of the Indies were put forward in 1681. Both of these ordinances were composed and written when most of the first colonial cities were already established and after some practical experience of the continent and city planning had been gained (Hardoy 1978). Systematic ideas, rules, and guidelines about how to perform this gigantic project of urbanization were therefore formulated after contact with different pre-European urban forms in the Americas.

Indigenous Populations outside Direct Colonial Control

A large part of the indigenous population connected to the Spaniards lived at sites outside immediate colonial control, but these settlements were rarely recorded in writing. In the case of El Pichao in the sub-Andean Calchaqui valleys in northwestern Argentina (map 6.1), the preconquest site is fairly large for the period and region in question, distributed over more than 100 hectares in a mountainous area with differences of more than 300 meters in altitude within the site (STucTav5). Field seasons from 1989 to 2004 were conducted as a multidisciplinary, binational project between Argentina and Sweden (Bengtsson et al. 2001; Cornell 1993; Cornell and Sjödin 1990, 1991; Medina and Cornell 2010). Remains of several buildings are still visible in the terrain, and there seem to have been more than sixty large habitation units in use during the fifteenth century. The archaeological assemblage is distinct and particular. The so-called Santa María urn is a salient feature, with a decoration corresponding to a human figure (DeMarrais 2001; Nastri 2008; Tarragó 2000). The remains of the habitation units are fairly large, often consisting of a large enclosure with dimensions of 600 square meters and several smaller structures

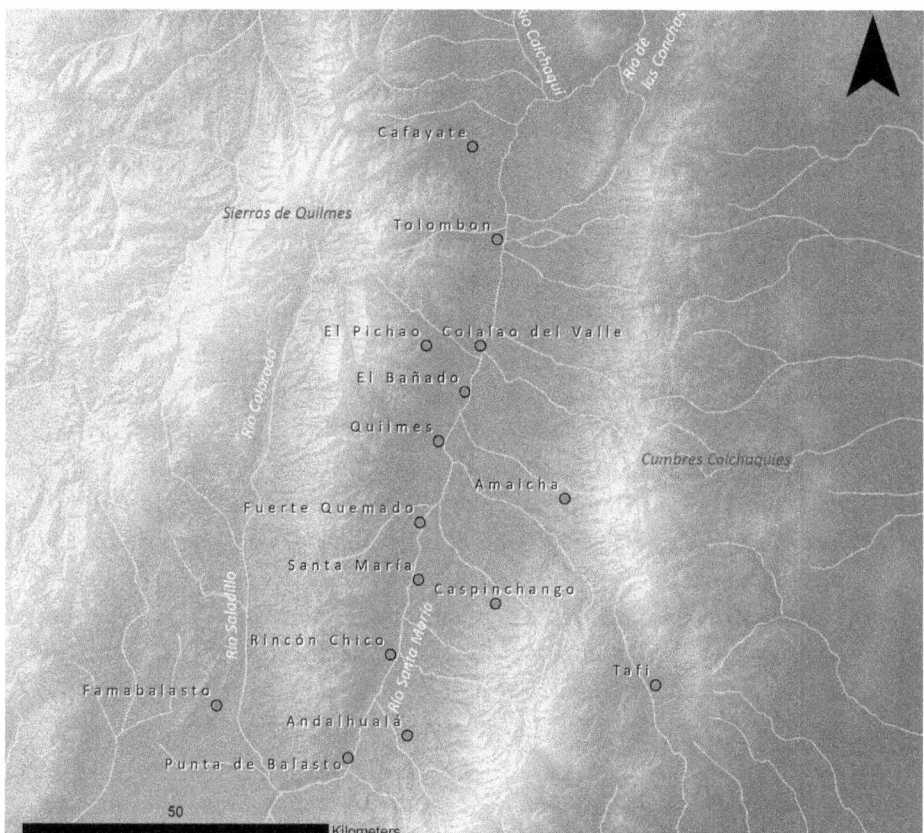

Map 6.1. Major sites in the southern Calchaqui highland valley, northwestern Argentina. Map produced as an open source by Per Cornell and Per Stenborg and graphically enhanced by Rich Potter in a project financed by the Swedish Research Council (VR) in collaboration with the Instituto de Arqueología, Universidad Nacional de Tucumán (its name at the time), Argentina.

linked to it. The walls are often double stone walls with a dirt filling between them. The domestic units in the core areas of Inca habitation are much smaller (the largest examples are perhaps 10 by 10 meters), and in certain regions they are even smaller, as in the Huánuco Pampa region in today's Peru. Thus, the Calchaqui area exhibits particular traits that merit more consideration.

What is of particular interest in the context of this volume is the dramatic change introduced in connection to the arrival of the Spanish in the region (Cornell 2007a and Lorandi et al. 1997). Prior to the Swedish-Argentinian project at the site, archaeological remains from the sixteenth and seventeenth centuries, the early period of contact between local populations and the Spaniards, were simply not known. However, we succeeded in identifying an indigenous settlement dated to the sixteenth and seventeenth centuries, located close to the pre-Hispanic site (Cornell and Johansson 1993; Johansson 1996; Stenborg 2002; also Medina 2002). This site exhibits material traits that differ substantially from those at the pre-Hispanic site. There are certain common elements in relation to particular design patterns on ceramics of limited occurrence and also, it seems, in the physical form of burials, which is a direct continuity from pre-Hispanic traditions. In the main, however, there are many differences. The houses are smaller and more hutlike, with much simpler wall construction. One of the most frequent ceramic types of the preconquest period, brick-red ware like that of the Santa María urn, was not present. Certain types much less common at the pre-Hispanic site dominate the postcontact site, and a few types, present in low numbers, were not found at the precontact site.

Although these differences are striking, there is another short phase between these two moments at the end of the fifteenth century when the Inca established some control over the Calchaqui valley system. However, we know very little about the exact nature of this control. At the Pichao site (map 6.2), there is little or no evidence of major settlement change at the pre-Hispanic site in relation to the Inca expansion. But there are indications of alterations within certain buildings in this phase, and new types of ceramics seem to be introduced (Cornell and Galle 2004; Cornell 2007b). Thus, the local context at the time of the arrival of the Spaniards should have been already marked by some kind of social change, and the Spanish arrival in the region must be seen in light of it. From the limited written sources available for the Calchaqui valleys in the period in question, we know that the Spaniards had great difficulties in coping with this region, and it was not until the end of the seventeenth century that they finally achieved some sort of dominance. The Pichao site may correspond to what is termed a *parcialidad Pichiao* in some Spanish documents, but that term may also include the Colalao unit. Both terms appear in several documents. For instance, a Spanish document from 1670 includes Pichao and Colalao as conquered groups that were to be included in an *encomienda*, which was a large parcel of land, including its population, granted and placed under control of a Spanish colonist (AGI 1670).

Map 6.2. El Pichao sites, Argentina. Site 5 is pre-Hispanic; site 7 is a sixteenth- and seventeenth-century indigenous site. Map by Cornell, Stenborg, and Potter.

I interpret the observed differences between pre-Hispanic sites and postcontact sites as related to the direct and indirect effects of the presence of the Spanish Crown and Spanish efforts to occupy this region, which led to the disintegration of pre-Hispanic social settings. It is plausible, though it remains to be demonstrated, that diseases played a major role here, decimating the population and making social inheritance difficult. The remaining population, who may also have received people running away from the Spaniards in other regions, had to find ways to address a new social setting. The large pre-Hispanic sites were highly vulnerable to attack, and a more distributed settlement pattern evolved, situated somewhat higher up in the mountains. The large cultivated fields were abandoned to a large extent in the process, and there was an intensified orientation toward hunting wild animals and herding llama. In terms of ceramics, some of the common types in the period of Spanish contact are similar to Inca day-to-day vessels, and this may be an important cultural feature. Actually, this type of "Inca"-inspired ceramics is more common in the period of Spanish contact than ever before in this particular region. This point may have major cultural implications.

It must be stressed that the new social form described here was not a direct continuation of previous forms. What is strikingly evident is that very few elements of European culture were incorporated. In burials, only a few objects of European origin, among them Venetian pearls and a pair of iron scissors, have been unearthed. But there is no evident European influence in the layout of settlements or in other salient material features of the settlement. Here we have an interesting and important case of indigenous social innovation. The Pichao case differs strongly from the cases discussed by Cipolla (this volume) and Mrozowski, Gould, and Law Pezzarossi (this volume), in which the use of European artifacts constitutes an important element of the indigenous (Lightfoot 2005). What is perhaps most interesting in the Pichao case is that something "new" was constructed without a direct use of European objects despite the wider colonial context. As to the question of "ethnic" or cultural continuity, it seems that ethnic markers at times were stronger among groups living within the colonial realm than outside.

At the foot of the mountains, some 100 kilometers from Pichao, the Spaniards tried to found a city, San Miguel de Tucumán at Ibatín (Noli 2012). This sixteenth-century city was repeatedly attacked by indigenous populations and also located in a difficult setting close to a seasonally shifting river. Thus, in 1680 the Spaniards moved the city to the location of today's San Miguel de Tucumán under royal command (AGI 1661). Some archaeological work has been done at Ibatín. The original city was built according to a strictly orthogonal, chessboard pattern. In the material record, certain European objects figure prominently, above all varied forms of ceramics. There is also an abundance of a special type of ceramic at times called Averrias by Argentine archaeologists that was produced by indigenous populations living at Spanish settlements (Silliman 2010 presents similar examples from another region). This kind of ceramic, which looks very different from European ceramics from this period, occurs frequently at Ibatín. A small percentage of this ceramic type has been found at the contact-period site at Pichao (STucTav7). Interestingly, this may indicate some kind of interaction between indigenous populations at Spanish sites and indigenous, non-Spanish sites. Concerning the presence of various ethnic groups, there are, according to historians, various indigenous ethnicities in the Calchaqui valleys in the later colonial period. But, as Lorena Rodrígues has stressed, discussing the Atacameños from the high *altiplano* (2008:137–160), we still know little about when and how this situation came about (also Noli 2005). It should be noted that the Pichao site does not seem to exhibit strong ethnic markers in this period.

It is interesting that some historians have noted an indigenous trade in the Andes during the colonial period. Estela Noli (2001, 2005), working on examples from the colonial region of Tucumán, has demonstrated how some indigenous groups, working as carpenters, enjoyed a certain independence within the system. There may even have been an indigenous trade in silver from the famous mine at Potosí. Silvio Zavala mentions examples of official Spanish complaints of indigenous theft of silver from the 1570s (1978:85; also Tandeter 1992:116). The end of the seventeenth century was, however, a period of decline in the production of silver and also, slowly, in the internal trade in the central Andean area (Assadourian 1994; Cardoso and Pérez Brignoli 1979:216–227).

Monte Polizzo and Iron Age Colonial Settings of the Mediterranean

As a contrast to the Pichao example, I will briefly mention a Mediterranean Iron Age case from the inland of the western part of the island of Sicily. It concerns the archaeological site of Monte Polizzo, located close to today's Salemi. The site mainly dates to the seventh and sixth centuries

BC. Since the site was abandoned in the sixth century, the archaeological material from these early urban periods is fairly easy to access. A multinational project involving Sweden, the United States, Italy, and Norway has worked on the site since the late 1990s using relatively detailed documentation by means of digital recording techniques. Katarina Streiffert-Eikeland (2006) and Christian Mühlenbock (2008) have produced interesting analyses and discussions of domestic units from the site. For the purposes of this chapter, I offer a broad overview of the site.

The period in question witnessed early projects of colonial establishments on the coast of Sicily, both from the Greek context (Magna Grecia e Sicilia in the Italian archaeology) (Cerchiai, Guzzo, and Pesando 2005; Greco 1992; Hodos 2006; Puliga and Panichi 2005; van Dommelen 2010) and from the Phoenician-Carthaginian context (Moscati 1986). The colonial projects are limited to relatively small settlements that exhibit particular types of architecture and cultural material in general. Archaeology for this period in Sicily has been frequently limited to these coastal settlements and mainly to the Greek settlements. Thus, the work on Monte Polizzo has introduced new kinds of data to the general discussion. The archaeological evidence from Monte Polizzo clearly demonstrates that this archaeological assemblage differs substantially from those of the coastal colonial settlements. The question of "ethnic" affiliation of the population at Monte Polizzo remains open, though some scattered information in historical sources may give clues. What interests me here, however, is the difference between this inland settlement and its contemporary sites on the coast. In the context of coastal colonial projects, the inland site is an "indigenous" site. Thus, this case is highly interesting for discussing colonial-indigenous relations for this period.

Looking closer at the evidence from Monte Polizzo, there are certain general resemblances between this site and the coastal ones. While the architectural design of the site is much less elaborate than the layout of some coastal sites, there are similarities, such as the existence of a larger temple and in certain elements of building techniques. There is also a limited but easily recognizable set of objects at Monte Polizzo that evidently stems from the coastal context and demonstrates some kind of contact between these populations. Still, the main impression of the material from Monte Polizzo seems to indicate a degree of independence, at least in terms of ceramics and in the use of natural resources that are predominantly from the local region. Just to take one example, hunting was evidently much more important at Monte Polizzo as compared to the coastal sites. There are no archaeological indications that the coastal sites had direct political control over the inland sites. The scenario seems to be one of a relative independence but with certain kinds of exchange and relations with the coastal settlements. There is no indication of any systematic intention to conquer the inland areas on the part of the coastal settlements, and this is of great significance in addressing this example of the relations between colonial and indigenous settlements. It is fairly evident that the differences with the Pichao case are striking, but there are also similarities, not least in the relative autonomy of certain indigenous settlements in the context of larger colonial projects.

Toward a New General History of the Colonial

An important lesson from the Pichao example is thus that the effects of a colonial project are not necessarily limited to direct acculturation or direct cultural continuity. There might be an important element of third space à la Bhabha (1994) or a hybridity in the sense of Canclini (1989) or a middle ground as outlined by White (1991). Perhaps Bhabha's approach is the most promising (Cornell and Galle 2004), but it is evident that the relations must always have been at least potentially dramatic, conflicted, and fairly closed. I would suggest that Lucas (2004:198) goes too far, however, when he speaks about the colonial as centripetal, dispersed, and fragmentary, since there were also advanced integrative processes in most large-scale colonial projects. Aguirre Rojas (2005) considers the subaltern culture to possess autonomy, lacking in the hegemonic; though perhaps also a bit extreme, he does address an underrepresented perspective. What matters most is the potential for a substantial element of social innovation in the margins of the colonial center, and this point is important to stress. It would be highly interesting to compare the Pichao case to the Cimarron or maroon settlements of escaped slaves in various tracts of Latin America (Ferreira and Funari, this volume; Funari 1999), particularly with regard to social innovation. Simple dual models discussing the colonial center vis-à-vis communitarian villages seem unproductive and will obstruct rather than facilitate productive analysis. Archaeologists studying colonialism are in need of new perspectives in which the cases like that of Pichao or the Cimarron are included in a different general history.

Thus, to summarize briefly, the Pichao case of colonial setting differs from the Monte Polizzo case. In the Monte Polizzo case, the indigenous site seems to have an independence that is not under direct threat of immediate conquest. In the Pichao case, there is a direct and immediate armed conflict and a permanent risk of conquest. In both cases, however, we have a relative autonomy in the indigenous setting. Not least in the Pichao case, the social innovation is remarkable.

It is important to develop more intensive studies on indigenous sites on the periphery of or outside colonial control. Such installations are part of the general history. They exhibit special traits, but their internal workings are still little known. Looking closely at such experiences means confronting the unknown and will probably force our practical and theoretical capacities to their limit, requiring new thinking about time and the social. I quote here Derrida, whose words appear in "Fors," a text related to an intricate reading of Freud and the case of the Wolfman (Derrida 1976:72–73, my translation). It is about a paleontologist, not an archaeologist; perhaps Derrida wished to discuss a scholar far removed from the discourse of "true Being." It might be an end, but also a new beginning: "I am thinking of the motion-less paleontologist, suddenly, in the sun, frozen by the delicate word-thing there, an abandoned stone instrument, like a tombstone burning in the grass, with the stare of a biface."

References Cited

Aguirre Rojas, Carlos
2005   Hegemonic Cultures and Subaltern Cultures: Between Dialogue and Conflict. *Review, Fernand Braudel Center,* XXVIII:187–210.
Andrews, Anthony P.
1984   The Political Geography of the Sixteenth Century Yucatán Maya. *Journal of Anthropological Research* 40:589–96.
Archivo General de Indias (AGI) [Seville]
1661   *Charcas*, 5:L.3.
1670   *Charcas*, 103:N.10.
Assadourian, Carlos Sempat
1994   Integración y desintegración regional en el espacio colonial. Un enfoque histórico. *Mercados e historia*, edited by Grosso and Riquer, pp. 141–64. Instituto Mora, Mexico City.
Bengtsson, Lisbeth, Per Cornell, Nils Johansson, and Susana Sjödin
2001   *Investigations at Pichao: Introduction to Studies in the Santa María Valley, North-Western Argentina.* BAR International series, 978. Hedges, Oxford, England.

Bhabha, Homi
1994   *The Location of Culture*. Routledge, London.
Bois, Guy
1976   *Crise du Féudalisme*. Presses de la fondation nationale de sciences politiques/ EHESS, Paris.
Bonfil Batalla, Guillermo
1992   *Identidad y pluralismo cultural en América Latina*. Fondo Editorial del Cehass, Buenos Aires.
Braudel, Fernand
1967   *Civilisation matérielle et capitalisme (XV–XVIIIe Siécle)*, vol. 1. Armand Colin, Paris.
Brenner, Robert
1993   *Merchants and Revolution*. Princeton University Press, Princeton, New Jersey.
Cabrera Vargas, María del Refugio
1995   El Indio en las relaciones geográficas del siglo XVI: La construcción de un significado. In *Diversidad étnica y conflicto en América Latina, vol. 2: El Indio como metáfora en la identidad nacional*, edited by Barceló, Portal and Sánchez, pp. 11–46, Plaza y Valdez, Mexico City.
Calnek, Edward E.
1972   Settlement Pattern and Chinampa Agriculture at Tenochtitlán. *American Antiquity* 37:104–115.
Canclini, Nestór
1989   *Culturas hibridas*. Grijalbo, Mexico City.
Cardoso, Ciro F. S., and Hector Pérez Brignoli
1979   *Historia económica de América Latina, 1: Sistemas agrarios e historia colonial*. Crítica, Barcelona.
Carmagnani, Marcello
1976   *Formación y crisis de un sistema feudal, América Latina*. Siglo XXI, Mexico, City.
Cerchiai, Luca, Pietro Giovanni Guzzo and Fabrizio Pesando
2005   Le regioni dell'Italia meridionale e le isole, In *L'Italia antica. Culture e forme del popolamento nel 1 millenio a.C.*, edited by Fabrizio Pesando, pp. 201–255. Carocci, Rome.
Chiaramonte, José
1983   *Formas de sociedad e economía en Hispanoamérica*. Grijalbo, Buenos Aires.
Colombres, Adolfo
1977   *La colonización cultural en América Latina*. El Sol, Quito.
Cornell, Per
1988   *Emergence and Growth of Centres*. GOTARC C:6, Department of Archaeology, University of Gothenburg, Sweden.
1993   *Early Centres and the Household*. GOTARC B:3, Department of Archaeology, University of Gothenburg, Sweden.
2007a   Relaciones socio-espaciales en el mundo andino centromeridional. In *Report from the Project Social Innovation in Indian Culture by the Time of European*

Contact, edited by Per Stenborg and Per Cornell, pp. 120–143. GOTARC D:67, University of Gothenburg, Sweden.
2007b Unhomely Space: Confronting Badiou and Bhabha. In *Encounters/Materialities/Confrontations*, edited by Per Cornell and Fredrik Fahlander, pp. 100–122. CPS, Newcastle.

Cornell, Per, and Hermann Galle
2004 El fenómeno Inka y su articulación local. Reflexiones desde el sitio de El Pichao, Valle de Santa María (Tucumán). In *Local, Regional, Global*, edited by Per Cornell and Per Stenborg, pp. 211–218. Anales N. E. 6, Ibero-American Institute, University of Gothenburg, Sweden.

Cornell, Per, and Nils Johansson
1993 Desarrollo del asentamiento del sitio STucTav5 (El Pichao), Provincia de Tucumán. Comentarios sobre dataciones de 14C y luminiscencia. *Publicaciones*, 2, pp. 31–43, Instituto de Arqueología, Universidad Nacional de Tucumán, Tucumán, Argentina.

Cornell, Per, and Charlotte Nilsson
2011 *Tracing Archaeology. Time and Other.* GOTARC, Department of Historical Studies, University of Gothenburg, Sweden.

Cornell, Per, and Susana Sjödin (editors)
1990 *El Pichao 1989. First report from the Project "Emergence and Growth of Centres."* GOTARC D:4, Department of Archaeology, University of Gothenburg, Sweden.
1991 *El Pichao 1990. Second report from the Project "Emergence and Growth of Centres."* GOTARC D:5, Department of Archaeology, University of Gothenburg, Sweden.

DeMarrais, Elizabeth
2001 La arqueología del Norte del valle Calchaqui. In *História argentina prehispánica*, edited by Eduardo Berbérian and Axel Nilsen, pp. 289–346. Brujas, Córdoba, Argentina.

Derrida, Jacques
1965–1966 De la grammatologie I–II. Critique. Revue génèrale des publications françaises et étrangères, 223, pp. 1016–1042; 224, pp. 23–53, Editions de Minuit, Paris.
1967 *L'écriture et la différence.* Seuil, Paris.
1976 Fors. Les mots anglés de Nicolas Abraham and Maria Torok. In *Cryptonomie. Le Verbier de l'homme aux loups,* edited by Nicolas Abraham and Maria Torok, pp. 7–73. Aubier-Flammarion, Paris.
2000 *Le toucher, Jean-Luc Nancy.* Galilée, Paris.

Derrida, Jacques, and P. Eisenman
1997 *Chora L Works.* Monacelli, New York.

Farris, Nancy
1984 *Maya Society under Colonial Rule.* Princeton University Press, Princeton, New Jersey.

Frank, André Gunder
1979 *Mexican Agriculture 1521–1630: Transformation of the Mode of Production.* Cambridge University Press, Cambridge, England.

Funari, Pedro Paulo A.
1999   Etnicidad, identidad y cultura material: un estudio del Cimarron Palmares, Brasil, Siglo XVII. In *Sed non satiata. Teoría social en la arqueología Latinoamericana contemporánea,* edited by Andrés Zarankin and Felix Acuto, pp. 77–96. Del Tridente, Buenos Aires.

García Targa, Juan
1995   Arqueología colonial en el área maya. *Revista Española de Antropología Americana,* 25:41–69.

Gasparini, Graziano
1991   The Law of the Indies. The Spanish-American Grid Plan: The Urban Bureaucratic Form. In *The New City. Foundations,* edited by C-F Lejeune, pp. 7–17. Princeton Architectural Press, Princeton, New Jersey.

Godelier, Maurice
1972   Anthropologie et économie. Paper presented at the conference L'unité de l'homme, Abbaye de Royaumont, France, 1972.

González Aragón, Jorge
1993   *La urbanización indígena de la ciudad de México. El caso del Plano en papel maguey.* Biblioteca Memoria Mexicana, Mexico City.

Greco, Emmanuele
1992   *Archeologia della Magna Grecia.* Laterza, Turin, Italy.

Hardoy, Jorge E.
1978   European Urban Forms in the Fifteenth to Seventeenth Centuries and Their Utilization in Latin America. In *Urbanization in the Americas from Its Beginning to the Present,* edited by Richard Schaedel, Jorge Hardoy, and Nora Scott-Kinzer, pp. 215–248. Mouton, The Hague.

Hodos, Tamar
2006   *Local Responses to Colonization in the Iron Age Mediterranean.* Routledge, London.

Johansson, Nils
1996   *Burials and Society.* GOTARC B:5, Department of Archaeology, University of Gothenburg, Sweden.

Kubler, George
1978   Open-Grid Town Plans in Europe and America. In *Urbanization in the Americas from Its Beginning to the Present,* edited by Schaedel, Hardoy, and Scott-Kinzer, pp. 327–342. Mouton publishers, The Hague.

Lightfoot, Kent
2005   *Indians, Missionaries, and Merchants.* University of California Press, Berkeley.

Lorandi, Ana María, Roxana Boixadós, Cora Bunster, and Miguel Angel Palermo
1997   El Valle Calchaqui. In *El Tucumán Colonial y Charcas,* edited by Lorandi, pp. 205–51. Facultad de Filosofía y Letras, Universidad de Buenos Aires, Buenos Aires.

Lucas, Gavin
2004   *An Archaeology of Colonial Identity. Power and Material Culture in the Dwars Valley, South Africa.* Kluwer/Plenum, New York.

Marder, Michael
2009   *The Event of the Thing: Derrida's Post-Deconstructive Realism*. Toronto University Press, Toronto.

Markman, Sydney David
1978   The Gridiron Town Plan and the Caste System in Colonial Central America. In *Urbanization in the Americas from Its Beginning to the Present*, edited by Schaedel, Hardoy, and Scott-Kinzer, pp. 470–490. Mouton, The Hague.

McAndrew, John
1965   *The Open-Air Churches of Sixteenth-Century Mexico*. Harvard University Press, Cambridge.

Medina, Maria Clara
2002   *Landless Women, Powerful Men*. Theses, 50, Department of History, University of Gothenburg, Sweden.

Medina, Maria Clara, and Per Cornell
2010   El proyecto Pichao 1989–2005: Apuntes de su historia e resultados. Rastros en el camino. Trayectos e identidades de una institución. In *Homenaje a los 80 años del IAM-UNT*, edited by Patricia Arenas, Carlos Aschero, and Constanza Taboada, pp. 245–55. Instituto de Arqueología y Museo, Universidad Nacional de Tucumán, Tucumán, Argentina.

Mörner, Magnus
1953   *The Political and Economic Activities of the Jesuits in the La Plata region. The Habsburg Era*. Ibero-American Studies, School of Economics, Stockholm.
1983   Economic Factors and Stratification in Colonial Spanish America with Special Regard to Elites. *Hispanic American Historical Review* 63:335–369.

Moscati, Sabatino
1986   *Italia Punica*. Bompiano, Milan.

Mrozowski, Stephen A., Katherine Hayes, and Anne P. Hancock
2007   The Archaeology of Sylvester Manor. *Northeast Historical Archaeology* 36:1–15.

Mühlenbock, Christian
2008   *Fragments from a Mountain Society. Tradition, Innovation and Interaction at Archaic Monte Polizzo*. GOTARC B:50, Department of Archaeology, University of Gothenburg, Sweden.

Nalda, Enrique
1998   El colapso y el nuevo orden político en las Tierras Bajas mayas. In *Los últimos reinos mayas*, edited by Enrique Nalda, pp. 7–22. Jaca Books, Mexico City.
2010   El clásico en el México antiguo. In *Nueva Historia General de México*, pp. 71–118. Colegio de México, Mexico City.

Nastri, Javier
2008   La figura de las largas cejas de la iconografía santamariana. Chamanismo, sacrificio y cosmovisión Calchaquí. *Boletín del Museo Chileno de arte Precolombino* 13:9–34.

Noli, Estela
2001   Indios ladinos del Tucumán colonial: los carpinteros de Marapa. *Andes* 12:139–172.

2005   Fronteras culturales? Pueblos de indios y estancias en el Curato de Chiquiligasta (mediados del S. XVII, comienzos del S. XVII). *Revista Andina*, 40:209–35.

2012   *Indios ladinos, criollos aindiados. Procesos de mestizaje y memoria* étnica *en Tucumán (Siglo XVII)*. Prohistoria, Rosario, Argentina.

Puliga, Donatella, and Silvia Panichi

2005   *Un'altra Grecia. Le colonie d'Occidente tra mito, arte e memoria*. Einaudi, Turin, Italy.

Quezada, Sergio

1993   Espacialidad indígena y poder colonial en Yucatán (Siglo XVI). In *Perspectivas antropológicas en el mundo maya*, edited by Iglesias Ponce de León and Liggred Perranor, pp. 419–432. Sociedad Española de Estudios Maya, Madrid.

Rodríguez, Lorena

2008   *Después de las desnaturalizaciones*. Antropofagía, Buenos Aires.

Rose-Redwood, Reuben S.

2008   Genealogies of the Grid: Revisiting Stanislawski's Search for the Grid-Pattern Town. *Geographical Review*, 98:42–58.

Roskams, Steve

2006   The Urban Poor: Finding the Marginalised. In *Social and Political Life in Late Antiquity*, edited by William Bowden, pp. 487–531. Brill, Leiden, Netherlands.

Sanders, William T.

1971   Settlement Patterns in Central Mexico. In *Handbook of Middle American Indians,* vol. 10, edited by Robert Wauchope, pp. 3–44, University of Texas Press, Austin.

Silliman, Stephen

2010   Indigenous Traces in Colonial Spaces. *Journal of Social Archaeology,* 10:29–59.

Socolow, Susan Migden, and Lyman L. Johnson

1981   Urbanization in Colonial Latin America. *Journal of Urban History* 8:27–59.

Sofri, Gianni

1969   *Il modo di produzione asiatico. Storia di una controversia marxista*. Einaudi, Turin, Italy.

Spalding, Karen

1984   *Huarochirí. An Andean Society under Inca and Spanish Rule*. Stanford University Press, Stanford, California.

Spivak, Gayatri Chakravorty

1999   *A Critique of Postcolonial Reason. Toward a History of a Vanishing Present*. Harvard University Press, Cambridge.

Stanislawski, Dan

1947   Early Spanish Town Planning in the New World. *Geographical Review*, 37:94–105.

Stenborg, Per

2002   *Holding Back History*. GOTARC B:21, Department of Archaeology, University of Gothenburg, Sweden.

Stern, Steve J.
1984   *Peru's Indian Peoples and the Challenge of Spanish Conquest. Huamanga to 1640.* University of Wisconsin Press, Madison.

Streiffert-Eikeland, Katarina
2006   *Indigenous Households: Transculturation of Southern Italy and Sicily in the Archaic Period.* GOTARC B:44, Department of Archaeology, University of Gothenburg, Sweden.

Tandeter, Enrique
1992   *Coacción y mercado. La minería de la plata en el Potosí colonial, 1692–1826.* Sudamericana, Buenos Aires.

Tarragó, Myriam
2000   Chacras y pucara. Desarrollos sociales tardíos. In *Nueva Historia Argentina*, vol. 1: *Los pueblos originarios y la conquista*, edited by Myriam Tarragó, pp. 259–300. Sudamericana, Buenos Aires.

van Dommelen, Peter
2010   *Material Connections in the Ancient Mediterranean: Mobility, Materiality, and Identity.* Taylor and Francis, Hoboken, New Jersey.

Velázquez, Adriana
2011   De la selva al mar: los mayas de Quintana Roo. In *Los mayas. Voces de piedra*, edited by Alejandra Martínez de Velasco y Vega, pp. 433–445. Ambar Diseño, Mexico City.

Wallerstein, Immanuel
1974–1980   *The Modern World System*, vols. 1–3. Academic Press, New York.

Watters, Britta M.
2001   *The Development of the Spanish American grid-plan town: A Survey of Archaeological Investigations at Early Spanish Colonial Sites in Latin America and the Caribbean.* Vanderbilt University, Nashville.

White, Richard
1991   *The Middle Ground. Indians, Empires, and Republics on the Great Lakes Region 1650–1815.* Cambridge University Press, Cambridge, England.

Wickham, Chris
2007   Memories of Underdevelopment: What Has Marxism Done for Medieval History, and What Can It Still Do? In *Marxist History-Writing for the Twenty-First Century*, edited by Chris Wickham, pp. 32–48. Oxford University Press, Oxford, England.

Zavala, Silvio
1941   *Ideario de Vasco de Quiroga.* Colegio de México, Mexico City.
1978   *El servicio personal de los indios en el Perú, I.* Colegio de Mexico, Mexico City.

Zúñiga, Jean-Paul
1999   La voix du sang. Du 'métis' à l'idée de 'métissage' en Amérique espagnole, *Annales Histoire, Sciences sociales*, pp. 425–452.

7

Rethinking Colonialism

Indigenous Innovation and Colonial Inevitability

STEPHEN A. MROZOWSKI, D. RAE GOULD,
AND HEATHER LAW PEZZAROSSI

In this chapter we argue for a rethinking of colonialism as a historical process. The evidence provided by our research suggests that the Nipmuc people of what is today Massachusetts and Connecticut continued to shape their own cultural and political destiny despite the powerful impact of European colonization. We present a historical narrative of indigenous innovation and cultural perseverance that runs counter to the inevitability inherent in the political discourse of the past two hundred years. Colonialism clearly resulted in struggles over territory, sovereignty, and cultural identity, but the archaeological evidence points to a narrative different than that underlying much of colonial and postcolonial discourse. Those struggles were not conceptualized as European versus indigenous identity or measured by comparison to some mythical prehistoric past but rather as generational choices involving older practices and newer practices. In this narrative we attempt to move beyond the notion of indigenous resistance to a new understanding of the role innovation played and continues to play in the production of contemporary indigenous society, particularly in New England.

In building our argument we have sought to incorporate the work of historians, anthropologists, and archaeologists who have contributed to a theoretical discourse that seeks to reimagine colonialism by drawing upon evidence of daily life over the past three hundred years that was not experienced as theory but rather through a vernacular lexicon of older practices and newer practices. The production and depiction of Native American history was itself written in still a third lexicon, that of an emergent "American" narrative in which Native American persistence played no role. Jean O'Brien (2010) has shown that the emplacement of indigenous people in New England's past occurred as part of the creation of an emerging Euro-American national historical narrative in the late eighteenth and early nineteenth centuries. This discourse held Native American authenticity to a model of presumed cultural apex in the moments just prior to the arrival of the English. Any departure from this static model was deemed as a loss or a weakening of Native legitimacy. The momentum of ongoing indigenous historical trajectories were ignored and invalidated. While some scholars have acknowledged the absurdity of this assumption (Baron, Hood, and Izard 1996; Cipolla 2013; Doughton 1997, 1999; Ferguson 2004; Gould 2010, 2013a; Handsman and Richmond 1995; Law 2008; Mrozowski et al. 2009; O'Brien 2006; Richmond 1994; Thee 2006; Weinstein 1994), federal policies for tribal recognition are still largely based on this rigid way of thinking about how the past is brought forward into the present (Cipolla, this volume; Hayes and Cipolla, this volume).

The issue of authenticity is also a major element in the politics surrounding federal recognition in the United States (Gould 2010, 2013b; Mrozowski et al. 2009). It has meant problems for contemporary indigenous groups in their dealings with public and private institutions that served as repositories for human remains and sacred artifacts. The Native American Graves Protection and Repatriation Act (NAGPRA) is one specific instance in which indigenous groups are forced to embrace a form of "strategic essentialism" (Spivak 1987, 1990) to demonstrate the shared cultural relationship demanded by the law. The essentialism that underlies many of the issues surrounding NAGPRA (Liebman 2008; Lovis et al. 2004; Trope and Echo-Hawk 2000) and federal recognition in the United States (Cipolla 2013; Daehnke 2007; Mrozowski et al. 2009) is reinforced by the false dichotomy between history and prehistory. In practice such a distinction promotes the separation of what would otherwise be viewed as a continuous history whose unfolding is characterized by a trajectory of concurrent change and continuity (Gould 2013a, 2013b; Mrozowski 2013).

In fact, the prehistory/history divide masks a profound contradiction in the narrative of the Native American past. Before "contact," any prehistory and specifically the "prehistory" of indigenous New England, has historically been organized around the Western notion of linear, inevitable progress toward a Western ideal. In this classic social evolutionary scheme developed by Louis Henry Morgan, innovation (brought in from outside) is rewarded with a higher cultural status. Prehistorians search intently for evidence of the development (adoption) of maize horticulture, Late Woodland (ca. 1000–400 BP) villages, task specialization, and political complexity because these are all milestones that presumably led populations toward a Western European–style civility. Scholars rely specifically on evidence of material innovation to mark and measure the advancement of "prehistoric" New England toward the Western ideal (Stein 2008 examines New England context; Pratt 1992, Fabian 1983, Wolf 1982 present general context). This problematic narrative is replaced by a contradictory one at the moment of colonial "contact," in which any further "advancement" or "innovation" is deemed evidence of cultural breakdown and illegitimacy. After that moment of contact, change is equal to loss, and stagnation is equal to continuity and legitimacy. Part of the problem is that Western conceptions of culture as bounded spatial entities hinder the imagination of the simultaneous continuity of separate historical trajectories once colonial power is emplaced (Clifford 1988; Gupta and Ferguson 1997). Such concepts of culture still rely on Morgan's model that assumes all historical trajectories eventually and inevitably merge into a single Western future (Hall and Du Gay 1996).

The result is a view of the Native American past as a deep, slowly changing prehistory truncated by European colonization. History is equated with the arrival of Europeans and the adoption of European technologies and religion that resulted in an overall loss of cultural authenticity when compared with a more essentialized perception of the prehistoric past (Gould 2013a; Silliman 2009). In essence the prehistory/history divide is a prime example of the kinds of critical temporalities to which Hayes and Cipolla refer in their introduction to this volume (as does Cornell, this volume). The prehistory/history narrative also has tended to mask the interdependence of the concepts of tradition and innovation, instead making them appear as opposites. Such a dichotomy contributes to a view of tradition as static and innovation as something new and modern and fresh that will lead to an inevitably shared future. But tradition and innovation, habit and ingenuity, replication and modification, and memory and anticipation are all active processes in which the future becomes the past and recedes as memory (Husserl 1928; Gell 1998:234–242). Acknowledging this process is an important step toward the goal of constructing critical temporalities that confront the dichotomous views of history blinding us to the growth of new cultural formations. This is precisely the point Cornell (this volume) raises in his discussion of the indigenous communities of El Pichao in northwestern Argentina. Rather than interpret the materiality of the inhabitants of the settlement as an outgrowth of indigenous-Spanish interaction, Cornell argues that it represents a form of innovation that needs to be conceptualized as something "new," something outside our own perceptions of a colonialism dominated by indigenous-Spanish interaction (Cipolla 2013:27–29 offers a similar example from North America).

In an effort to counter a dichotomized view of Native American history and to provide the temporal depth often ignored in historical archaeology, we provide examples illustrating the importance of drawing connections in the present, recent past, and deeper history. We draw on research from Magunkaquog and Hassanamesit, two "Christian Indian" communities in Massachusetts, to explore the intellectual confines imposed by the false distinction between history and prehistory. These two postcontact communities provide evidence that links religious and cultural practices to a deeper past, demonstrating that Nipmuc cultural practices involve elements of deep antiquity and simultaneous, continuous change. Rather than a picture of a static society upended by European colonization, the portrait that emerges is one in which tensions between older practices and newer practices were a part of daily life in a way that did not result in a loss of cultural identity. In this regard the evidence of long-term spiritual practice may represent a prime example of what Pauketat (2001) suggests are deep practices that prove to be more easily woven into newer practices. In the examples discussed below the practices involve some elements of Nipmuc religion undergoing change as some aspects of Christianity were being adopted by the Nipmuc of Massachusetts and Connecticut during the seventeenth and eighteenth centuries.

This research has developed through collaboration between the Fiske Center for Archaeological Research at the University of Massachusetts Boston and the Nipmuc Nation. Over the past two decades archaeological and documentary research has focused on the Nipmuc communities of Magunkaquog and Hassanamesit that are located in what are today Ashland and Grafton, Massachusetts, respectively (map 7.1). Documentary research and excavations carried out at the former site of Magunkaquog (Mrozowski et al. 2005, 2009), the Sarah Boston farmstead as part of the Hassanamesit Woods project (Law, Pezzarossi, and Mrozowski 2008;

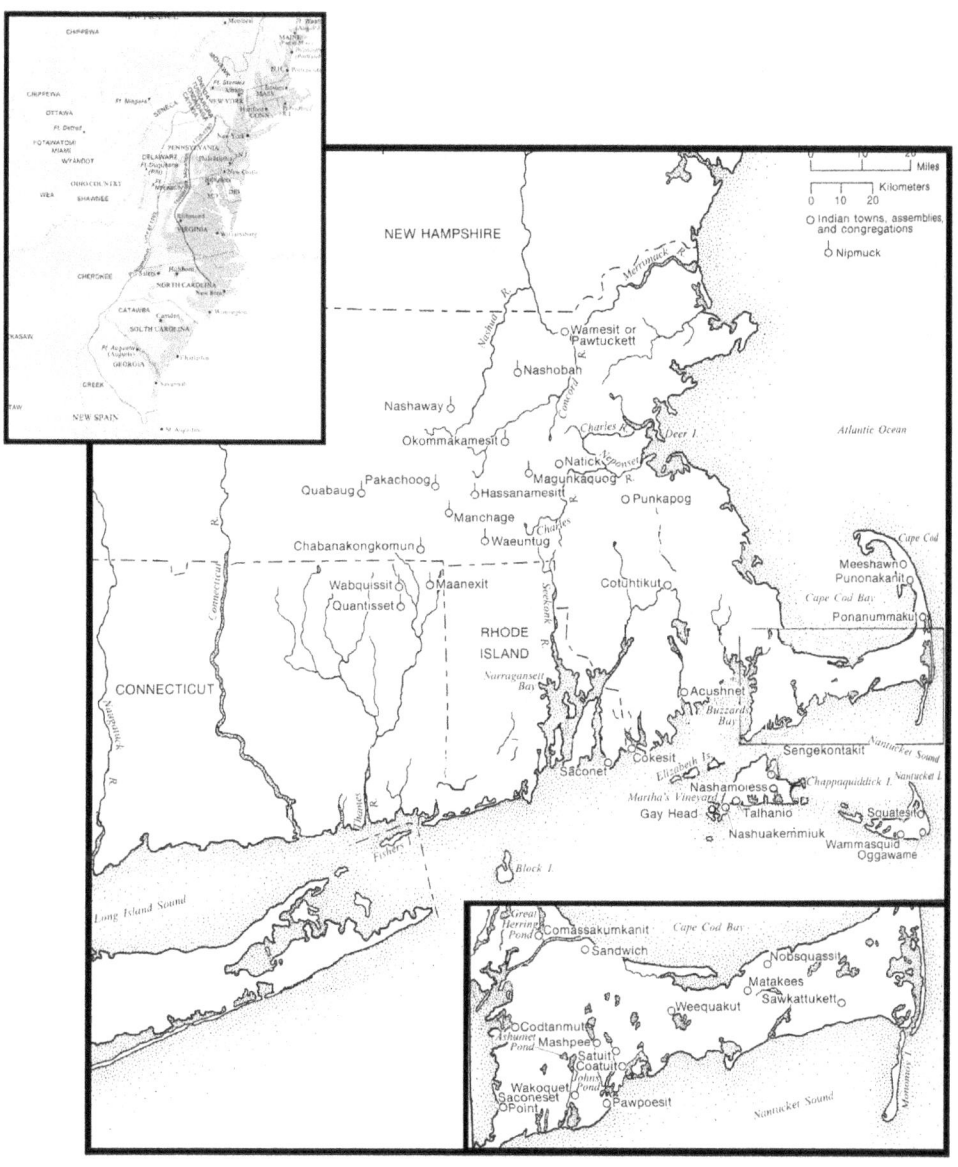

Map 7.1. Location of the "Praying Indian" communities of Natick, Magunkaquog, and Hassanamesit in Massachusetts and Connecticut. Map by the Fiske Center for Archaeological Research, University of Massachusetts Boston, reproduced with permission.

Law Pezzarossi and Mrozowski 2014), and the Printer-Cisco property that today serves as the Nipmuc Hassanamisco Reservation (Gould 2010, 2013a, 2013b) have contributed to a new, more refined understanding of the events that have shaped Nipmuc history over the past three hundred years. The results of these continuing investigations form the corpus of our discussion.

Magunkaquog and Hassanamesit

This chapter focuses on the Nipmuc communities of Hassanamesit and Magunkaquog, two of fourteen settlements incorporated in English missionary John Eliot's early attempts to Christianize Native peoples of southern New England during the seventeenth century. The first such community, Natick, was established in 1650 through Eliot's efforts, followed by his efforts to Christianize Nipmuc people at Hassanamesit a few years later. Magunkaquog, the seventh such community, was acknowledged in 1669 as a Christian Indian settlement. By the 1670s, Eliot's influence was felt in fourteen settlements across Massachusetts and northeastern Connecticut.

Each of these communities was different, yet all shared a connection to Eliot's larger enterprise of converting Native peoples to Christianity. Eliot had a particular vision of religious conversion that was part of an eschatology that held that the conversion of all non-Christian believers would happen during the latter stages of the seventeenth century (Cogley 1999:9–22). This process was to follow a particular path, with Jews and Muslims converting first. Like many religious figures of this period, Eliot was not sure where Native peoples of North America fit into this larger scheme. Therefore, he chose a particular path for their conversion that began with their adopting the cultural practices of the English into their own daily lives. This was the primary purpose of what would come to be called the "Praying Indian" communities in Massachusetts and Connecticut (map 7.1). The outbreak of war in 1675 between the Native peoples of southern New England and the English, commonly known as King Philip's War, or Metacom's Rebellion, temporarily halted Eliot's work. Once the war ended in 1676, he returned to working with the communities including many whose daily lives were severely disrupted by the war. Magunkaquog, which never had been much larger than fifty to sixty people, did not regain its prewar vitality, although it seems to have remained viable until the middle of the eighteenth century (Mrozowski et al. 2005, 2009).

At the conclusion of King Philip's War, the English governments of the Massachusetts and Connecticut colonies moved to limit the remaining Native American communities from controlling their own destinies. Most importantly, they passed laws that established state-appointed guardians for many Indian communities to handle the legal and commercial affairs of the various groups and manage proceeds of land sales and other economic activities. Magunkaquog and Hassanamesit worked with guardians, but there is little in the documentary record concerning Magunkaquog before the eventual takeover of the community's lands by Harvard College—today Harvard University—in 1719. Harvard leased some of this land to English settlers in the 1720s to provide the college with income (Mrozowski et al. 2009).

Excavations conducted at Magunco Hill revealed the remains of a dry laid foundation built into the sloping hillside. It appears the building could be entered either at ground level or through the lower room or cellar opening on the northeast, downhill side of the yard (figure 7.1). The building appears to have been constructed after 1650 and was occupied for several generations. Excavations of the foundation and surrounding yard unearthed a rich assemblage of material culture that extended into a small yard area north of the foundation. Much of the assemblage was composed of items manufactured in Europe, primarily Britain. There was also a small but highly significant collection of artifacts that exhibited evidence of Native technology. Based on the manufacturing dates of the ceramics discovered on the site and other diagnostic artifacts, it appears to have been established sometime during the second half of the seventeenth century—documents suggest circa 1669—with occupation ending by the middle of the eighteenth century (Mrozowski et al. 2005, 2009).

There was no evidence for an interior hearth; however, an exterior hearth contained charred faunal remains and a substantial assemblage of lithic debitage, primarily from heated quartz cobbles. In his initial description of Natick, Eliot referenced the "fair house" at that site as a place where valuables would have been stored (Whitfield 1834 [1652]:138–143); a fair house referred to a well-built, substantial structure in seventeenth-century England (Steane 2004:50–51). It seems safe to assume that among those items that Eliot would have considered valuable would have been

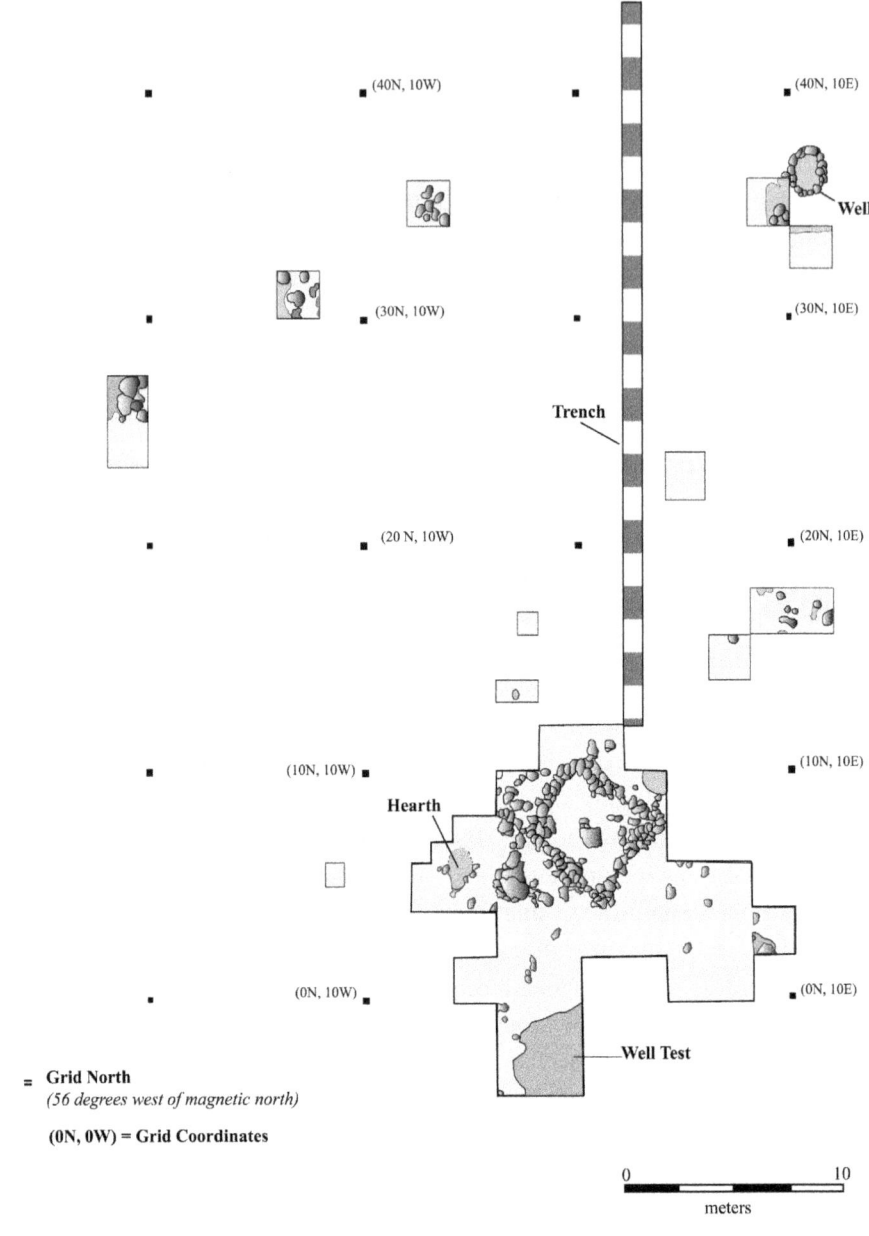

Figure 7.1. Magunco Hill site, foundation of Magunkaquog meeting house, Ashland, Massachusetts. This was one of fourteen "Praying Indian" communities gathered in the seventeenth century by John Eliot. Image by the Fiske Center for Archaeological Research, University of Massachusetts Boston.

the English material culture stored in such a building. The material culture recovered from Magunkaquog included items associated with furniture such as bed-curtain rings, ornamental chair tacks, and matching drawer pulls for a chest with possibly a single drawer. Harness hardware from a saddle and bridle were recovered as well as a discrete assemblage of eight identical thimbles. Much of the remaining assemblage included ceramics, glassware, faunal material, and lithic artifacts including several gunflints, quartz debitage, and quartz crystals (Mrozowski et al. 2005, 2009). The orientation of the foundation as well as the specific items recovered from inside it and the yard area to the north of the structure suggests that the architectural remains are the community's meetinghouse.

It is possible that the foundation discovered on Magunco Hill could have also served as a dwelling for either Ponhamen or Job, the spiritual leader and teacher for the community, respectively. It appears as well to have served as a gathering place where activities such as teaching young Native American women how to sew—evidenced by the assemblage of thimbles—may have taken place. More than likely this building and its surrounding yard served as the locus of a combination of activities, as Native American gathering spaces often do.

As a central place in the settlement, the meetinghouse would have served many purposes, but chief among them appears to be an outward expression of English ways, much the way the Cisco Homestead at Hassanamesit did more than a hundred years later. The recovery of quartz crystals that were placed in three corners of the foundation suggests a more hybridized reality in which the spiritual power of quartz appears to have been woven into the construction of a building that may have incorporated elements of English construction practices as well. These crystals were extracted from larger quartz cobbles that were heated in the hearth immediately outside the foundation. If the building on Magunco Hill served as a teaching place for the most pious of the community, the presence of the crystals suggests that the lessons here were steeped in a Native spirituality of greater antiquity, possibly as deep as four thousand years ago (Mrozowski 2013). We are not suggesting that indigenous spirituality had not changed in four thousand years, but the incorporation of quartz crystals into the construction of the building probably represents a hybridized reality that was itself emblematic of indigenous spirituality when the building was constructed. In this regard we are dealing with practices consistent with Pauketat's notion of tradition as "a practice brought from the past into the present" (2001:2), a practice that changes or drifts with its routine performance, allowing for local variation and regional unity simultaneously. In this way, tradition indeed brings the past into the future, not by being rigid but by providing a bundle of constraints within which a spectrum of practices and possible innovations can take place (Pauketat 2001:3). In time and through countless reiterations of tradition, even the constraints that define it can change. This allows us to identify traditions without demanding literal homogeneity either across space or through time. In fact, Pauketat suggests that the "deepest" traditions are those that lend themselves best to negotiation in practice.

Connections of practices that could potentially span thousands of years argue for the importance of critical temporalities (Hayes and Cipolla, this volume) that eliminate the practice of bounding history and prehistory as separate. The bulk of material culture recovered from the foundation may easily be interpreted as coming from an English household. Such an assumption misses the more obvious reality that European manufactured items used by indigenous people are indigenous items (Silliman 2009). The presence of quartz crystals, as well as an assemblage of quartz gunflints that Luedtke (1999, 2000) and Murphy (2002) ascribe to Native lithic technology, reveal an even more complex picture. Through a review of archaeological evidence of quartz crystals recovered from burial and other contexts, Murphy's analysis suggests a potential link between the quartz crystals at Magunkaquog and their deeper role in the religious practices of the Native peoples of southern New England covering a period of four thousand years (Mrozowski 2013). The adoption of specific technologies such as metal cooking vessels and English ceramic pots by Native groups throughout southern New England (Bragdon 1996; Crosby 1988) represents actions designed to incorporate new elements into a cultural lexicon with deep but not static roots. In this example, objects like quartz crystals and metal cooking vessels are not the mere products of tradition; they are imperfect material iterations of tradition executed by people who each bring a unique set of experiences, perspectives, habits, knowledge, skills, and opinions to bear on the construction or use of the object. The identification of an agent-driven performance even within the practice of tradition reveals an opportunity to further illustrate the codependence of innovation and tradition (Gell 1998).

The combination of indigenous and European manufactured items at Magunkaquog suggests that the Nipmuc who lived there incorporated both older and newer technologies into their daily practices. This practice continued for centuries, as demonstrated by the Sarah Boston and Cisco Homestead sites at Hassanamesit. Most importantly, it continues into the present as well. Rather than signifying a loss of Native American identity, this supports a different narrative of colonial history, one in which English colonization was not preordained domination but rather an unfolding of events in which the inevitability of the future was clear to no one. Instead of a history in which the Native peoples of New England would become extinct, they survived and have now entered a new phase of history in which their political and economic power has been reestablished to a varying degree as part of a future very different than that envisioned in the narratives of New England history produced by Western-trained scholars and local historians.

Silliman (2009) provides comparable examples from his work on the Eastern Pequot Reservation in Connecticut, noting that archaeologists have helped perpetuate the view that colonization resulted in cultural changes that marked the loss of Indian identity, especially when compared with an essentialized prehistoric baseline of unchanging continuity. Instead, he finds strong material evidence that Pequot households adopted European material culture without losing their cultural identity.

For Silliman the central issue is memory and its links to materiality similar to that outlined by Joyce (2003) and Meskell (2003). It may be simple to identify remembrance in things like texts or monuments, but material acknowledgements of the past become more subtle when we attempt to identify them on the quotidian scale (Joyce 2003). The materials recovered from Magunkaquog and Hassanamesit were once part of dwellings, intimate spaces that served to "localize" memories. Within these contexts things acted as mnemonic triggers, some of which extended back generations, others maybe only moments, but each contained a link to another time and another place (Bachelard 1964:8). In the next section we challenge an understanding of the materiality of memory in a discussion of an object found in a Nipmuc household context of the late eighteenth to early nineteenth century, with a connection to an especially deep past. We ask, How durable is social memory, and how can its materiality contribute to a counternarrative that transcends the history/prehistory divide?

Hassanamesit

The sale of much of Hassanamesit to colonial settlers in 1727 resulted in the allotment of land parcels to prominent members of the remaining Hassanamesit community in what is today Grafton, Massachusetts. One such plot was allotted in 1727 to the daughter of a Nipmuc leader, a woman named Sarah Robins (map 7.2). The history of these 106 acres is a testament to the persistence of Sarah's family and the larger Native community at Hassanamesit. By tracing the ownership of the land from 1727 to 1837, when the death of Robins's great-granddaughter Sarah Boston appears to have marked the end of daily occupation of the property, it is clear that a strong tradition of matrilineal naming and inheritance of land was observed by several generations of Nipmuc women. The land passed from Robins to her daughter Sarah Muckamaug, from Muckamaug to her daughter Sarah Burnee, and finally to Burnee's daughter Sarah "Boston" Phillips. These women all faced aggressive colonial land encroachment

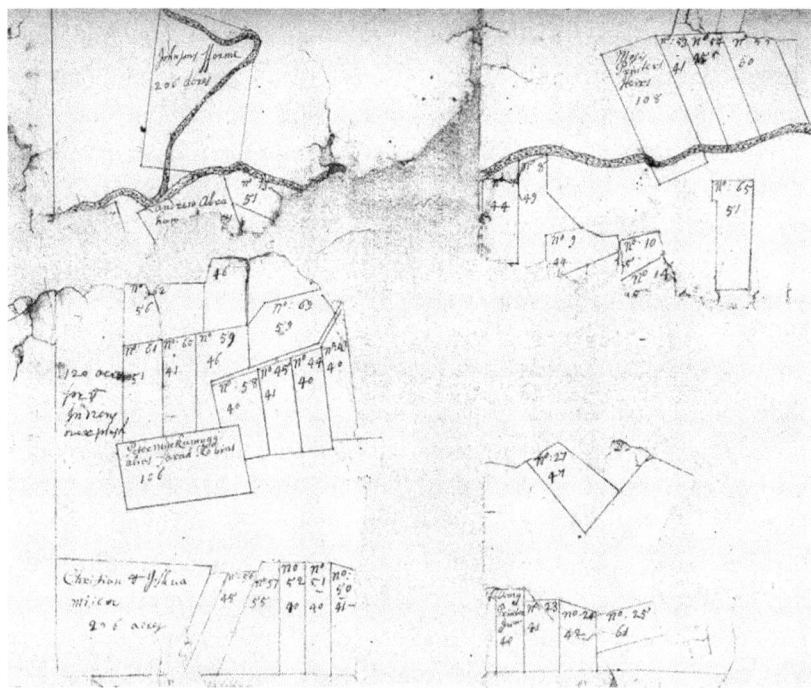

Map 7.2. A 1727 land redistribution map showing the Sarah Robins and Peter Muckamaug lot and the Moses Printer lot. Courtesy American Antiquarian Society, Worcester, Massachusetts.

Figure 7.2. Foundation of the Sarah Burnee Phillips–Sarah Boston farmstead, Grafton, Massachusetts. Photograph by Heather Law Pezzarossi.

in the form of patriarchal challenges to their matrilineal rights. Issues of race and class challenged their gender roles even further. In spite of these trials, Sarah Burnee and her daughter Sarah remained on the property for a total of more than 125 years (Law 2008; Law and Pezzarossi 2008; Pezzarossi, Kennedy, and Law 2012).

The bulk of the material culture recovered from the site dates to the period 1750–1840 (figure 7.2), when the household was run first by Sarah Burnee Phillips and then her daughter Sarah "Boston" Phillips. One of the more noteworthy attributes of the site assemblage is the large number of eating utensils—more than seventy knives, forks, and spoons, as well as serving dishes, and drinking vessels—many more than normally found on Anglo sites—that suggests the household served as a community gathering place for the local Hassanamisco (Law 2008; Law, Pezzarossi, and Mrozowski 2008; Pezzarossi, Kennedy, and Law 2012). Such a setting would have allowed for the creation and maintenance of Nipmuc social memory, where collective remembrance was performed and transformed among the material surrounds of the Burnee-Boston homestead. In this setting, bowls, cups, and knives—many of Euro-American manufacture—

could be drawn into the performance and renewal of Nipmuc tradition. Similar processes occurred among the Eastern Pequot in Connecticut (Silliman 2009).

One notable exception to a materiality consistent with an Anglo middle-class household is the remains of a soapstone crucible or small bowl. The bowl fragments were recovered from a midden containing European ceramics and other material culture including metals that date to the late eighteenth to early nineteenth centuries. Precisely how the bowl may have functioned is unclear; however, its presence raises questions concerning the "authenticity" of this object and the memory it represents. Is this an example of an item kept in one family for hundreds of years? Was it found by one of the residents of the household and kept because it represented some conscious link to the past? Or was it an old technology that was understood as such? Instead of claiming the presence of some unwaveringly accurate and ancient memory, perhaps we should acknowledge what Meskell calls the fiction of memory's inherent authenticity and instead embrace the "waning, renewal, and revisioning of memory [that] might prove potentially even more compelling" (2003:51). Regardless of the specific context and use of the steatite bowl, we can say that this family employed the object in the active reconstruction of the "prehistoric" past in terms of the family members' own present, effectively extending their historical narrative back and, in theory, forward as one continuous historical trajectory. In looking at it this way, we recognize not only the inevitability of forgetting but also the role of imagination and innovation in the process of remembrance (Pezzarossi, Kennedy, and Law 2012). Excavations at Eastern Pequot households revealed a similar experience: precontact artifacts—an argillite projectile point, stone celt, and soapstone bowl fragment—located in a clearly early-nineteenth-century deposit signaling the reincorporation (and perhaps reappropriation) of these items in a Native American household millennia after their initial creation and use (Silliman 2009:223). As with the items at Hassanamesit (soapstone bowl) and Magunkaquog (quartz crystals), the exact meanings, uses, and connections to these artifacts in the postcontact period will never be clear.

Rather than view the adoption of European technologies by Native Americans as a loss of identity, we agree with those who have argued that the merging of technologies can be viewed as evidence of the innovative character of indigenous populations throughout the New World (Cornell and Stenborg 2003; Hayes 2013; Liebman 2008; Lomawaima 1989; Mills

2008; Mrozowski 2013). Not all of these innovations involve a merging of technologies, however. As Cornell (this volume) notes, there are also examples of indigenous innovation that are not directly linked to interactions with European colonists, as his own case study from Argentina demonstrates. His case serves as a reminder of the variability that characterized colonialism across the earth and throughout time. There is no denying that European colonialism was a historically transformative event, yet as the Nipmuc example reveals, the unfolding of that history differed depending upon the context. By looking at more recent Nipmuc history, the connections between past and present practices reveal a cultural vibrancy that has traveled a distinctly Native path.

The Cisco Homestead

Another site at Hassanamesit provides a second example of innovation, hybridity, and the melding of English and Native practices, in the form of a two-hundred-year-old structure now known as the Cisco Homestead (figure 7.3). Originally constructed in 1801 as a sixteen-by-twenty-foot English-style home for Lucy Gimbee on her family land, this homestead has been the focus of an ongoing research project and provides another example of how New England Native people—and Nipmucs in particular—define their own history and cultural practices based on which ones they have chosen (or been able) to continue from their past combined with newer ones integrated into their dynamic cultures. It is an example of Native people embracing transformation and change, adopting new customs and materials, and modernizing as times and technologies change. The project conducted at this site has included documentary and archival research, an archaeological survey to better understand land use and change over time, a detailed architectural study of the building and oral history. The archaeological phase of the project was able to link the date of landscape alterations with the expansion of the house. This information was then combined with oral histories of the property to generate the picture of innovation and change noted above.

The parcel on which the homestead was constructed traces to a 1727 allotment at Hassanamesit to Lucy's ancestor Moses Printer (map 7.2). As an English-style Native American dwelling, it represents as authentic an indigenous practice as other, more "recognizable" elements may be to outsiders. The 1801 structure provided the foundation for contemporary

Figure 7.3. Cisco Homestead, Hassanamisco Reservation, Grafton, Massachusetts. Photograph by Margaret Haynes from the second author's collection, courtesy of the Nipmuc Nation Archives.

cultural practices as it expanded to a ten-room building over 150 years and became the focal point of Nipmuc gatherings, political activism, cultural practices, and tribal identity.

The parcel on which the homestead sits has never belonged to anyone except Nipmuc people, back into precolonial times. Conscious choices by occupants of the homestead in the mid-nineteenth century—when it became the last Nipmuc parcel at Hassanamesit still occupied by tribal members—enabled the preservation of the land and the house. The collective memory and mnemonic triggers associated with this place clearly connect contemporary Native people to their past for generations back (Gould 2010 presents an in-depth discussion of the Cisco Homestead).

In the twenty-first century, this place connects modern-day Nipmuc tribal members to their history and past, as they define them; memory, place, and practice provide a critical element to the continuity of contemporary Native culture. Although outwardly an expression of the incorporation of English ways tied to colonial hegemony, the Cisco Homestead is more an example of the change and hybridity Nipmuc people were able to incorporate into their daily practices over the centuries and, at the same time, their cultural and spiritual continuity, reflective of their continuous identification as Native American.

Conclusion

Ultimately the archaeology of New England's Praying Indian communities and their successive settlements provides concrete evidence of a history that was altered but not ended, an unfolding of events that was shaped by older and newer traditions. This is how we have come to view this past, not as a historical moment ruptured by an irresistible force that would eventually result in the loss of indigenous identity but rather as a blending of old and new ways. In doing so we attempt to employ a lexicon that we assume would have been consistent with that employed by the people whose histories we seek to better understand. From the vantage point of the present, the past may have seemed inevitable even to academics who study the past. This nonindigenous perspective may point toward an inevitability that may seem credible to us as academics, but the Nipmuc of Massachusetts and Connecticut probably did not see it that way. They more likely measured their lives as most of us do, as daily negotiations between past and present in the hope of securing a more stable, predictable future for our descendants. The future that unfolded is probably quite different than the Nipmuc of the eighteenth century would have imagined, a future shaped by collaboration and the rewriting of histories. Yet it remains a present in which indigenous history is contested terrain. As Cipolla's chapter in this volume attests, the issue of federal recognition in North America remains one of the most divisive forces in Indian country. For the residents of Brothertown, Wisconsin, their history remains interwoven with multiple pasts. The same appears to have been true for the Nipmuc of the eighteenth and nineteenth centuries, as it remains for them today. Their history continues to be contested, caught between strongly contrasting views of how the past shaped the present. Yet archaeology has given new voice to a past that has long been silenced by a historical narrative in which indigenous peoples were inevitably headed toward extinction. This inevitability never materialized. Instead, with the help of archaeology, a different history is being rediscovered. We hope that history portends a future that is far from inevitable.

References Cited

Bachelard, Gaston
1964   *The Poetics of Space*. Orion Press, New York.

Baron, Donna K., J. Edward Hood, and Holly V. Izard
1996   They Were Here All Along: The Native American Presence in Lower-Central New England in the Eighteenth and Nineteenth Centuries. *William and Mary Quarterly*, 3rd series, 53(3):561–86.

Bragdon, Kathleen J.
1996   *Native People of Southern New England 1500–1650*. University of Oklahoma Press, Norman.

Cipolla, Craig N.
2013   *Becoming Brothertown: Native American Ethnogenesis and Endurance in the Modern World*. University of Arizona Press, Tucson.

Clifford, James
1988   *The Predicament of Culture: Twentieth-Century Ethnography, Literature, and Art*. Harvard University Press, Cambridge.

Cogley, Richard W.
1999   *John Eliot's Mission to the Indians before King Philip's War*. Harvard University Press, Cambridge.

Cornell, Per, and Per Stenborg (editors)
2003   Local, Regional, Global: Prehistoria, Protohistoria e Historia en Los Valles Calchaquíes, *Anales*, Nueva Época No. 6. Instituto Iberoamericano, University of Gothenburg, Sweden.

Crosby, Constance A.
1988   From Myth to History, or Why King Philip's Ghost Walks Abroad. In *The Recovery of Meaning: Historical Archaeology in the Eastern United States*, edited by M. P. Leone and P. B. Potter, pp. 193–209. Smithsonian Institution Press, Washington, D.C.

Daehnke, Jon D.
2007   A Strange Multiplicity of Voices: Heritage Stewardship, Contested Sites, and Colonial Legacies on the Columbia River. *Journal of Social Archaeology* 7(2):250–275.

Doughton, Thomas L.
1997   Unseen Neighbors: Native Americans of Central Massachusetts, a People Who Had "Vanished." In *After King Philip's War: Presence and Persistence in Indian New England*, edited by Colin G. Calloway, pp. 207–230. University Press of New England, Hanover, New Hampshire.

1999   Like the Shadows in the Stream: Local Historians, the Discourse of Disappearance, and Nipmuc Indians of Central Massachusetts. Paper presented at the American Antiquarian Society, Worcester, Massachusetts.

Fabian, Johannes
1983   *Time and the Other: How Anthropology Makes Its Object*. Columbia University Press, New York.

Ferguson, T. J.
2004   Academic, Legal, and Political Contexts of Social Identity and Cultural Affiliation Research in the Southwest. In *Identity, Feasting, and the Archaeology of the Greater Southwest*, edited by Barbara J. Mills, pp. 27–41. University of Colorado Press, Boulder.

Gell, Alfred
1998   *Art and Agency: Towards a New Anthropological Theory*. Clarendon Press, Oxford, England.

Gould, D. Rae
2010   Contested Places: The History and Meaning of Hassanamisco. Ph.D. dissertation, Department of Anthropology, University of Connecticut, Storrs.
2013a   Cultural Practice and Authenticity: The Search for Real Indians in New England in the "Historical" Period. In *The Death of Prehistory*, edited by Peter R. Schmidt and Stephen A. Mrozowski, pp. 241–66. Oxford University Press, Oxford, England.
2013b   The Nipmuc Nation, Federal Acknowledgment, and a Case of Mistaken Identity. In *Recognition, Sovereignty Struggles, and Indigenous Rights in the United States: A Sourcebook*, edited by Jean O'Brien and Amy E. Den Ouden, pp. 213–31. University of North Carolina Press, Chapel Hill.

Gupta, Akhil, and James Ferguson
1997   Beyond "Culture": Space, Identity, and the Politics of Difference. In *Culture Power Place: Explorations in Critical Anthropology*, edited by A. Gupta and J. Ferguson, pp. 33–51. Duke University Press, Durham.

Hall, Stuart, and Paul Du Gay
1996   *Questions of Cultural Identity*. Sage, London.

Handsman, Russell G., and Trudie Lamb Richmond
1995   Confronting Colonialism: The Mahican and Schaghticoke Peoples and Us. In *Making Alternative Histories: The Practice of Archaeology and History in Non-Western Settings*, edited by Peter R. Schmidt and Thomas C. Patterson, pp. 87–117. School of American Research Press, Santa Fe, New Mexico.

Hayes, Katherine H.
2013   *Slavery before Race: Europeans, Africans, and Indians on Long Island's Sylvester Manor Plantation, 1651–1821*. New York University Press, New York.

Husserl, Edmund
1928   *On the Phenomenology of the Consciousness of Internal Time (1893–1917)*. J. B. Brough, translator. Kluwer, Dordrecht, Netherlands.

Joyce, Rosemary A.
2003   Concrete Memories: Fragments of the Classic Maya Past (500–1000 AD). In *Archaeologies of Memory*, edited by Ruth M. Van Dyke and Susan E. Alcock, pp. 104–125. Blackwell, Oxford.

Law, Heather
2008   Daily Negotiations and the Creation of an Alternative Discourse: The Legacy of a Colonial Nipmuc Farmstead. Master's thesis, Department of Anthropology, University of Massachusetts Boston.

Law, Heather, Guido Pezzarossi, and Stephen A. Mrozowski
2008   Archaeological Intensive Excavations: Hassanamesit Woods Property, The Sarah Boston Farmstead, Grafton, Massachusetts. Andrew Fiske Memorial Center for Archaeological Research, Cultural Resource Management Study No. 26, University of Massachusetts, Boston.
2014   Final Report of the Archaeological Investigations of Hassanamesit Woods: The Sarah Boston Farmstead. Cultural Resource Management Report No. 64. Andrew Fiske Memorial Center for Archaeological Research, University of Massachusetts Boston.

Liebmann, Matthew J.
2008   Postcolonial Cultural Affiliation: Essentialism, Hybridity, and NAGPRA. In *Archaeology and the Postcolonial Critique*, edited by Matthew J. Liebmann and Uzma Z. Rizvi, pp. 73–90. AltaMira, Walnut Creek, California.

Lomawaima, Hartman H.
1989   Hopification, a Strategy for Cultural Preservation. In *Columbian Consequences*. Vol. 1: *Archaeological and Historical Perspectives on the Spanish Borderlands West*, edited by David H. Thomas, pp. 93–99. Smithsonian Institution Press, Washington, D.C.

Lovis, Willam A., Keith W. Kintigh, Vincent P. Steponaitis, and Laurie G. Goldstein
2004   Archaeological Perspectives on the NAGPRA: Underlying Principles, Legislative History, and Current Issues. In *Legal Perspectives on Cultural Resources*, edited by J. R. Richmond and M. P. Forsyth, pp. 165–184. AltaMira, Walnut Creek, California.

Luedtke, Barbara E.
1999   Gunflints in the Northeast. *Northeast Anthropology* 57:27–43.
2000   Gunflints from Magunco. Paper presented at the Annual Meetings of the Society for Historical Archaeology, Quebec City, Canada, January 4–9, 2000.

Meskell, Lynn
2003   Memory's Materiality: Ancestral Presence, Commemorative Practice, and Disjunctive Locales. In *Archaeologies of Memory*, edited by Ruth Van Dyke and Susan E. Alcock, pp. 34–55. Blackwell, Malden, Massachusetts.

Mills, Barbara
2008   Colonialism and Cuisine: Cultural Transmission, Agency, and History at Zuni Pueblo. In *Cultural Transmission and Material Culture: Breaking Down Boundaries*, edited by Miriam Stark, Brenda Bowser, and Lee Horne, pp. 245–262. University of Arizona Press, Tucson.

Mrozowski, Stephen A.
2013   The Tyranny of Prehistory and the Search for a Deeper History. In *The Death of Prehistory*, edited by Peter R. Schmidt and Stephen A. Mrozowski, pp. 220–240. Oxford University Press, Oxford, England.

Mrozowski, Stephen A., Holly Herbster, David Brown, and Katherine L. Priddy
2005   Magunkaquog: Native American Conversion and Cultural Persistence. In *Eighteenth-Century Native Communities of Southern New England in the Colonial*

Context, edited by Jack Campsi, pp. 57–71. Occasional Paper No. 1. Mashantucket Museum and Research Center, Mashantucket, Connecticut.
2009   Magunkaquog Materiality, Federal Recognition, and the Search for a Deeper History. *International Journal of Historical Archaeology* 13(4):430–463.

Murphy, John P.
2002   Crystal Quartz from Magunco. Master's thesis, Department of Anthropology, University of Massachusetts Boston.

O'Brien, Jean M.
2006   "Vanishing" Indians in Nineteenth-Century New England: Local Historians' Erasure of Still-Present Peoples. In *New Perspectives on Native North America: Cultures, Histories, and Representations*, edited by Sergei A. Kan and Pauline Turner Strong, pp. 414–432. University of Nebraska Press, Lincoln.
2010   *Firsting and Lasting: Writing Indians out of Existence in New England*. University of Minnesota Press, Minneapolis.

Pauketat, Timothy
2001   A New Tradition in Archaeology. In *The Archaeology of Traditions: Agency and History before and after Columbus*, edited by Timothy Pauketat, pp. 1–16. University Press of Florida, Gainesville.

Pezzarossi, Guido, Ryan Kennedy, and Heather Law
2012   "Hoe Cakes and Pickerel": Cooking Traditions and Community at a Nineteenth Century Nipmuc Farmstead. In *The Menial Art of Cooking: Archaeological Studies of Cooking and Food Preparation*, edited by S. Graff and E. Rodriguez-Alegria, pp. 201–230. University of Colorado Press, Boulder.

Pratt, Mary Louise
1992   *Imperial Eyes: Travel Writing and Transculturation*: Taylor and Francis, London.

Richmond, Trudie Lamb
1994   A Native Perspective of History: The Schaghticoke Nation, Resistance, and Survival. In *Enduring Traditions: The Native Peoples of New England*, edited by Laurie Weinstein, pp. 103–112. Bergin and Garvey, Westport, Connecticut.

Silliman, Stephen W.
2009   Change and Continuity, Practice and Memory: Native American Persistence in Colonial New England. *American Antiquity* 74(2):211–230.

Spivak, Gayatri C.
1987   Subaltern Studies: Deconstructing Historiography. In *Other Worlds: Essays in Cultural Politics*, edited by Gayatri C. Spivak, pp. 197–221. Routledge, New York.
1990   Strategic Essentialism, Political Power, Strategy. In *The Post-Colonial Critic: Interviews, Strategies, Dialogues*, edited by S. Harasym, pp. 1–16. Routledge, New York.

Steane, Mary A.
2004   Building in the Climate of the New World: A Cultural or Environmental Response. *Traditional Dwellings and Settlements Review* 15(2):49–60.

Stein, Ninian R
2008   Dichotomies and the "Maize Debate" in Late Woodland and Contact Period

Southern New England. In *Current Northeast Paleoethnobotany II*, edited by J. P. Hart, pp. 61–72. New York State Museum, Albany.

Thee, Christopher J.

2006   Massachusetts Nipmucs and the Long Shadow of John Milton Earle. *New England Quarterly* 79(4):636–654.

Trope, Jack F., and Walter R. Echo-Hawk.

2000   The Native American Graves Protection and Repatriation Act: Background and Legislative History. In *Repatriation Reader: Who Owns American Indian Remains?*, edited by Devon A. Mihesuah, pp. 123–168. University of Nebraska Press, Lincoln.

Weinstein, Laurie (editor)

1994   *Enduring Traditions: The Native Peoples of New England*. Bergin and Garvey, Westport, Connecticut.

Whitfield, Henry

1834 [1652]   Strength out of Weakness; or a Glorious Manifestation of the Further Progress of the Gospel among the Indians in New England. *Massachusetts Historical Society Collections*, 3rd series, 4:149–196.

Wolf, Eric R.

1982   *Europe and the People without History*. University of California Press, Berkeley.

8

Materializations of Puritan Ideology at Seventeenth-Century Harvard College

CHRISTINA J. HODGE, DIANA D. LOREN, AND PATRICIA CAPONE

Seventeenth-century Harvard College in Cambridge, Massachusetts, was an intercultural space where English and Native American lives intermingled and authority was shared. Through material experiences of co-residence and education, this unique, dynamic, and hybrid colonial community pushed against imperial distinctions between English and Native American. The archaeology of early Harvard reveals a textured process of colonialism specific to Puritan New England. The dynamics of these relations cannot be captured within a binary model of domination and resistance, colonizer and colonized. As a materializing practice, archaeology plays a focal role in the collaborative recovery and remembrance of seventeenth-century Native American and English students. In this chapter, we consider how Puritan ideologies materialized at early Harvard through the questioning of material hybridity in an institutional context in order to foster a critical perspective on colonial lives and their continuing legacies. Although Puritan beliefs were a driving force of English colonization, this project draws out the multiple, creative ways Native and English people extracted the empowering potential of these same ideologies, best represented by literacy, printing, and the Harvard Indian College.

Established in 1636, Harvard College opened in 1638 with one master and nine English students, all of whom lived in a house facing out to Braintree Street (now Massachusetts Avenue) just up the bank from the Charles River in Cambridge (CSM 1935; Morison 1935, 1936). Harvard struggled financially soon after its establishment and was revived by funds for Native American education at Harvard from the English Society for the Propagation of the Gospel in New England (SPGNE). The 1650 Harvard Charter dedicated the institution to "the education of the English & Indian Youth of this Country in knowledge: and godlines[s]." Following the charter's issue, in 1655, Harvard Indian College building, a two-story brick structure, was built.

With its completion, the Harvard campus then had four buildings: three wooden structures and the brick Indian College constructed to house Native American students. The wooden structures included the multipurpose Old College building, and two street-front domestic structures which had been used by the College for various purposes including for housing English-colonial students as well as for academic purposes. Native American students were educated to become Puritan ministers. A total of five Native American students resided at the Indian College building between 1661 and 1675 (the year of King Philip's War), learning, eating, and worshipping alongside English-colonial peers. While there were no more than two Native students attending the college at one time, class sizes in the seventeenth century were often no more than ten students (Sibley 1881). Two of the nine graduating students (22 percent, a substantial minority) in the class of 1665 were Native: Caleb Cheeshahteaumuck and Joel Iacoomes, both Wampanoag from Martha's Vineyard. Of the five Native American students who attended Harvard, only Cheeshahteaumuck graduated. Joel Iacoomes completed degree requirements and was recognized as an exceptional scholar, but he tragically died in a shipwreck prior to commencement. Iacoomes was not considered a graduate of the college until 2011, when he was awarded a posthumous degree (A Degree Delivered 2011).

An important figure in the history of Native American education in New England and at Harvard especially was missionary John Eliot (also discussed in Cipolla, this volume; and Mrozowski, Gould, and Law Pezzarossi, this volume). Eliot, a member of the SPGNE, not only was instrumental in the establishment of the Harvard Indian College but also was responsible for translating and printing several religious works in the local Algonquian language. Literacy across languages and cultures was integral to Protestant religious expression and a key component of proselytizing. Harvard aimed to perfect Native American students' English, Greek, Latin, and Hebrew skills toward edification and ministerial potential. To this end, bringing Native students to live at the college made sense because founders believed that an "advantage to Learning acrue's by the multitude of persons cohabitating for Scholastical communication, whereby to actuate the minds of one another" (in Bunting 1985:16). Through co-residence with Native scholars, the institution similarly aimed to expose their English counterparts to Native American languages, improving their ability to serve the proselytizing goals of both Harvard and its benefactor, the SPGNE: "what you propound from the honorable corporation about six hopeful Indians to be trained up in the college under some fit Tutor that preserving their own language they may attain the knowledge of other tongues and disperse the Indian tongue in the College we fully approve as a hopeful way to further the work [of Native conversion]" (Connecticut Commissioners to Edward Winslow, SPGNE, September 24, 1653, in Littlefield, 1907:187). This stance led Eliot and the SPGNE to print the first Bible in British North America not in English but in the local Algonquian language family. The volume was produced at Harvard in 1663 at the first printing press in North America, which was for a time housed in the Indian College.

One of the more notable individuals involved with the Indian College and press was Nipmuc Indian James Printer, also known as Wowaus, whose home community was Hassanamesit in central Massachusetts. Printer earned his English surname for the skill he displayed as a printer's "devil" (apprentice) at Harvard. There, he laid the type for the 1663 "Indian Bible" and many other works. For several subsequent decades, Eliot and other assistants translated more than twenty religious tracts into Algonquian; the Harvard press produced these and other religious and official English products.

The colonial initiative to educate Native Americans at Harvard ended just after King Philip's War (1675–1676), when its building was devoted to printing. By 1693, with the building in ruins, the press was removed from the Indian College (Bunting 1985:13). In 1695 the SPGNE declared, "Whereas the President & Fellows of ye College In Cambridge have Proposed & Desired that ye Bricks belonging to ye Indian College wch is gone to decay & become altogether Useless may be Removed & Used for an Additional Building to Harvard College" (CSM 1925:lxxxiv). In 1698 the Indian College's empty and crumbling building was dismantled. Some of its bricks were used to build a new dormitory, itself torn down in 1781. The political abandonment of the Indian College mission, along with its unique vision for cooperative Native-white relations, was signaled by the dismantling of its physical structure. The Indian College and its students became a footnote in Harvard's institutional histories as well as the larger histories of colonial New England.

The Harvard Yard Archaeology Project

As part of the commemoration of the 350th anniversary of the 1655 Indian College building, the Peabody Museum of Archaeology and Ethnology, Harvard University Native American Program (HUNAP), and Department of Anthropology began an ongoing partnership that includes Harvard students and faculty and other scholars, neighboring Native American communities, and state and local history representatives. We study seventeenth-century Harvard and the material lives of Native American and English students who lived there. Our work both within and beyond the Harvard Yard archaeology fieldwork course is collaborative, utilizing a community-based notion of heritage and the involvement of stakeholders —including students—in order to be successful. We view our work in Harvard Yard as a way to educate the public at Harvard and beyond on the importance of the university's unique multicultural past and of the preservation of this past for a variety of stakeholders. We collaborate to promote new insights and add new voices to stories of colonial history and its present legacies. Throughout our work, we maintain and revisit inclusiveness as well as critique to provide space for diversity of culture and thought.

Relationships of collaborators with each other and the past are themselves the topics of scholarly and community research. For example, through conversations with Wampanoag, Nipmuc, and other Native representatives, project participants have learned that genealogy and family histories, community oral histories, and seventeenth-century written accounts are still actively intertwined with the continuation of tribal identities. There are a number of individuals and families who acknowledge direct ancestral relationships with seventeenth-century Native American students—primarily Cheeshahteaumuck and Iacoomes—who were born on Martha's Vineyard. Some Nipmuc individuals similarly recall James Printer's place in their lineage and role within community history; among them, Moses Printer figures in Mrozowski, Gould, and Law Pezzarossi (this volume).

There is a sense, based on robust documentary and material data, that

Native Americans at colonial Harvard were exceptional individuals. At the same time, their experiences at the college were an example of the varied and diverse colonial entanglements and exchanges that took place throughout New England and the New World. Their experiences within a system of Native education support the conclusion that English authorities sought to "set the limits on Algonquian participation in English society" but complicate assertions that Eliot "insisted on" Native Americans' physical distance from the English (Wyss 2003:17). The individual stories of Iacoomes and Cheeshahteaumuck also play an active role in present-day Native American communities, individual and familial identities, and the complicated issue of indigenous sovereignty. Their legacies extend into popular imagination as fictionalized by Geraldine Brooks in *Caleb's Crossing* (2011) and by Susan Power in the short story "First Fruits" (2002).

Archaeological explorations of the physical and intellectual place of the Indian College building in Harvard's history commenced in 2005 (Stubbs et al. 2010). Over the past several excavation seasons, the Harvard Yard Archaeology Project has actively sought to locate the Indian College building's footprint and other material culture associated with seventeenth-century Harvard. Our first glimpse at the Indian College building occurred in the 2007 field season, when a seventeenth-century feature was encountered in a test unit. When we expanded this area in 2009, students revealed a seventeenth-century foundation trench, associated with the Indian College building by its location, architectural contents, date, and printing type. In September 2011 and again in 2014, the next cohorts of student excavators returned to the area to continue excavations, revealing more of this shallow north-south trench and adjacent land surfaces.

To broach the complex cultural context of these finds, we draw inspiration from Bhabha's (1994) discussion of mimicry as a form of colonial discourse that encourages colonial subjects to "mimic" the colonizer. He expounds that "the reforming, civilizing mission" has at its heart "the *ambivalence* of mimicry (almost the same, *but not quite*)"; he finds that "the *menace* of mimicry is its *double* vision which in disclosing the ambivalence of colonial discourse also disrupts its authority" (123, 126, emphasis original). In colonial contexts, that authority was shored in part through imperial categories of personhood—understood as sociomaterially produced and inscribed difference or as supposedly fixed and ordered subjectivities—upon which colonial stability was assumed to depend (Stoler 2009). Seventeenth-century Harvard was centrally concerned with knowledge and godliness among an emergent category of "Christian Indians." The college desired Native students to follow the behaviors of English students and eventually to become ministers within Christian Native communities. The laws of the college, structure of the curriculum, and layout of the physical space all reinforced homogenization within the collegiate community. Nevertheless, Bhabha persuasively argues that rather than a simple reproduction of colonizer, "to be Anglicized is *emphatically* not to be English" (1994:125, emphasis original).

For Bhabha, however, the result is a blurred copy, which he discusses in terms of mockery, failure, inauthenticity, and irony. This tone is captured by Mary Rowlandson, the wife of Puritan minister Joseph Rowlandson, in her 1682 firsthand narrative of captivity by Wampanoag and Narragansett during King Philip's War. Written several years after her eleven-week imprisonment, Rowlandson's account is replete with descriptions of Algonquian people she encountered. Rowlandson made little distinction between Praying Town Indians and other Native peoples in describing Native people as "savages" and their behavior as "cruel." Even when wearing English clothes, she writes, they were decidedly non-Puritan:

> My heart skipped within me, thinking they had been Englishmen at the first sight of them, for they were dressed in English apparel, with hats, white neckcloths, and sashes about their waists; and ribbons upon their shoulders; but when they came near, there was a vast difference between the lovely faces of Christians, and foul looks of those heathens, which much damped my spirit again. (Rowlandson 1828 [1682]:50)

The posture espoused in her narrative is present in others of the period, which also suggest the incomplete mapping of English culture on Native peoples (Breitwieser 1990; Vaughan and Clark 1986); they are never truly English in manner, speech, action, or dress. This discourse and materialization is, however, not present at Harvard.

Our interpretation of the archaeological record from seventeenth-century Harvard has been informed by current discussions of material hybridity in a variety of colonial contexts (for example, Dietler 2010; Hantman 2010; Voss and Casella 2012). Numerous archaeologists attending to the materiality of hybridity recognize, as do we, the limitations of Bhabha's privileging of ideology, arguing that there are context-specific material nuances to manifestations of colonialism. Focusing on material practices enables archaeologists to frame the materiality of colonialism not as a choice between being European and being Native but as the conscious, creative, and complex entanglement of different forms of material culture to generate new practices and identities. Nor are archaeologists complacent with Bhabha's language, especially given present-day political agendas of sovereignty and self-determination. Instead they prefer a corrective discourse of creativity, perseverance, adaptation, and continuity (Cipolla, this volume; Ferreira and Funari, this volume; Hodge 2005, 2013; Loren 2007, 2013; McBride 1990; Mrozowski, Gould, and Law Pezzarossi, this volume; Silliman 2009).

Most often these new ways of being are addressed at sites of known Native American occupation through the concurrence of Native materials or technologies within a partially or predominantly Euro-American assemblage. The material practices typically involved spirituality, dress and adornment, architecture and residence, memorialization, and foodways (Cipolla, this volume; Ferreira and Funari, this volume; Loren 2007, 2013; McBride 1990; Mrozowski, Gould, and Law Pezzarossi, this volume; Silliman 2009). In this colonial "mess," recovered non-European materials or practices become powerfully emblematic of Native cultural persistence and innovation—and rightly so. Through documentary records, we understand colonial Harvard as a hybrid Native-European space during the years of the Indian College (Hodge 2013). Yet, in this institutional setting, there is no Native material culture to stand as an icon for hybridizing practices.

At this colonial institution, archaeological evidence indicates little difference in the material culture of daily life at the Indian College from the rest of the college, suggesting a homogeneity of practice and experience noted elsewhere (Cipolla, this volume; Hayes, this volume; Hodge 2013; Mrozowski, Gould, and Law Pezzarossi, this volume; Silliman 2009). Similar tableware, tobacco pipes, dress accoutrements, and other items are found without spatial distinction across the Old College and Indian College buildings. The primary distinction between the two buildings is architectural, with the evidence for the printing press at the Indian College also setting the building apart. Our investigations have revealed that the Indian College, built of brick, was more robust than any other early structure at the college, even though its sill-on-ground construction was similarly ill suited to the sandy subsoil and high water table of this marshy former cow yard. The material qualities of brick underlie seventeenth-century accounts, which describe the structure as "strong and substantial" and "plaine but strong and durable" (Bunting 1985:13). Embellished brick is part of the archaeological evidence, indicating that the Indian College space was physically a better-appointed space than the Old College; it marked a segregated space that conveyed a substantial commitment to Native American education beyond simple words within the charter. The location of the printing press in the Indian College building as well as the work of a number of the Native Americans at the college, including James Printer, indicates the influence of local Native American communities in this early dedication to literacy.

At least sixteen pieces of seventeenth-century printing type have been recovered from excavations in Harvard Yard. The fonts of some of these letters have been matched to surviving seventeenth-century products of Harvard's early press, initially housed in the President's House before being moved to the Indian College. During a 1979 excavation in the vicinity of the President's House, a piece of print type bearing a double pica (22 points) italic "l" was unearthed (Graffam 1982; Stubbs 1992:571–572). This type piece was matched to the preface to *The Indian Grammar* (1666), written by John Eliot. A brevier (8 points) italic "o" excavated in 1980 was matched to the English chapter summaries in the 1685 edition of what came to be known as the "Eliot Bible."

At Harvard, we do not find material or documentary residues of non-European practices. This situation undermines the usual role of archaeology in colonial settings: to complicate the interpretation of European material culture through recovering and discussing concurrent materializations of non-European practices. We are forced to rethink both Bhabha's and archaeologists' interpretations of hybridity and its legacies. What we do find at Harvard, however, is the materialization of a cultural intangible: language. The presence of Native students and the authoritative role of the Indian College press were sanctioned manifestations of Native language, specially privileged and yoked to the authorizing structures of Puritan colonialism (conversion, missionizing, literacy, testimony). Early Harvard concentrates the materialization of Puritan ideology. Its careful consideration offers new perspectives on the intangibles of colonial identity and authority and complicates the notions of personhood and authenticity that were part of the Puritan colonizing project.

These material finds are inspiring two primary avenues of inquiry among students, researchers, and stakeholders concerned with the experiences of seventeenth-century Native American and English students. Given the institutional and religious context of their lives, the printing type, in particular, has spurred consideration of, first, the power of the written word to combine higher education with religious conversion and, second, the ways Native American communities have actively used education for self-determination, in both the past and the present (Brooks 2008; Wyss 2003).

Education and Conversion

The ways Native American and English individuals were differentiated from each other formed a crucial component of colonizing discourses that legitimated European power. English New World colonizing strategies forwarded peaceful conversion (at least initially) as a means to establish a mercantile base for England. Through peaceful conversion in New England, Puritans sought to distance themselves from what was viewed as the cruelty of Spanish colonial efforts and the ineffectiveness of French rule (Lepore 1999:9–11). Moreover, Puritans fostered "social capitalism" in which economic development would result from industrious behavior, piety, and a proper education (Innes 1995:7–10).

The Puritan doctrine of predestination posited a world where one never truly knew if he was among the saints or the sinners. English authorities thus deduced religious adherence through observed states of body and soul, which were scrupulously attended to, both individually and communally (Loren 2014; Rivett 2011; St. George 1998). Spiritual status—ever precarious and aspirational—was recognized via embodied practice and shaped by material cultures of dress, comportment, and religious ritual. In this context, Native people were recognized as non-English and non-Puritan through a state of irreligion, among many other practical and material distinctions like those Mary Rowlandson depicted in her captors. Daniel Gookin (1970 [1792]:5), first superintendent of the Praying Indians in the Massachusetts Bay Colony, described Native people as "subjects upon which our faith, prayers, and best endeavours should be put forth, to reduce them from barbarism to civility; but especially to rescue them out of the bondage of Satan, and bring them to salvation by our Lord Jesus Christ." This framework situated Native peoples as passive, godless subjects, but through the mechanism of conversion, it held within it the possibility for an empowering and disruptive Christian transformation.

Although Christianity did not change the overall hierarchy of New England's colonial society (Rivett 2011:17), Native Christianity offered a new kind of middle ground.

Literacy and religion were two fundamental axes along which categories of English and Native American were drawn. Therefore, the codependent logics of racial and religious difference were substantially transformed by Harvard's Native American students. They had segregated living quarters at the Indian College, but their lives were otherwise structured identically to those of English students with whom they formed this collegiate community. Spiritual identities were mapped onto all Harvard students as they behaved more or less like devout Puritans. Native students' daily practices inscribed shared, idealized Puritan ideologies through bodily movements to and from class and prayer, educational achievement through study and recitation, pious dress and respectful behavior, and multilingual literacy that matched and surpassed that of their English-colonial peers through their knowledge of Algonquian. Cheeshateaumuk, Iacoomes, and other Native scholars thus transgressed identities of race, destabilizing the colonial project through daily practices. Archaeological evidence of a broadly shared material culture of drinking, dining, and residence underscores this point (Hodge 2013:218–222).

Literacy was a crucial mechanism of Puritan faith and religious observances and therefore integral to imperial conversion efforts. Ministers advocated literacy among Native North Americans, as they did among their English congregations. The Harvard Indian College and press were created to further this mission. In the rooms of the Indian College and through the products of its press, encounters of English and Native American people were structured along lines of formal intellectual exchange and religious study. The Indian College conflated English and Native American literacies within its walls. Its press produced and distributed, in Algonquian Bibles and other works, a material opportunity for New England's Native people to empower themselves, albeit within English-initiated values, through literacy and Puritan indoctrination. These social and material processes both entangled and destabilized identities of Native American, English, Christian, and non-Christian (Hodge 2013). The small, iconic bars of lead printing type recovered by archaeologists were part of this material engagement. Although the Indian College afforded a distinct space for the practical project of Native American conversion, it was never wholly within English control until the building was demolished.

Self-Determination through Education

Harvard became a place—for a time the only place—where a handful of brilliant young Native American men were invited to come, live, and learn. The two Native American scholars of the Class of 1665 were Cheeshahteaumuck and Iacoomes. Overseer Gookin knew Iacoomes personally and described him as pious, learned, grave, sober, diligent, and reverent: an ideal Puritan. Iacoomes was also the highest-ranked scholar in his class. Having an official place in the College allowed Iacoomes, Cheeshahteaumuck, and others to work against hierarchies of race in favor of a hierarchy of intellectual achievement and religious aptitude. Native American scholars would never be authentically English, remaining "mimic men" as articulated by Bhabha. But with their achievements, the boundary between English and Native American, savageness and civility slipped, if it ever clearly existed at all (Hodge 2013).

In a sense, these Native American students colonized Harvard. As Algonquian speakers and teachers, they joined James Printer in signaling that Native American people could direct the flow of resources within English communities and effect change within their own communities. They both enforced and undermined foundational logics of English colonialism. And they were present at Harvard because of the Indian College. Recent work by Abenaki scholar Lisa Brooks (2008), among others, emphasizes the active role of colonial Native American communities in pursuing literacy and education. Native American traditions of oration and negotiation actively adopted and incorporated written modes of communication in petitioning land rights and other issues of sovereignty. Seventeenth-century indigenous written texts, however rare, demonstrate accomplishment, mastery, and active pursuit of the tools of literacy and education.

The setting of Harvard College exposes the hybridized political construction of knowledge of and through multicultural colonial subjects. Seventeenth-century Native American students were recognized as authoritative brokers of indigenous language and other knowledge, and they simultaneously became, at least to an extent, a mimetic embodiment of

English Puritan ideals. Harvard's Indian College facilitated these transformations by materializing Puritan aspirations as a physical location and as a center of knowledge production and distribution. One of the project's contributions to the archaeology of colonialism is to draw out circumstances of hybridity even in the absence of non-European material practices. Given the charged role of literacy, in particular, we should address intangibles like language and education more broadly within frameworks of indigenous materiality. A fuller conceptualization of English and Native American colonial entanglements will result.

Reflection

The Harvard Yard Archaeology Project operates with the conviction that past colonial experiences, recovered on a micro scale, have influenced present structural relations between Euro-Americans and Native Americans, between sovereign tribes and the U.S. government, and in terms of the role of universities in civic life. Furthermore, our current institutional context has been shaped by the colonial contexts we study and, in turn, shapes the future (an important dimension in all the chapters in this volume). In 2010, Harvard Native American students involved in the archaeology project raised a *wetu* (an indigenous northeastern American shelter) at the Indian College site under the guidance of neighboring Wampanoag artists (figure 8.1). Through the *wetu* project, the students commemorated the 360th anniversary of Harvard's charter, which had committed the college to education of "English and Indian youth." Harvard Native American students, in the form of organized campus clubs and groups, associated themselves with the archaeology project. Their initial associations were formally encouraged through invitations to the project's community events. Soon, informal contacts and information networks became active. Their formation was facilitated by HUNAP in the form of announcements and public events to make information about the field course and its public archaeology format available to students. HUNAP's activation of campus energy around commemorating the Indian College and interrogating Harvard's charter facilitated Native American student commitment to raising consciousness about the Indian College.

Furthermore, HUNAP's engagement with the topic extended beyond campus through a 2005 symposium with invited participation by Native American neighbors. Present-day Native American tribes whose seven-

Figure 8.1. Commemorative *wetu* at the location of the Harvard Indian College built in 1655. The *wetu* was installed by members of the undergraduate student organization Native Americans at Harvard College (NAHC) in 2010. Courtesy of President and Fellows of Harvard College, Peabody Museum of Archaeology and Ethnology, Harvard University, PM# 2014.0.11 (digital file #99110007).

teenth-century predecessors had sent their students to the Indian College, families whose ancestors were connected to the Indian College, or Native American scholars who had considered related topics gathered to discuss the Indian College and its legacies. This symposium is just one example of the ways in which the archaeological field project fostered a community of interest and, while under way, became a formal and informal gathering place for project updates and conversation for students and other interested parties.

The *wetu* project was largely student-driven with support and guidance from various campus entities, including HUNAP and the Peabody Museum–Harvard Yard Archaeology Project. Growing from the emerging community of interest, students made contact and sought advice beyond campus with regard to cultural, architectural, and artistic aspects of the proposed *wetu* installation. They clearly articulated the goal to develop their vision of it in a culturally and technically appropriate manner and to raise awareness of these facets of the project. The students became apprentices, especially to the Wampanoag artists who welcomed student involvement in the building process. The students led the commemoration and memory making, from crafting the saplings that formed the internal support of the *wetu* to creating an installation ceremony and public programming that was culturally appropriate as well as meaningful to their vision.

The *wetu* project was overt in its awareness-raising goal by referencing the archaeologically confirmed location of the Indian College as a symbol of the university's commitment to Native American students and indigenous studies revised for the twenty-first century. Intangible heritage was made tangible through a structure envisioned by students and permitted by university administration. Students made a successful case and were permitted to construct the *wetu* in a campus area where structures are not usually allowed. By formally articulating the goals and the program in meetings with university administration, with HUNAP and Peabody Museum–Harvard Yard Archaeology Project representatives also at the table, students not only gained the necessary permission but also expanded the circle of stakeholders as the administrators became parties to activating Harvard's history. University deans, their staff members, and operations specialists came together to guide the students in a workable plan that would maintain the vision as well as address concerns such as safety code requirements and intra-university policies regarding public space and gathering. At the *wetu*, the Harvard Native American student community engaged the public and Harvard communities in dialogue about the past as well as contemporary indigenous issues; as a result they engaged in collective memory making. Similarly, individual identity and memory making unfolded as they utilized the *wetu* as something like a temporary student center.

Recovered printing type also links past and present, inciting memory and deep personal connections among individuals. In speaking with students and the public in the context of the excavation and the exhibit development process, Bruce Curliss, a Nipmuc Nation member and vital Harvard neighbor today, invoked the legacy of his ancestor James Printer as a respected, authoritative Native American individual working and living among different colonial communities. These engagements widened the circumference of stakeholders in a shared past and generated attention to updating the university's commitment to indigeneity and diversity in twenty-first-century education and democratic institutions.

One of the challenges of this volume has been to articulate the long-term consequences of colonialism in both New and Old World contexts. At Harvard we work with collaborators to overcome an absence in the present-day cultural landscape. There is no physical Indian College to manifest these histories and forward contemporary conversations and engagements, and the desire for (and efficacy of) such a tangible location is manifested by the *wetu* project. In contrast, the monumental masonry of Hadrian's Wall discussed by Hingley (this volume) is a lodestone for stakeholder and community engagement. Hadrian's Wall is a symbol for inspiring public dialogue around notions of outsiders and insiders. It offers a different view of community and colonial legacies and reminds us to revisit and embrace inclusiveness as part of colonialism's legacies. Harvard's colonial past and problematic aspects of indigenous education in this setting further conversations about today's relevance of colonial legacies and generated ideas about justice for indigenous cultures.

Harvard's archaeological narrative clarifies the unique inflection of Puritan colonialism, which privileged literacy and anxiously evaluated bodies and souls. It also contributes to comparative colonialism on a broad scale. Closer to home, it aims to decolonize Harvard's story of itself. Archaeology provides critical opportunities to remember, critique, and edit Harvard's established narrative. The archaeology project's focus on the seventeenth century foregrounds the underrepresented story of Native American education at Harvard and provides a platform for reflecting on the shape and aims of today's educational community as well as its relationships to Native American neighbors. We challenge historical and contemporary conceptions of seventeenth-century Cambridge and Boston by highlighting Harvard's first indigenous scholars and the legacy of indigenous literacy in colonial and contemporary New England.

References Cited

Bhabha, Homi K.
1994   *The Location of Culture*. Routledge, New York.
Breitwieser, Mitchell Robert
1990   *American Puritanism and the Defense of Mourning: Religion, Grief, and Ethnol-*

ogy in Mary White Rowlandson's Captivity Narrative. University of Wisconsin Press, Madison.

Brooks, Geraldine
2011   *Caleb's Crossing*. Viking, New York.

Brooks, Lisa Tanya
2008   *The Common Pot: The Recovery of Native Space in the Northeast*. University of Minnesota Press, Minneapolis.

Bunting, Bainbridge.
1985   *Harvard: An Architectural History*, edited and compiled by Margaret Henderson Floyd. Belknap Press of Harvard University Press, Cambridge.

Colonial Society of Massachusetts (CSM)
1925   *Harvard College Records*. Vol. XV. CSM, Boston.
1935   *Collections: Harvard College Records III*. Vol. 31. CSM Boston.

A Degree Delivered
2011   *Harvard Gazette*, May 26. Electronic document, http://news.harvard.edu/gazette/story/2011/05/a-degree-delivered/, accessed May 24, 2014.

Dietler, Michael
2010   *Archaeologies of Colonialism: Consumption, Entanglement, and Violence in Ancient Mediterranean France*. University of California Press, Berkeley.

Gookin, Daniel
1970 [1792]   *Historical Collections of the Indians in New England; of Their Several Nations, Numbers, Customs, Manners, Religion and Government, before the English Planted Here*. Towtaid, Boston.

Graffam, Gray
1982   A Discovery of Seventeenth-Century Printing Types in Harvard Yard. *Harvard Library Bulletin* 30(2):229–213.

Hantman, Jeffrey L.
2010   Long-Term History, Positionality, Contingency, Hybridity: Does Rethinking Indigenous History Reframe the Jamestown Colony? In *Across a Great Divide: Continuity and Change in Native North American Societies, A.D. 1400–1900*, edited by Laura L. Scheiber and Mark D. Mitchell, pp. 42–60. University of Arizona Press, Tucson.

Hodge, Christina J.
2005   Faith and Practice at an Early-18th-Century Wampanoag Burial Ground: The Waldo Farm Site in Dartmouth, Massachusetts. *Historical Archaeology* 39(4):65–86.
2013   "A Small Brick Pile for the Indians": The 1655 Harvard Indian College as Setting. In *Archaeologies of Mobility and Movement*, edited by Mary C. Beaudry and Travis G. Parno, pp. 217–236. Springer, New York.

Innes, Stephen
1995   *Creating the Commonwealth: Economic Culture of Puritan New England*. W. W. Norton, New York.

Lepore, Jill
1999   *The Name of War: King Phillip's War and the Origins of American Identity.* Vintage Books, New York.
Littlefield, George Emery
1907   *The Early Massachusetts Press, 1638–1711.* Vol. 1. The Club of Odd Volumes, Boston.
Loren, Diana DiPaolo
2007   *In Contact: Bodies and Landscapes in the 16th- and 17th-Century Eastern Woodlands.* AltaMira Press, Walnut Creek, California.
2013   Considering Mimicry and Hybridity in Early Colonial New England: Health, Sin, and the Body "Behung with Beades." *Archaeological Review from Cambridge* 28(1):151–168.
2014   Bodily Protection: Dress, Health, and Anxiety in Colonial New England. In *Archaeologies of Anxiety*, edited by Jeffrey Fleisher and Neil Norman. Springer, New York.
McBride, Kevin
1990   The Historical Archaeology of the Mashantucket Pequot. In *The Pequots: The Fall and Rise of an American Indian Nation*, edited by Laurence M. Hauptman and James D. Wherry, pp. 96–116. University of Oklahoma Press, Norman.
Morison, Samuel Eliot
1935   *The Founding of Harvard College.* Harvard University Press, Cambridge.
1936   *Harvard College in the Seventeenth Century.* 2 vols. Harvard University Press, Cambridge.
Power, Susan
2002   First Fruits. In *Roofwalker*, pp. 111–137. Milkweed Editions, Minneapolis.
Rivett, Sarah
2011   *The Science of the Soul in Colonial New England.* University of North Carolina Press for the Omohundro Institute of Early American History and Culture, Chapel Hill.
Rowlandson, Mary
1828 [1682]   *A True History of the Captivity and the Restoration of Mrs. Mary Rowlandson.* Carter, Andrews, London.
Sibley, John Langdon
1881   *Biographical Sketches of Graduates of Harvard University, in Cambridge, Massachusetts: Volume 2, the Classes of 1659–1677.* Massachusetts Historical Society, Boston.
Silliman, Stephen W.
2009   Change and Continuity, Practice and Memory: Native American Persistence in Colonial New England. *American Antiquity* 74(2):211–230.
St. George, Robert Blair
1998   *Conversing by Signs: Poetics of Implication in Colonial New England Culture.* University of North Carolina Press, Chapel Hill.

Stoler, Ann L.
2009   *Along the Archival Grain: Epistemic Anxieties and Colonial Common Sense*. Princeton University Press, Princeton, New Jersey.
Stubbs, John D.
1992   "Underground Harvard: The Archaeology of College Life." Unpublished Ph.D. dissertation, Department of Anthropology, Harvard University, Cambridge.
Stubbs, John, Patricia Capone, Christina J. Hodge, and Diana DiPaolo Loren
2010   Campus Archaeology at Harvard University, Cambridge, Massachusetts. In *Beneath the Ivory Tower: The Archaeology of Academia*, edited by Russell Skowronek and Kenneth Lewis, pp. 99–120. University of Florida Press, Gainesville.
Vaughan, Alden T., and Edward W. Clark
1986   *Puritans among the Indians: Accounts of Captivity and Redemption, 1676–1724*. Harvard University Press, Cambridge.
Voss, Barbara, and Eleanor Conlin Casella
2012   *The Archaeology of Colonialism: Intimate Encounters and Sexual Effects*. Cambridge University Press, New York.
Wyss, Hilary E.
2003   *Writing Indians: Literacy, Christianity, and Native Community in Early America*. University of Massachusetts Press, Amherst.

9

Working with Descendant Communities in the Study of Roman Britain

Fragments of an Ethnographic Project Design

RICHARD HINGLEY

> The notion that archaeology's subjects are dead is slowly moving from a position of orthodoxy to an outmoded and unethical stance few could validate.
>
> Lynn Meskell, *Archaeological Ethnography*

The achievements and limitations of the so-called "postcolonial" movement in Roman archaeology have interested me for some time. Postcolonial Roman archaeologies (PCRA) constitute the work of scholars who have been exploring ways of approaching the Roman past explicitly through critique in order to move beyond colonial thinking (Gardner 2013; Hingley 2000; Mattingly 2006, 2011; Webster and Cooper 1996). The postcolonial movement is part of a broader reevaluation of the colonial legacy of past theory and practice in archaeology (Atalay 2012; Gero 2008; Gosden 2001). The aim of decolonizing Roman archaeology appears particularly apposite in Britain, since the British drew directly upon Roman models in their imperial and colonial actions during the late nineteenth and twentieth centuries. This had a deep and lasting influence on the types of archaeological approaches that were developed (Hingley 2000:xi–xii). PCRA suggest that we can move forward to address new themes and topics that avoid the baggage of the colonial past, but is this actually possible?

PCRA's agendas include the exploration of the political context of past ideas about classical Rome and the undermining of simplistic ideas of the impact of Rome as "progress" from barbarism to civilization. PCRA have sought to demonstrate the colonial concepts incorporated in these images and to create new, more complex and critical accounts of the Roman Empire. I suggest below that it is debatable whether images of Romans communicated by the media have moved on in a comparable manner. Popular television renditions of Roman Britain continue to emphasize images of imperial Rome as having civilized the people of southern Britain. This may help to perpetuate collective assumptions about the continuing legitimacy of the philosophy that lies behind colonial activities (Hingley 2015). It is easy to be critical of the media for promoting outdated images, but the issue that drives this chapter is that PCRA have not engaged directly with the public at all. I propose that we should seek to commence a broader discussion about the contemporary meanings of the Roman past that spans the division between the academy and the public.

The exploration of public attitudes to the ancient monuments of Roman Britain should enable archaeologists and heritage practitioners to assess the intangible ideas that link to tangible heritage (Smith and Akagawa 2009). Some of the theories and methods developing within heritage studies may help in this regard by addressing the complex relationships that mediate present views of the past. This chapter addresses how those in the academy and heritage practice might take studies of Roman Britain forward by engaging more fully with the public (Atalay 2012; Meskell 2012). My argument draws on new work that is addressing the major frontier structure of Roman Britain, Hadrian's Wall (Hingley 2012a). I seek to establish the context for a new project that will address the "ethnography of the Wall" but also to explore the important international context of this debate. A broader program of work exploring the views of the current populations living along the extensive Roman frontier works in different countries (map 9.1) is likely to raise significant issues about the valuation of Roman culture throughout a vast and variable territory in Europe, North Africa, and the Middle East (Hingley 2012b). In the context of this international situation, the creation of PCRA within the territory of one previously dominant Western imperial nation may, in itself, be seen to raise problematic issues that draw contrasts and comparisons with the case studies explored by other authors in this volume, particularly in the chapters by Hodge, Loren, and Capone and by Mrozowski, Gould, and Law Pezzarossi.

I shall address the critique of the progressive model of Romanization that has been outlined by PCRA and then explore the extent to which

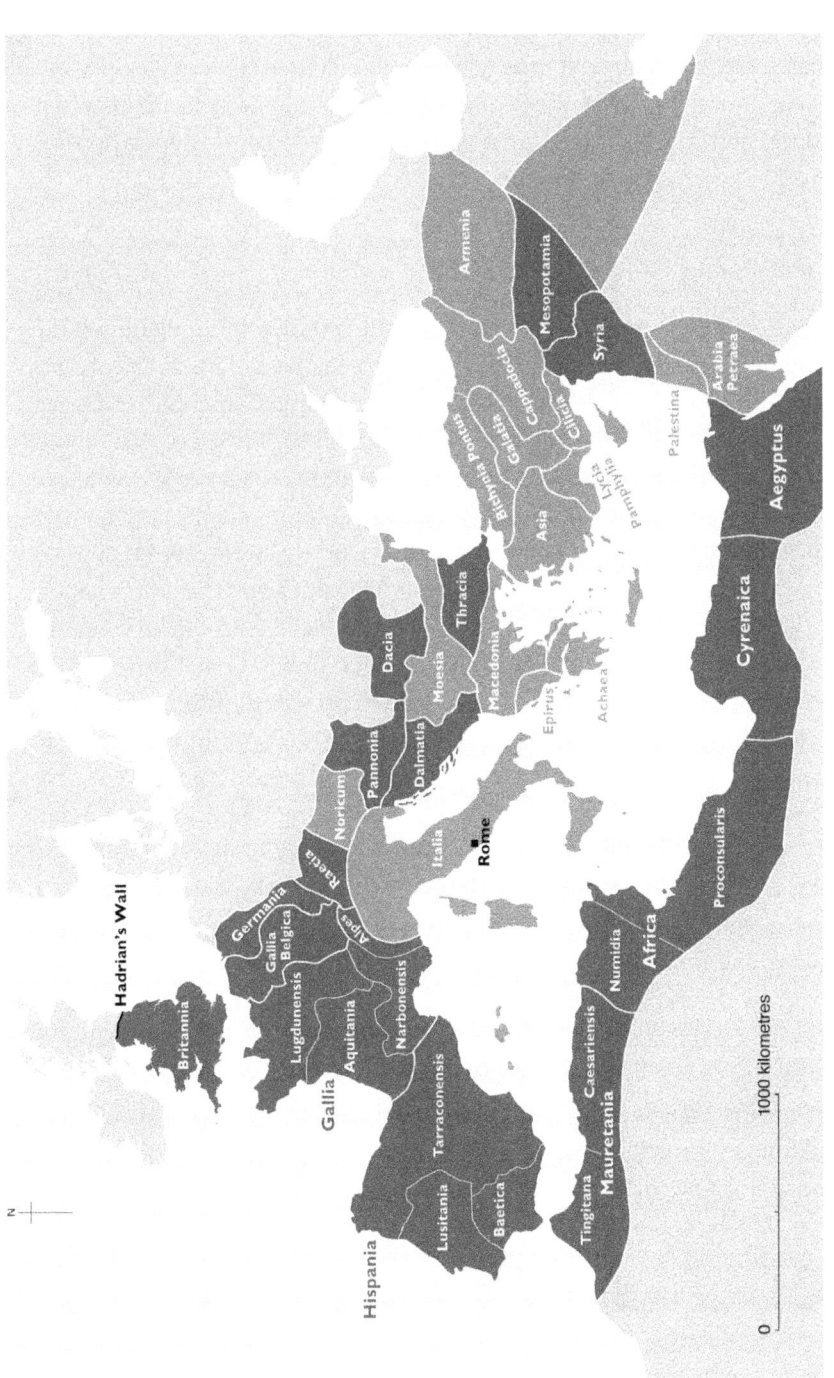

Map 9.1. Frontiers of the Roman Empire. The more darkly shaded areas represent territories from which soldiers were recruited to serve on Hadrian's Wall. Created by Christina Unwin using information provided by Robert Witcher.

such ideas appear to be perpetuated in some of the recent accounts of Roman Britain developed for the television. I will then explore the relevance of the concept of descendant communities for people in the British Isles, addressing issues arising from postcolonial archaeologies that have developed in other parts of the world.

Colonial and Postcolonial

The Roman colonization of Britain during the early first millennium AD has long been supposed to have introduced "civilization" to the peoples of lowland Britain living to the south of Hadrian's Wall (map 9.2). Classical authors established the view of the passing on of Mediterranean culture from the Roman invaders to the lowland Britons. From the late sixteenth century to the twentieth, this idea of the inheritance of civilization by the ancient barbarian population was used as a powerful imperial tool in the conceptualization of the actions of the British as an expanding nation, as illustrated by the figure of Agricola in an eighteenth-century engraving (figure 9.1) (Hingley 2008:59–67). It was drawn upon during the late sixteenth to nineteenth centuries to help to provide a justification for the subjugation and incorporation of the peoples of the northern and western peripheries of the British Isles (Wales, Scotland, and Ireland) into the expanding metropolitan order. It was used by the English to help define their feelings about the superiority of their own civilization in the context of the supposed continuing barbarity of communities living in northern and western Britain. It was also drawn upon to justify the conquest and incorporation of indigenous peoples across the extensive overseas territories to which the British wished to lay claim (Hingley 2000). This image of ancestral civilization continues today in the media and presumably, to at least some extent, in the public mind.

During the late nineteenth and early twentieth centuries, this powerful image was articulated through the concept of the Romanization of the indigenous population of the southern and eastern British Isles (Hingley 2000), a concept that shared much of its logic with early theories of acculturation in historical and colonial archaeology (Funari, Jones, and Hall 1999:4). This tradition emphasized the importance of the "Roman" aspects of the province—cities, forts, villas, and roads—and downplayed the lives of women, slaves, and peasants (Hingley 1999) and the extensive evidence for armed violence and the imposition of the dictatorial rule of

Map 9.2. Britain, with the locations of Hadrian's Wall, the Antonine Wall, York, and London. Created by Christina Unwin.

Rome (Mattingly 2006:4). Roman military studies tended to address the creation of military order and discipline on the frontiers of civilization, policies deemed necessary to impose imperial peace (James 2002). The idea of ancestral Romanization was particularly apposite in Britain during the late nineteenth and early twentieth centuries due to the scale and value of its imperial territories. The idea that this ancient act of Roman colonization led directly to the contemporary international standing of the British was used to justify acts of violence and oppression aimed against many of the indigenous peoples across the British Empire (Hingley 2000). In such colonial images of Roman Britain, Hadrian's Wall formed a vital element, a well-defined boundary to the area occupied by the Romanized population (Hingley 2008:85).

Britain's territorial possessions mostly gained independence during the middle decades of the twentieth century, and it is felt to some extent

Figure 9.1. *Agricola* by J. Goldar. This illustration is from E. Barnard's *The New, Comprehensive, Impartial, and Complete History of England* (1790). It shows the Roman governor Agricola bringing gifts of civilization to the ancient Britons in the first century AD (Hingley 2005, 24–25). Engraving in possession of the author.

that we now live in a postcolonial world (although, as the introduction to this volume emphasizes, not all agree). PCRA have recognized that the world has changed significantly since the 1960s and has developed new approaches and interpretations about the Roman past. Relevant studies have explored how colonial thinking was exported by Western colonial powers across Europe and the Mediterranean, including David Mattingly's 1996 seminal study of French and Italian archaeology in the Maghreb. PCRA have also transformed the agenda to address the complex responses of indigenous people in Britain to Roman conquest and incorporation (Mattingly 2006). Much of the focus has been to problematize the largely positive image of the Roman conquest and assimilation of the indigenous peoples (4). This has been achieved by building more complex understandings that address the oppressive—in addition to the beneficial—aspects of imperial incorporation, including slaughter and enslavement. Influential approaches have adopted ideas of hybridity, creolization, discrepant experiences, and diaspora (Eckardt 2011; Mattingly 2006; Webster 2001). A wider range of archaeological sites has been excavated, some of which appear to be less apparently Roman in character than the villas, forts, and cities that were formerly the focus of scholarly attention (Hingley 1999 and a supporting argument in Fulford and Holbrook 2011). PCRA have also developed to address the influence of Rome in other areas of Europe, the Mediterranean and parts of the "New World" (Dietler 2010; Funari et al. 2008; Garraffoni and Funari 2012; Jiménez Díez 2008; Totten and Lafrenz Samuels 2012).

Recent media accounts of classical Rome continue, however, to project a favorable image of imperial civilization, drawing upon the ideas that dominated scholarly accounts until the 1990s. A consideration of images of Roman Britain in two popular recent television programs suggests a great degree of continuity in the Eurocentric models that PCRA have sought to critique. This raises the issue of what we might consider to represent "official" views of Roman Britain: Are the ideas of the Roman past communicated by PCRA examples of official interpretations (Mattingly 2006), or are the Eurocentric interpretations communicated by popular television programs and books more representative of official heritage? Television programs evidently seek to entertain and interest people without a strong educational remit, but many people may gain their understanding of the past from these sources, especially where the views of experts are drawn upon.

Media Images of Roman Britain

The highly popular television series *What the Romans Did for Us* was shown on the BBC in 2000. It explored the innovations supposedly introduced by the Romans to Britain. This program led to a published volume produced by the researcher who developed the series (Wilkinson 2000). The programs and the book emphasize the Roman innovations of cities, roads, and villas (elite country residences) and directed very little attention to factors of Roman imperial rule that might be viewed poorly, such as the slaughter of Britons during the process of conquest, their enslavement, or the impact on the lives of the agricultural population. By drawing a close connection between classical Rome and modern Britain, it ignored the intervening centuries between the collapse of Roman rule during the fifth century and the rediscovery of classical cultural models during the sixteenth century. Perhaps more significantly, the series and the book sidelined the large-scale immigration of people to Britain from overseas from ancient times by stressing the stability of "our island story" from the Roman period on (Runnymede Trust 2013; Tolia-Kelly 2011). This media agenda closely reflects the narrative of Romanization that has been critiqued by PCRA. It emphasizes the ways of life of the elite and the well connected, linking aspects of modern civilization directly to the ideas and materials introduced to Roman Britain during the first few centuries of the first millennium AD. Comparable with Romanization narratives that have characterized past scholarship, this unquestioning emphasis on progress links the Romans directly to our present time in a way that is familiar from other colonial discourses that address innovation and tradition in strictly binary terms. As Cornell and as Mrozowski, Gould, and Law Pezzarossi indicate in this volume, colonialism does not inevitably lead indigenous people to adopt innovations wholesale, and the process of cultural change in colonial situations requires complex negotiations; but there is little sign of such processes in *What the Romans Did for Us*.

The equally popular and long-running television series *Time Team* followed a comparable approach. The general editor, Tim Taylor, published a book in 2006 that drew on the knowledge of the experts featured in the program. This publication summarizes the results of the excavations undertaken over the years. Addressing the Roman period, Taylor (2006:112) emphasizes that

> Time Team has dug at over 20 Roman sites, including Hadrian's Wall, Arbeia Roman fort [and] large villa sites . . . We have searched for remnants of Roman roads, temples and forts and have been lucky enough to find many beautiful objects, including rings and high-status pottery.

The emphasis here is again on the progress of the province under Roman rule. For example, Taylor explains that

> the dark peat floors inside the [Iron Age] roundhouse in which we found bone tools and pottery are in marked contrast to the mosaic pavements and concrete floors found on Roman sites. The technological advances that accompanied the Roman invasion have been emphasized by our reconstructions. (Ibid.)

The Roman invasion did result in substantial technical innovations, but the emphasis placed on this in such popular accounts simplifies the processes of change and continuity in a Roman territory where the majority of the population lived in a comparatively humble way in the countryside (Hingley and Miles 2002). Earthen floors strewn with bone and broken pottery were very common in the Roman countryside, while mosaic pavements were comparatively rare.

Taylor (2006:113) discusses the hypocausts (underfloor heating systems) and villas explored by *Time Team*, emphasizing mosaic floors as works of art. Along with "luxury artefacts," he argues that these mosaics make us aware of the "tremendous" increase in consumer goods that resulted from Roman occupation. *Time Team's* expert on Roman topics told Taylor that much of what we know about the Roman period has "stayed fairly constant since the early part of the twentieth century" (ibid.). Indeed, *Time Team* focused attention on the same types of monuments that fascinated Victorian and Edwardian excavators—the cities, forts, roads, and villas (Hingley 2000:149–152). There is no mention in Taylor's book of aspects of Roman society such as slavery, prostitution, and exploitation, while the rather un-Roman-style life of many rural dwellers across the province is sidelined. The issues of the lives of the less-Roman or non-Roman populations of the British Isles represent much more of a focus for PCRA but are effectively written out of these popular accounts, with the indigenous peoples fully acculturating themselves to Roman rule.

Taylor (2006:114) discusses the military aspect of the Roman province, drawing on the work undertaken by *Time Team* with the Ermine Street Guard reenactment group. Roman reenactment groups are highly popular in Britain and are often employed by English Heritage and the National Trust to provide entertainment and live action for visitors at Roman monuments (figure 9.2) (Giles 2012). Taylor (2006:114) notes that "seeing them in action makes you realize that the Roman army's planning and technological advances were on a different scale to the Iron Age."

Figure 9.2. The Living Frontier event at Corbridge, Northumberland, England, on May 30, 2009. Photograph by Robert Witcher.

Not all commentators agree about the extent to which the Roman army represented an advance over the pre-Roman situation, since the Roman invasion led to an increased technology of violence. The Romans were not a peace-keeping force but a ruthless mechanism of imperial enslavement. Graham Appleby, who is a Roman re-enactor turned archaeologist, has argued that Roman reenactments "pander to popularized notions of Roman culture, replete with red tunics, togas, shiny helmets and armour" (Appleby 2005:257). He has also observed that the performances tend to focus more on the military and the elite and less on more mundane aspects of life in the Roman province. Appleby argues that "public expectations are pandered to rather than challenged." Thus, Roman military re-enactors present a rather one-sided view of life in Roman Britain. They do not explore major issues of provincial life such as slavery and violence. The performances of Roman re-enactors sanitize a violent and dangerous past.

It is possible to put these media reflections on Roman Britain into context by considering other more critical forms of reception. For example, the films *Centurion* (2010) and *The Eagle* (2011) present more reflective views of the role of Rome in Britain, building upon a cinematic tradition of portraying the darker side of the Roman Empire (Mattingly 2011:5; Cyrino 2005). Both films reflect public concerns in Britain and the West about recent military action in other parts of the world; they represent Roman soldiers and civilian populations in a more critical fashion than the television programs. Howard Brenton's notorious play *The Romans in Britain*, first performed in 1980, provided a more critical reflection on Roman rule. It directly links the actions of Roman colonists in Britain with the activities of the contemporary British army in Ireland. Tim Brennan's performance art (2005) raises the theme of the relationship of the Roman frontier in Britain to attempts to prevent movement between peoples in today's world. Brenton's and Brennan's accounts are united in their fictionalization of the Roman past, but neither has become mainstream in media terms. They draw upon a far more critical tradition in reflecting upon modern and ancient acts of colonialism (Hingley 2011:624–626).

In answering the contention that we need to provide more critical views of the Roman past for television, one response is that studying the adverse side of Roman conquest could lead to less successful programs. Another stock response is to argue that the public would not engage with the nuanced nature of the past as communicated by archaeological writings and is likely to favor simpler and more linear versions of history. Appleby (2005:258) has observed, "To propose to Roman re-enactors that they should consider theoretical issues such as identity, hybridization or creolization, would, I am sure, have the majority running for cover!" Appleby also suggests, however, that archaeologists should engage with re-enactors to explore a more complex and critical interpretation of the Roman past. The rise of "Indigenous archaeologies" and "descendant archaeologies" clearly communicates that people feel strongly about the past (Atalay 2012), and it is becoming increasingly evident that archaeologists across Britain may need to develop a more open agenda in order to be able to communicate their arguments.

Indigenous Voices

The consideration of indigenous and descendant archaeologies in the New World raises issues about the degree to which official versions of the Roman past interact with the views and interests of various publics. Television programs like *Time Team* and *What the Romans Did for Us* reach far larger audiences than the writings of PCRA. Although David Mattingly has attempted to develop a more accessible postcolonial version of Roman Britain in his book *An Imperial Possession* (2006), the impressive level of detail may discourage all but the most enthusiastic member of the public from reading this entire volume. PCRA have paid very little attention to the interests of the public, and future research should address this topic. I argue that although we have no "Indigenous groups" in the legal sense in Britain, we do have people who draw deeply on associations with the ancient communities who built our monuments. The voices of these people might potentially enable Roman archaeologists in Britain to reorient their aims, theories, and methods.

Postcolonial Archaeology of the New World and the Old

A fundamental issue here relates to the contrasting character of postcolonial archaeology in the Old and New Worlds (Hingley 2015). The basic tenets of archaeology in the New World and Australia have been challenged through engagement with the thoughts and beliefs of indigenous peoples. For the purpose of this paper, the term "indigenous" is used to address occupants of a single area whose communities appear to have had a long-term history connected with that particular place, although we need to note the complexity of this concept (Hayes, this volume). By contrast, "Indigenous" has a more specific definition (Smith and Wobst 2005:7), relating to contemporary communities living in seventy-two countries who are in a disadvantageous position with regard to the dominant population; they include the Indigenous peoples of North America, Oceania, New Zealand, and Australia. In these parts of the world, the discipline of archaeology has developed a powerful postcolonial movement as a result of the intellectual and political conflicts that have occurred with Indigenous peoples. As a result, archaeologists have increasingly engaged with alternative ways of interpreting the right of access by these communities to human remains, cultural property, and land (Gero 2008; Smith 2004; Smith and Wobst 2005). This has gradually led to a more open agenda that draws in communities that can be identified as "descendant." Theresa Singleton and Charles Orser (2003:143) define descendant communities as "broadly speaking, present-day groups of people whose heritage is under investigation at an archaeological site or who have some other historical, cultural, or symbolic link to the site." They also observe that too many archaeologists imagine that descendant communities are simply those who are the biological descendants of the people who occupied the site (144). Descendant communities might be defined in more abstract terms to include people who draw historical, cultural, or symbolic associations from an archaeological site or from the concept of a link to a perception of life in the past (Colwell-Chanthaphonh and Ferguson 2008:8). Archaeologists have increasingly worked to involve indigenous and descendant communities more fully in excavations and research (Atalay 2012; Meskell 2012; Smith and Wobst 2005).

A basic issue in the British Isles is that, if we adopt the strict legal definition, we have no Indigenous communities. No individual or community can demonstrate a direct claim to descent from the members of a pre-Roman or Roman population. The populations of the British Isles have been highly mixed since immigration began in prehistory that may have accelerated during the Roman period and at various times since the early fifth century (Eckardt 2011; Tolia-Kelly 2011). Many people in the British Isles have imagined a continuity of population from the ancient past to the present day, but there is a powerful myth that the English are descended from the Anglo-Saxons (Young 2008). Archaeologists today generally feel that it is likely that the modern population of the entire area of the British Isles, like that of many nations, has complex genetic origins. It is likely that some of the prehistoric and Roman populations that lived across southern Britain have descendants living in England today. DNA studies suggest a certain amount of population stability in some areas and changing populations elsewhere (Oppenheimer 2006).

There are many people across the British Isles who feel a deep spiritual connection with the past populations who lived in Britain, and it is possible to consider these present-day people as descendant communities. They include pagan groups, members of Iron Age (Celtic) and Roman re-enactment groups, and communities that live close to or identify with particular ancient monuments.

Iron Age and Roman Descendant Communities in England

There is no legal requirement for archaeologists to obtain permission to excavate from local people across much of western Europe unless they own the land on which a project is to be undertaken (Gosden 2001:256). This lack of engagement ignores the powerful attachment that some local communities have to their sites and landscapes. This is increasingly being addressed under the banner of "community archaeology" (Smith and Waterton 2009), but research on Iron Age and Roman heritage remains extremely limited. As a result, we really do not have very much information about the range of attitudes held by the public about the legacy of ancient Britain and classical Rome. It is unknown to what extent school and media presentations of Roman Britain influence the public and to what degree other contrasting ideas about the past may occur. Future work with the public might investigate this issue, but in the absence of any detailed information on how the public perceives ancient monuments, I shall explore some ideas considered by archaeologists to represent unofficial heritages.

Contemporary pagans, who draw upon ancient sources in a wide variety of ways for their beliefs, have presented a formidable challenge to the official ideas of ancient heritage. An important element in these pagan religions is the concept of the "sacred site," which Blain and Wallis (2007:28) have argued is derived by pagans partly from the claims of indigenous communities for their own rights with regard to the repatriation of artifacts and the reburial of human remains. Monuments in the British countryside sacred to pagan individuals and communities include stone circles, barrows, standing stones, "rock art," Iron Age forts, Roman-period temple sites, and holy wells. Religious performances in these places are often marked by votive offerings such as flowers, food, drink, candle wax, and coins (ibid.:38, 42). Attention has been focused mainly on the activities of pagans at Stonehenge and Avebury (Bender 1999, 2001; Stout 2008), and some contemporary Druids draw on an association with these and other megalithic monuments. This is a tradition with a long ancestry. A number of eighteenth-century antiquaries drew upon classical texts to elaborate tales that connected historical writings about Druids to places (Chippindale 2004:82–95; Smiles 1994:80–82). Nineteenth-century painters continued this tradition by associating Stonehenge with Druids (Hutton 2013:24; Smiles 1994, figures 42, 48, 60). Druidic performance at Stonehenge commenced in the early twentieth century and drew upon these earlier ideas about the character of the monument and its association with the Druids (Chippindale 2004:172–174; Stout 2008:126–153). Only when archaeological dating techniques started to develop was it realized that the construction of megalithic monuments predated the historically attested Druids by several millennia. Archaeologists have often used this knowledge to argue that such "unofficial" forms of heritage can have no place in a scientific understanding of the human past (Blain and Wallis 2007:34–63; Stout 2008:163–165).

The archaeological response to Druidic worship at Neolithic sites has modified considerably in the past two decades, and many pagans and archaeologists are now united in efforts to protect and promote these sites (Wallis and Blain 2011). It is generally accepted that public support assists with the promotion and protection of these remains, even if archaeologists and pagans cannot strictly agree about their values and meanings. Since Stonehenge, Avebury, and other henge monuments did not physically disappear during later prehistory, subsequent populations have continued to interact with them; it is likely that some may still have been perceived as sacred places when the Romans came to Britain (Hutton 2011:12–13). The scientific bias of analytical archaeology may have led to the exclusion of ephemeral evidence for the later significance of these surviving remains.

I shall not address in detail some of the problems that arise through the use of Celts, Druids, and the ancient Britons as national ancestor figures, although it has been suggested that such narratives about ancient populations may sometimes draw upon the embittered narratives of the extreme right (Wilson 2013:213; also Kenrick and Lewis 2004; Kuper 2003). A number of studies, however, address the ways in which spiritual beliefs in ancient monuments can come into conflict with the attitudes and interests of local people. Pagans from outside the region often leave offerings at wells and megaliths in Cornwall, and these activities are sometimes considered by local people to represent inappropriate claims to the past (Hale 2002:161–163). Paul Basu (2007:211–216) has explored heritage tourism by people traveling to Scotland from Australia, observing that visitors with family ties to northern Britain often draw upon debates about aboriginal rights to sacred sites in order to conceptualize their own relationships to places they consider to be sacred in the highland landscape. This author's case study of the building of a "prehistoric" stone circle in Glen Innes in New South Wales, Australia, demonstrates the potential for concepts of "Celtic" heritage to be used in exclusionary ways.

Pagan activities also occur at Roman-period sites across Britain and draw on ostensibly Celtic gods and spirits. Marion Bowman (1998) has explored the city of Bath (England) as a contemporary center of pagan religion, healing, and pilgrimage. Bath has a rich mythical history, and pagan and New Age influences are discernable at the reconstructed Roman baths focused around the sacred pool (ibid.:27). Roman dedications and offerings of coins, curses, and other objects at this spa relate to the twinned goddess Sulis Minerva. Minerva is the Roman goddess in this pairing and Sulis is believed to represent a pre-Roman or Celtic goddess who may have been worshiped here before Roman times, although there is no clear evidence for an Iron Age shrine. Recent events draw on the idea of Bath as a Celtic religious center and Bowman notes that "offerings, blessings and the odd curse are still occasionally thrown into the waters of the Roman Baths" (ibid., 27). These activities focus on the idea that the Romans found an existing pre-Roman cult center focused on the baths. The contemporary pagan cult also focuses on the mythical history of the spa, drawing on the medieval and early modern tale of King Bladud and his association with the Druids (Bowman 1998:28; the story of Bladud is presented in Hingley 2008:194–201). The cult site at Bath is integrated with the concept of holistic healing that draws upon the Roman and modern tradition of the spa waters (Bowman 1998:29). Bowman argues that "in contemporary Bath there are undoubtedly those for whom such legend is lived experience" (30).

Bath is by no means the only place in Britain at which Celtic and other pagan spirits are celebrated. Although there has been no thorough survey of the available information, there is evidence for pagan activity at a number of Roman ritual sites along Hadrian's Wall. Just to the west of the Roman fort at Carrawburgh, Northumberland, there was a cluster of small Roman temples constructed in a waterlogged valley. The only structure visible today is the temple dedicated to the eastern god Mithras. This was rediscovered and excavated in 1949–1950 (Breeze 2006:219–222). Close by was a temple dedicated to the nymphs and the *genius loci* (the spirit of place), and just to the north was a shrine now called Coventina's Well. Coventina was a nymph or water goddess whose cult focused around a natural spring (ibid.). Her shrine was located and excavated in 1876 and produced a wealth of offerings, including a number of evocative images (figure 9.3).

The Mithraeum at Carrawburgh contains three concrete reproductions of altars connected with the worship of Mithras. Offerings left by visitors on the central altar most commonly feature modern coins, drawing on a tradition of leaving coins in wet places in the British countryside. Other objects placed on this altar include flowers, sweets and other food items, golf balls, plastic dinosaurs, a modern wooden writing tablet and, two Ten Commandment tokens (figure 9.4). The latter items, produced by the company "needGod.com," are commonly left in places where the dedicator feels that people need to reflect on the presence of God. Perhaps the offerings on Mithras's altar are at least partly directed at the cult of Coventina, since she is highly popular on the Internet. In February 2013, a search with Google produced 129,000 websites with references to Coventina, referencing her in a wide variety of ways. Her cult appears to draw upon associations comparable to that of Sulis Minerva at Bath. There is no obvious present-day place in which to leave offerings to Coventina, and it is possible that the altar at the Mithraeum constitutes a convenient place to commemorate her healing spirit. On the other-hand, Mithras also has quite a cult following in the present day, and the offerings may partly represent his continued worship.

These examples demonstrate that the Roman invasion and settlement of Britain has a living relevance to some people in Britain today. These particular activities may seem to be rather marginal in reflecting beliefs that few specialists would accept as in any way relevant to understand-

Figure 9.3. One of the commemorative stones from Coventina's Well, now at Chesters Museum, Northumberland, England. Photograph by Richard Hingley, reproduced by permission of English Heritage.

Figure 9.4. Offerings on the Roman altar at Carrawburgh, Northumberland, England, in 2012. Photograph by Richard Hingley.

ing the past, but they also provide challenges to media images of Roman culture as progress. They may suggest that unofficial heritages exist in a variety of forms across Britain, partially spread by digital media, although more research is required to assess this suggestion.

Archaeological Ethnographies

In the absence of any detailed research on public attitudes to Roman monuments in Britain, an ethnographic study of the contemporary population of Hadrian's Wall is planned to be undertaken over the next few years. This proposal builds on the earlier project Tales of the Frontier that ran from 2007 to 2014 and has already addressed the afterlife of this major Roman frontier system (Hingley 2012a). The Wall was a complex frontier structure within the northern borderlands of the Roman province of Britannia. Constructed during the 120s AD, it was occupied for most of the Roman period until the early fifth century, when imperial control of southern Britain collapsed (Breeze 2006). This monument has continued to have a dramatic physical presence and has been deeply drawn upon for cultural and political reasons, including ideas about nationhood and empire. Tales of the Frontier explored aspects of the contemporary relevance of Hadrian's Wall (Hingley 2012a:304–326; Tolia-Kelly 2011; Witcher 2011), but the main emphasis of study was placed upon the history of this substantial monument, and it was not possible to consider in any detail the attitudes of people who live along the line of the wall today or of visitors to the remains.

When heritage managers arrange for the public to be interviewed about their experiences of archaeological sites in the British Isles, questions usually focus on issues relating to the marketing of monuments. It has not been common to explore ideas of the sense of place focusing around particular sites (Warnaby, Medway, and Bennison 2010). For example, a recent survey of actual and potential visitors to Hadrian's Wall incorporated four aims that related to identifying the needs of visitors and whether these were being met (Mills 2013:171). Such surveys are linked to the idea of generating increased income from better-informed visitors (Warnaby, Medway, and Bennison 2010:1365). This approach does not seek to identify the extent to which various forms of "official" knowledge of Roman Britain might have influenced the ideas of people who live close to and of those who visit the monument. Such surveys also fail to address the complex variety of views and attitudes that are held by local residents about ancient places (ibid.:1379). Recent developments in heritage practice relating to the debates about descendant communities help to point toward a different approach to the assessment of the public views to ancient monuments.

Heritage practice has been changed across much of the world as a result of the political debates arising from indigenous responses to established heritage measures (Atalay 2012; Smith 2004). In some cases the outcome has been a healthy engagement among heritage practitioners, academics, and some members of particular communities. As a result, new concepts of valuation have been developing (Atalay 2012:3). Comparable considerations have had a deep impact in the museum world in Britain, partly as a result of the multitude of items held by British museums that were derived from indigenous peoples across much of the former British Empire (Benton and Watson 2010). These debates, however, have not had so much influence on the consideration of the intangible aspects of ancient heritage (Hassard 2009), especially the unofficial views of heritage that may well be held by local communities across Britain.

Various approaches have been developed in heritage practice to assess and communicate the associative values inherent in ancient monuments and places (Atalay 2012; Giaccardi 2012; Hollowell and Nicholas 2009; Kurtz 2010; Labadi 2007; Orange 2011; Smith and Waterton 2009), including in other chapters in this volume. These works are intended to inform and enrich heritage practice, but they also have value in influencing how "specialists" view the historical resources they explore. Some relevant work has been undertaken in Britain, often drawing upon intangible heritage and heritages that have formerly been marginalized (Harrison 2010, 2011; Watson 2011). The proposed project on Hadrian's Wall is meant to assess the significance of the monument as a living landscape and to explore the ways people view and value the areas—both rural and urban—that constitute the monument today. Part of this assessment will explore the ways official views derived from education and the media have influenced people's appreciations of the wall. There is a general feeling that public images of the monument relate to the masculine fixation on the idea of the Roman centurion, derived from the city of Rome, marching up and down a ruined stone frontier wall (figure 9.2). There are many other ways this monument can be appreciated, from the image of the wall as a bastion of Western civilization (Kipling 1906) or as an analogy for contemporary efforts to re-create the European Union as a "gated community" (Carr 2012) to ideas of the enforced imposition of a divisive military frontier on an unwilling indigenous population (Hingley 2012a:320–321) or those that draw upon the gods, goddesses, and famous people who formerly inhabited these landscapes.

Mythical ideas are highly variable in character and relate tales of a variety of figures, from giants who may have built the stone curtain wall to legendary tales of King Arthur (Hingley 2012a:180–181, 211). Although some survived into the middle of the nineteenth century, it is not apparent whether these tales live on in the landscape of Hadrian's Wall. It is likely that many folk tales have ceased to circulate as a result of the development of official notions of Roman heritage over the past 150 years (ibid.:231–254). Initial interviews with a number of individuals suggest that many such tales still adhere to the wall. Nevertheless, further fieldwork will be required to assess the extent to which such stories may still exist, and perhaps they could be reintroduced following the ethnographic fieldwork proposed here. Other ideas, such as the cult of Coventina, have been revived as a result of Victorian archaeological discoveries, and these could be supplemented through additional archaeological fieldwork at a range of archaeological sites.

It is also possible to draw on the potential of recent debates about the establishment of the Frontiers of the Roman Empire World Heritage Site (Breeze and Jilek 2008). Hadrian's Wall has been a United Nations World Heritage Site since 1987, but over the past decade this monument has been incorporated into a transnational World Heritage Site that includes the Antonine Wall in Scotland and the Roman frontier works along the rivers Rhine and Danube in Germany. Other European sections of the Roman frontiers are under discussion as potential extensions to this site, but relatively little progress has been made in considering sections of the Roman frontier in North Africa and the Middle East (Hingley 2012a:321–324). An ambitious plan for the future would be to link the proposed ethnographic cases of Hadrian's Wall to comparable fieldwork in other sections of the former Roman frontier areas of Europe, the Middle East, and North Africa. Politicians often consider the Roman Empire as ancestral to modern Europe, but this is a Eurocentric concept, since classical Rome also incorporated extensive areas of the Mediterranean rim. This Eurocentric notion of imperial Rome reflects its appropriation as a fundamental symbol of civilization by Western nations. Exploring the broader agenda of the Frontiers of the Roman Empire, including areas where attitudes to Roman imperialism may well be more critical, should enable the creation of a whole series of locally based ethnographies, accounts that could address a variety of local, regional, and global issues (Lafrenz Samuels and Totten 2012). This might, in turn, enable the development of a broad-based, inclusive, and challenging agenda—a transformative and descendant-based postcolonial Roman archaeology (Moser et al. 2002:221). This approach might also be used to reflect back on the notions of the Roman and pre-Roman past across western Europe and in the New World (Hingley 2011, 2012b), with an aim to challenge the worrying rise of new nationalisms (Wilson 2013).

Conclusion

The prime aim of the future development of the proposed contemporary ethnographic study will be to build some participatory work into the ways archaeologists assess Hadrian's Wall. It would contribute to the official policy intended to build a more collegial approach of bringing together the interests and concerns of the public, heritage practitioners, and those in the academy (Mills 2013). It would build on the more directly cultural approach developed through Tales of the Frontier in order to focus on people's sense of place in the landscapes making up the wall zone today. Given the character of the PCRA that have arisen over the past two decades, as described early in this chapter, the project should also aim to address a critical focus on contemporary geopolitics by exploring the cross-cultural and cross-temporal potential of Hadrian's Wall as a source of reflection on frontiers and the movement of people in the contemporary world (Hingley 2012a:324–325; also Cooper and Rumford 2013). As in the case of the Harvard project (Hodge, Loren, and Capone, this volume), the aim should be to decolonize the ways the past is received by those in the academy, by local people, and by visitors—to situate and interrogate our colonial narratives by articulating the relationship between ancient and modern worlds.

What purposes does the idea of Rome play in the views of people along and across this Roman frontier zone today? The example of pagan beliefs at Carrawburgh would suggest a critical anti-Roman (or antistate) stance for some visitors, and Iron Age and Celtic re-enactment groups may project a comparable image; it should be noted, however, that Roman re-enactment groups are far more common than their Celtic counterparts. What is the balance of interpretations in contemporary views about the wall? To what extent should PCRA of Hadrian's Wall seek to prioritize a critical reflection on academic traditions, and to what extent should it seek to absorb multivocality and cosmopolitanism? These are issues that remain to be addressed in firming up this fragmentary research proposal; they are also ideas that resonate with a number of other papers in this volume. The messy business of comprehending values for the Frontiers of the Roman Empire should reflect the complexity of current views as well as the genealogy of how these attitudes have come into being. It should also direct a focus toward how to include and influence the public that inhabits the wall's landscapes along the entire Frontiers of the Roman Empire.

Acknowledgments

My thanks to David Breeze, Claire Nesbitt, David Mattingly, Nigel Mills, Sarah Semple, Ahmed Shams-el-Din, Michael Shanks, Veronica Strang, Christina Unwin, Rob Witcher, Christopher Young, the Hadrian's Wall Management Plan Committee, and the session organizers for discussing the issues raised in this chapter. This original research derives from the Tales of the Frontier project, funded by the Arts and Humanities Research Council (2007–2014) (Hingley 2012b). For access to relevant data, one may contact the author.

References Cited

Appleby, Graham A.
2005   Crossing the Rubicon: Fact or Fiction in Roman Re-Enactment. *Public Archaeology* 4:257–65.

Atalay, Sonya
2012   *Community-Based Archaeology: Research with, by and for Indigenous and Local Communities*. University of California Press, London.

Basu, Paul
2007   *Highland Homecomings: Genealogy and Heritage Tourism in the Scottish Diaspora*. Routledge, Abingdon, England.

Bender, Barbara
1999   *Stonehenge: Making Space*. Berg, London.
2001   Introduction. In *Contested Landscapes: Movement, Exile, and Place*, edited by Barbra Bender and Margot Winer, pp. 1–18. Berg, Oxford.

Benton, Tim, and Nichola J. Watson
2010   Museum Practice and Heritage. In *Understanding Heritage in Practice*, edited by Susie West, pp. 127–165. Manchester University Press, Manchester, England.

Blain, Jenny, and Robert J. Wallis
2007   *Sacred Sites: Contested Rites/Rights*. Sussex Academic Press, Eastbourne, England.

Bowman, Marion
1998   Belief, Legend, and Perception of the Sacred in Contemporary Bath. *Folklore* 109:25–31.

Breeze, David
2006   *J. Collingwood Bruce's Handbook to the Roman Wall*. 14th edition. Society of Antiquaries of Newcastle upon Tyne, England.

Breeze, David, and Sonja Jilek (editors)
2008   *Frontiers of the Roman Empire: The European Dimension of a World Heritage Site*. Historic Scotland, Edinburgh.

Brennan, Tim
2005   Performing Northumbria: Empire. Live art performance. Electronic document, http://archive.balticmill.com/index.php?itemid=33859, accessed February 12, 2013.
Brenton, Howard
1989 [1980]   *The Romans in Britain.* In *Plays:* [vol.] 2, vii–xvi, 2–57. Methuen, London.
Carr, Matthew
2012   *Fortress Europe: Dispatches from a Gated Community.* Hurst, London.
Chippindale, Christopher
2004 [1983]   *Stonehenge Complete.* Reprint, Thames and Hudson, London.
Colwell-Chanthaphonh, Chip, and T. J. Ferguson
2008   Introduction: The Collaborative Continuum. In *Collaboration in Archaeological Practice: Engaging Descendant Communities,* edited by Chip Colwell-Chanthaphonh and T. J. Ferguson, pp. 1–33. AltaMira, Plymouth, England.
Cooper, Anthony, and Chris Rumford
2013   Monumentalizing the Border: Bordering through Connectivity. *Mobilities* 8(1):107–124.
Cyrino, Monica Silveria
2005   *Big Screen Rome.* Blackwell, Oxford, England.
Dietler, Michael
2010   *Archaeologies of Colonialism: Consumption, Entanglement and Violence in Ancient Mediterranean France.* University of California Press, Berkeley.
Eckardt, Hella
2011   Introduction: Diasporas in the Roman World. In *Roman Diasporas: Archaeological Approaches to Mobility and Diversity in the Roman Empire,* edited by Hella Eckardt, pp. 7–12. Supplementary Series No. 78, *Journal of Roman Archaeology.*
Fulford, Michael, and Neil Holbrook
2011   Assessing the Contribution of Commercial Archaeology to the Study of the Roman Period in England, 1990–2004. *Antiquaries Journal* 91:323–346.
Funari, Pedro Paulo A., Sîan Jones, and Martin Hall
1999   Introduction: Archaeology in History. In *Historical Archaeology: Back from the Edge,* edited by Paulo Pedro A. Funari, Martin Hall, and Sîan Jones, pp. 8–20. Routledge, London.
Funari, Pedro Paulo A., Renata S. Garraffoni, and Bethany Letalien (editors)
2008   *New Perspectives on the Ancient World: Modern Perceptions, Ancient Representations.* British Archaeological Reports, International Series 1782, Archaeopress, Oxford, England.
Gardner, Andrew
2013   Thinking about Roman Imperialism: Postcolonialism, Globalisation, and Beyond? *Britannia* 44:1–25.
Garraffoni, Renata S., and Pedro Paulo A. Funari
2012   The Uses of Roman Heritage in Brazil: Traditional Reception and New Critical Approaches. *Heritage and Society* 5(1):53–76.

Gero, Joan
2008   The History of the World Archaeological Congress. Electronic document, http://www.worldarchaeologicalcongress.org/about-wac/history/146-history-wac, accessed, May 12, 2013.

Giaccardi, Elisa (editor)
2012   *Heritage and Social Media: Understanding Heritage in a Participatory Culture.* Routledge, London.

Giles, Howard
2012   *A Brief History of Re-Enactment.* Electronic document, http://www.eventplan.co.uk/page29.html, accessed August 26, 2013.

Gosden, Chris
2001   Postcolonial Archaeology: Issues of Culture, Identity, and Knowledge. In *Archaeological Theory Today*, edited by Ian Hodder, pp. 241–261. Polity, Cambridge, England.

Hale, Amy
2002   Whose Celtic Cornwall? The Ethnic Cornish Met Celtic Spirituality. In *Celtic Geographies: Old Cultures, New Times*, edited by David C. Harvey, Rhys Jones, Neil McInory, and Christine Milligan, pp. 157–171. Routledge, London.

Harrison, Rodney
2010   Heritage as Social Action. In *Understanding Heritage in Practice*, edited by Susie West, pp. 240–276. Manchester University Press, Manchester, England.
2011   Counter-Mapping: Heritage, Communities and Places in Australia and the UK. In *Local Heritage, Global Context: Cultural Perspectives on Sense of Place*, edited by John Schofield and Rozy Szymanski, pp. 79–98. Ashgate, Farnham, England.

Hassard, Frank R.
2009   Intangible Heritage in the United Kingdom: The Dark Side of the Enlightenment? In *Intangible Heritage*, edited by Laurajane Smith and Natsuko Akagawa, pp. 270–288. Routledge, London.

Hingley, Richard
1999   The Imperial Context of Romano-British Studies and Proposals for a New Understanding of Social Change. In *Historical Archaeology: Back from the edge*, edited by Paulo Pedro A. Funari, Martin Hall, and Sîan Jones, pp. 137–150. Routledge, London.
2000   *Roman Officers and English Gentlemen: The Imperial Origins of Roman Archaeology.* Routledge, London.
2005   *Globalizing Roman Culture: Unity, Diversity, and Empire.* Routledge, London.
2008   *The Recovery of Roman Britain 1586–1906: "A Colony So Fertile."* Oxford University Press, Oxford.
2011   Iron Age Knowledge: Pre-Roman Peoples and Myths of Origin. In *Atlantic Europe in the First Millennium BC: Crossing the Divide*, edited by Tom Moore and Xosê-Lois Armada, pp. 617–637. Oxford University Press, Oxford.
2012a   *Hadrian's Wall: A Life.* Oxford University Press, Oxford.
2012b   Commentary: Inheriting Roman Places. In *Making Roman Places, Past and Pres-*

ent, edited by Darian Marie Totten and Kathryn Lafrenz Samuels, pp. 171–176. Supplementary Series 89, *Journal of Roman Archaeology*.
2015   Colonial and Post-Colonial Archaeologies. In *The Oxford Handbook of Archaeological Theory*, edited by Andrew Gardner, Mark Lake, and Ulrike Sommer. Oxford University Press, Oxford.

Hingley, Richard, and David Miles
2002   The Human Impact on the Landscape: Agriculture, Settlement, Industry, Infrastructure. In *Short Oxford History of the British Isles: The Rome Era*, edited by Peter Salway, pp. 141–172. Oxford University Press, Oxford.

Hollowell, Julie, and George Nicholas
2009   Using Ethnographic Methods to Articulate Community-Based Conceptions of Cultural Heritage Management. *Public Archaeology* 8(2–3):141–160.

Hutton, Ronald
2011   Romano-British Reuse of Prehistoric Ritual Sites. *Britannia* 42:1–22.
2013   Druids in Modern British Fiction. In *Mysticism, Myth, and Celtic Identity*, edited by Marion Gibson, Shelley Trower, and Garry Tregidga, pp. 23–37. Routledge, Abingdon, England.

James, Simon
2002   Writing the Legions: The Development and Future of Roman Military Studies in Britain. *Archaeological Journal* 159:1–58.

Jiménez Díez, Alicia
2008   *Imagine Hibridae: Una aproximación postcolonialista al estudio de las necrópolis de la Betica*. Instituto de Historia, Madrid.

Kenrick, Justin, and Jerome Lewis
2004   Indigenous Peoples' Rights and the Politics of the Term "Indigenous." *Anthropology Today* 20:4–9.

Kipling, Rudyard
1906   *Puck of Pook's Hill*. Macmillan, London.

Kuper, Adam
2003   The Return of the Native. *Current Anthropology* 44(3):389–402.

Kurtz, Matthew
2010   Heritage and Tourism. In *Understanding Heritage in Practice*, edited by Susie West, pp. 205–239. Manchester University Press, Manchester.

Labadi, Sophia
2007   Representations of the Nation and Cultural Diversity in Discourses on World Heritage. *Journal of Social Archaeology* 7(2):147–170.

Lafrenz Samuels, Kathryn, and Darian Marie Totten
2012   Roman Place-Making: From Archaeological Interpretation to Contemporary Heritage Contexts. In *Making Roman Places, Past and Present*, edited by Darian Marie Totten and Kathryn Lafrenz Samuels, pp. 11–32. Supplementary Series 89, *Journal of Roman Archaeology*.

Mattingly, David
1996   From One Colonialism to Another: Imperialism and the Maghreb. In *Roman Imperialism: Post-Colonial Perspectives*, edited by Jane Webster and Nick Coo-

per, pp. 49–70. No. 3, School of Archaeological Studies, University of Leicester, England.
2006   *An Imperial Possession: Britain in the Roman Empire.* Penguin, London.
2011   *Imperialism, Power, and Identity: Experiencing the Roman Empire.* Princeton University Press, Princeton, New Jersey.

Meskell, Lynn
2012   Archaeological Ethnography: Materiality, Heritage, and Hybrid Methodologies. In *Anthropology and Archaeology*, edited by David Shankland, pp. 133–144. Bloomsbury, New York.

Mills, Nigel (editor)
2013   *Presenting the Romans: Interpreting the Frontiers of the Roman Empire World Heritage Site.* Boydell Press, Woodbridge, England.

Moser, Stephanie, Darren Glazier, James E. Phillips, Kamya Nasser el Nemr, Mohammed Saleh Mousa, Rascha Nasr Aiesh, Susan Richardson, Andrew Conner, and Michael Seymour
2002   Transforming Archaeology through Practice: Strategies for Collaborative Archaeology and the Community Archaeology Project at Quseir, Egypt. *World Archaeology* 34(2):220–248.

Oppenheimer, Stephen
2006   *The Origins of the British.* Constable, London.

Orange, Hilary
2011   Exploring Sense of Place: An Ethnography of the Cornish Mining World Heritage Site. In *Local Heritage, Global Context: Cultural Perspectives on Sense of Place*, edited by John Schofield and Rozy Szymanski, pp. 99–119. Ashgate, Farnham, England.

Runnymede Trust
2013   Consultation Response by the Runnymede Trust in Conjunction with Operation Black Vote and Supported by a Coalition of Race Equality Organisations to the Proposed Changes to the National Curriculum in England History Key Stages 1–4. Electronic document, http://www.rota.org.uk/webfm_send/210, accessed August 26, 2013.

Singleton, Theresa A., and Charles H. Orser
2003   Descendant Communities: Linking People in the Present to the Past. In *Ethnical Issues in Archaeology*, edited by Larry J. Zimmerman, Karen D. Vitelli, and Julie Hollowell-Zimmer, pp. 143–152. AltaMira Press, Oxford, England.

Smiles, Sam
1994   *The Image of Antiquity: Ancient Britons and the Antiquarian Imagination.* Yale University Press, London.

Smith, Claire, and H. Martin Wobst (editors)
2005   *Indigenous Archaeologies: De-Colonizing Theory and Practice.* Routledge, London.

Smith, Laurajane
2004   *Archaeological Theory and the Politics of Cultural Heritage.* Routledge, London.

Smith, Laurajane, and Natsuko Akagawa (editors)
2009   *Intangible Heritage*. Routledge, London.
Smith, Laurajane, and Emma Waterton
2009   Introduction: Heritage and Archaeology. In *Taking Archaeology out of Heritage*, edited by Emma Waterton and Laurajane Smith, pp. 1–9. Cambridge Scholars, Newcastle upon Tyne, England.
Stout, Adam
2008   *Creating Prehistory: Druids, Ley Hunters, and Archaeologists in Pre-War Britain*. Blackwell, Oxford, England.
Taylor, Tim
2006   *The Time Team: What Happened When*. Channel 4 Books, London.
Tolia-Kelly, Divya P.
2011   Narrating the Postcolonial Landscape: Archaeologies Of Race at Hadrian's Wall. *Transactions of the Institute of British Geographers* 36:71–88.
Totten, Darian Marie, and Kathryn Lafrenz Samuels (editors)
2012   *Making Roman Places, Past and Present*. Supplementary Series 89, *Journal of Roman Archaeology*.
Wallis, Robert J., and Jenny Blain
2011   From Respect to Reburial: Negotiating Pagan Interest in Prehistoric Human Remains in Britain, through the Avebury Consultation. *Public Archaeology* 10(1):23–45.
Warnaby, Garry, Dominic Medway, and David Bennison
2010   Notions of Materiality and Linearity: The Challenges of Marketing the Hadrian's Wall Place "Product." *Environment and Planning* 42:1365–1383.
Watson, Sheila
2011   "Why Can't We Dig Like They Do on Time Team?" The Meaning Of The Past Within Working Class Communities. *International Journal of Heritage Studies* 17(4):364–379.
Webster, Jane
2001   Creolizing the Roman Provinces. *American Journal of Archaeology* 105:209–225.
Webster, Jane, and Nicholas Cooper (editors)
1996   *Roman Imperialism: Post-Colonial Perspectives*. No. 3, School of Archaeological Studies, University of Leicester, England.
Wilkinson, Philip
2000   *What the Romans Did for Us*. Boxtree, London.
Wilson, Andrew Fergus
2013   From Apocalyptical Paranoia to the Mythic Nation. In *Mysticism, Myth, and Celtic Identity*, edited by Marion Gibson, Shelley Trower, and Garry Tregidga, pp. 199–215. Routledge, Abingdon, England.
Witcher, Robert
2011   The Fabulous Tales of the Common People, Part 1: Representing Hadrian's Wall. *Public Archaeology* 9:211–238.
Young, Robert J. C.
2008   *The Idea of English Ethnicity*. Blackwell, Oxford, England.

10

The Archaeology of Slavery Resistance in Ancient and Modern Times

An Initial Outlook from a Brazilian Perspective

LÚCIO MENEZES FERREIRA AND PEDRO PAULO A. FUNARI

Since the early days of archaeology, the study of social relations in general and of slavery in particular has been, at best, a small business. Indeed, since the beginning of the discipline in the early nineteenth century there has been an interest in the grandiose, leaving aside ordinary people—including slaves. However, since those early days, there have been studies of inscriptions referring to slaves or freedmen. There also has been a great deal of attention paid to artifacts made and handled by slaves, such as amphorae, bricks, and tiles, contributing to a whole new area of archaeological research on humble materials, the so-called *instrumentum domesticum* (personal or home belongings and the like). However, it would take much longer for classical archaeologists to study slave quarters, and that is still not quite common. In any case, though, slaves were more often mentioned in classical archaeology than in other branches of the discipline, particularly since the 1960s, as is the case of the pioneering works by Carandini and colleagues (Carandini and Ricci 1985). There has also been a recent surge in interest in the materiality of slavery in ancient Greece and Rome (Bodel 2005; De Souza 2011; Fentress 2005, 2011; Fentress, Goodson, and Mauiro 2011; Thompson 2003).

Historical archaeology started in the United States as the study of the elites in the 1960s, more than a hundred years after the archaeological studies of early classical slave material. Historical archaeology paid attention to slavery only gradually from the 1970s starting in the United States. It then picked up in other places including Brazil and South Africa and spread to several countries in the wake of the Cold War (1946–1989), reaching Cuba, Colombia, Venezuela, and Argentina as well as French Guyana, Mauritius, and other parts of the world (Ferreira 2010; Singleton and Souza 2009). The main thrust from classical scholarship came from comparative studies such as the pioneering study by Moses Finley (1912–1986) on *Ancient Slavery and Modern Ideology* (1980), which has been seminal for rethinking the relationship between modern and ancient slavery. Historical archaeologists dealing with modern slavery started to look anew at classical archaeologists' studies of slave material culture (Orser and Funari 2001; Small 1995).

In this chapter, we start by discussing the history of slavery and resistance in Brazil, before considering the influential role that classical archaeology played in shaping archaeological studies of this topic. After that we discuss the early studies on maroon archaeology in Brazil and then turn to recent developments and outlooks in the field. The overall thrust of our argument is that the colonized situation of Brazil enabled classical archaeology to play a unique role in shaping progressive archaeology, including the study of slavery and resistance. We base this argument on the continued importance of Roman heritage in the country and the lasting slave and patrimonial social relations (Garraffoni and Funari 2012). To be clear, our focus is on the developing practice of archaeology in Brazil; the constraints of space in this chapter do not allow for great detail of the contexts of slavery and maroon communities themselves beyond the brief overview that follows.

Slavery and Resistance in Brazil

The enslavement of Africans and African descendants reigned in Brazil from the start of Portuguese colonization in 1500 until emancipation in 1888. Slaves comprised the vast majority of the population in almost all regions of Brazil (Karasch 2000; Mattoso 1987). It is estimated that 4,500,000 African slaves arrived in Brazilian ports (Curtin 1969; Curto and Lovejoy 2004; Eltis and Richardson 2010). They were the hands and feet of the Brazilian economic system (Gorender 1980). So far the still-incipient archaeology of slavery in Brazil shows that even in a subordinate position, slaves were active participants in the creation of new cultural forms. They plied the cosmology and material culture they brought from Africa and mixed them with the cultural repertoire present in the Brazilian regions (as examined, for example, in Agostini 1998, 2002; Souza 2007; Souza and Symanski 2009; Symanski 2007). In doing so, they reinforced their identity, that is, their humanity.

This everyday reinvention of culture was a form of resistance. It can be said that the constant effort of a slave was to cease to be a slave. Therefore, the history of the African diaspora refers mainly to the experiences and processes of slave resistance (Singleton and Souza 2009), which they had already initiated on slave ships (Behrendt, Eltis, and Richardson 2001). Slaves rarely acted freely. Thus, the acquisition, production, and use of artifacts by slaves in the diaspora almost always resulted in social actions and processes of resistance against the surveillance devices and oppression organized by slave masters (Ferreira 2010; Singleton 1999; Weik 2009).

As stated by two Brazilian historians (Reis and Gomes 1996:9), where there was slavery, there was resistance, negotiation for autonomous spaces, and strategies for coping with slave masters. In Brazil, the most typical form of resistance was the collective escape of slaves who, from the late sixteenth century, formed settlements known as *quilombos* or *mocambos*. Even after emancipation, maroon villages remained common in Brazil and were recognized by the national constitution of 1988 as traditional settlements to be preserved and protected with land rights (Leite 2008). According to some Afro-Brazilian social groups and the Brazilian government, there are more than four thousand maroon descendant communities in Brazil; six hundred of them are currently in the process of getting their land rights recognized (Ministério da Educação 2005). Therefore, in Brazil the *quilombo* was and continues to be a module of radical resistance to slavery and mainly to the ideological values of the landowners. The sociologist Clóvis Moura conceptualized this process as *quilombagem* (Moura 2001). Indeed, the Brazilian *quilombos* help archaeologists to understand slavery as a diachronic process (Miller 2012; Stahl 2008:39) and to realize the long-lasting consequences and legacies of slavery for contemporary maroon communities and their descendants. Thus, the *quilombos* are precious archaeological objects for the study of slave resistance in Brazil.

The Role of Classical Archaeology in Developing Modern Slavery Archaeology in Brazil

Classical archaeology developed first as an aristocratic and reactionary endeavor (Funari 1997), particularly during the latest dictatorship (1964–1985), as the eulogy of military-controlled academy attests (Menezes 1967). However, it was a key factor in shaping a democratic and progressive development of archaeology in Brazil since restoration of civilian rule, as discussed in detail by Funari (2013). It also contributed to the discussion of historical archaeology beyond modernity, again from a colonized perspective (Funari 1999; Funari and Hall 1999). In this chapter we explore the role that archaeological studies of Roman slavery played in the process, starting by discussing the epistemological relationship between historical and archaeological studies of Roman slavery. In her 2010 article on diaspora, Jane Webster stresses that an ancient history of slavery is well established in Europe, the Old World, while the archaeology of Roman slavery is almost absent. This is not the case in Brazil, and this is explained by the peripheral and colonial context of the country and its scholarship. As we argue here, the mixed situation has led this area of scholarship in new and creative directions.

Ancient history as well as mainstream archaeology were most reactionary scholarly endeavors in Brazil during military rule. Since amnesty in 1979, free state elections in 1982, the restoration of civilian rule in March 1985, and the new constitution in 1988, there has been a gradual but huge movement from conservative tenets to a diversified approach to both history and archaeology. However, archaeology was still controlled by the old guard for several years, and still today some of the most senior archaeologists are those who worked with the military. Several archaeologists kept powerful positions after the demise of the dictatorship, and their agenda included empiricism and conservatism (Funari 2002a, 2003). The discipline of ancient history also took several years to distance itself from conservative approaches, making the study of slavery in ancient history a recent endeavor, for the most part beginning in the 1960s (Wiedemann 2005). The study of Roman graffiti played a unique role in this scholarship. It was discussed as archaeological evidence of popular culture, including slave identities, soon after the restoration of freedom in Brazil (Funari 1989, 1993, 1995; Garraffoni 2008; Garraffoni and Funari 2009).

It is no coincidence that it was this Roman archaeological concern with slavery that led to the major thrust toward the archaeology of maroons in Brazil in the early 1990s.

Since then, and as a result of the changes in classical archaeology, Brazilian scholars of both ancient history and historical archaeology started to pay attention to slavery as a serious scholarly subject (Funari 2006; Funari and Carvalho 2012; Funari, Zarankin, and Salerno 2009). In epistemological terms, archaeology's lead is in contrast to the overall trend in former colonial powers (Funari 2002b), as emphasized by Jane Webster in several works (Webster 2005, 2008, 2010). Classical archaeology had this unique role because in the colonial situation of Brazil the leading positions and academics were conservative and even authoritarian scholars, including both ancient historians and archaeologists (Funari and Garraffoni 2008). This meant that new trends and ideas in these disciplines were left to the young Turks and challengers of the status quo. Roman graffiti and other evidence served to deal with the originality of popular culture in the past and the present, or the other way around (Cavicchioli 2008; Feitosa 2008; Feitosa and Garraffoni 2010; Garraffoni 2012; Garraffoni and Funari 2009). Again, it is no coincidence that the World Archaeological Congress and the discussion of indigenous peoples, colonialism, and exploitation were introduced by classical archaeologists in Brazil; still today their leading role is evident, even if democracy led to a positive development beyond the original thrust of classical archaeology.

Colonialism has been the main reason classical archaeology has played this uniquely social role in Brazil. Dictatorship in Brazil was part of the Cold War, and the ultrareactionary role of ancient history and archaeology is evinced by the persecution that progressive scholars endured from fellow archaeologists and ancient-historians, several of whom were still in academic power. The new and free generations of scholars result from the struggle against authoritarian rule; Roman graffiti and archaeologies of slavery were thus improbable scholarly weapons due to those particular colonial contexts.

Archaeologies of Roman and Brazilian Slavery

Moses Finley's 1980 classic is widely used in Brazil in its Portuguese-language translation and is a reference for archaeologists and historians of modern and ancient times. However, as Jane Webster (2008:104) stresses, classical archaeology is not always keen on comparative analysis, and that is also the case in Brazil. Classical archaeology in Brazil, though, has dealt with ordinary people since the demise of dictatorship in the mid-1980s (Funari 1997), just as the archaeology of Brazilian slavery was being established. A comparative approach is thus a clear, open avenue, most promising in two main aspects. First, the study of maroons in Brazil is at the forefront of progressive historical archaeology, offering a plethora of possible suggestions for classical archaeologies of slavery. The archaeological study of classical slavery is not particularly developed, as emphasized by Jane Webster (2010), and mostly deals with slaves in captivity rather than with rebel communities. Maroons in Brazil attest to a diversity of ethnic groups in rebel polities, a suggestion that could prove very promising in relation to the ancient Mediterranean. Second, Brazilian classical archaeology's focus on evidence from people, including slaves, may prove very useful for the study of slave and/or freedman graffiti and drawings. There has been some study of slave and maroon drawings, scarifications (Guimarães 1992), and other art forms (Orser 1996). Although these approaches are still in their infancy, they are very promising.

Early Studies of Maroon Archaeology in Brazil

The restoration of democratic rule in Brazil in 1985 supported increasing research interest in maroons, since many scholars considered the study of fugitive slaves and their descendants a key part of the struggle for social justice in the country (Funari and Carvalho 2005). A military coup in 1964 led to the long dictatorship under which some dissenters suffered persecution and exile and others went missing. Little maroon research was accomplished during this period. However, in the 1980s, with the return of civilian rule, the large Palmares *quilombo* was declared a national heritage site just a few months after the restoration of civil liberties. In addition, the democratic constitution of 1988 established the right of maroons to their own lands; several federal, state, and town laws not only protected maroons but also fostered the archaeological study of maroons as part of cultural resource management activities. Their distinct political status interestingly articulates with the intersections of diasporic and indigenous (in the sense of sovereign) identities, as discussed by Hayes (this volume). Furthermore, increasing scholarly interest in the subject led to a huge upsurge in historical, anthropological, sociological, and archaeological studies of maroons, again as part of the ongoing struggle for freedom, diversity, and human rights (Schmitt, Turatti, and de Carvalho 2002).

In the 1970s, Carlos Magno Guimarães undertook a pioneering archaeological study of maroons in the state of Minas Gerais, a historical mining area. Guimarães was a Marxist historian and archaeologist who opposed the military and whose previous undergraduate course in history included ancient history and the struggle of slaves. The study of maroons was a consequence of his own struggle for academic freedom. Guimarães used the many historical documents that referred to runaway slave settlements to propose an archaeological study of their remains. Guimarães (1992) revealed the construction techniques of the *quilombo* of Ambrósio; he studied the dietary remains of the maroons and made surprising discoveries such as the remains of rock art located in the Quilombo da Cabaça, in Diamantina, Minas Gerais.

From his findings it became clear that runaways lived in areas surrounding colonial towns and were well integrated into the towns' economic, social, and cultural activities (Guimarães 1992, 1996; Guimarães and Lanna 1980). This yet implies that despite their official persecution, runaways were able to create relationships with many ordinary people, including small traders and the inhabitants of slave quarters. The interpretations of Guimarães, in this way, are consistent with those made by other researchers (Ferreira 2009; Funari 2012): the maroons, as shields of resistance to slavery, were places of cultural exchange, multicultural spaces that brought together the outcasts of the slave societies of America (Baram 2008; Linebaugh and Rediker 2008; Weik 2008).

A growing interest in African and African Brazilian issues has produced a significant amount of scholarly literature since the 1980s (Costa e Silva 1996, 2002, 2003, 2005). Thus, in recent decades, maroons have received more attention than ever before (Reis and Gomes 1996). Palmares has been at the forefront of maroon studies in general and of maroon archaeology in particular. Palmares was studied archaeologically for the first time in the 1990s. The initial research, a joint Brazilian and international endeavor, was conceived as a political statement for freedom and against oppression. Two senior Marxist archaeologists, Charles E. Orser

Jr. (American) and Michael Rowlands (English), joined the second author of the present chapter to work on the project.

Orser is a pioneer in the study of African American material culture, slavery, and racism in the United States. He reshaped the field of historical archaeology from a critical perspective (Orser 1988, 1996) and encouraged researchers to focus on workers, slaves, and other oppressed peoples. Rowlands has a special interest in theoretical issues of domination and resistance (Miller and Rowlands 1989) and also specializes in the African continent, particularly in unique patterns of symbolism associated with African cultures (Rowlands and Warnier 1988). Funari published the first Brazilian handbook on archaeology (1988), defining it as the study of power, as well as another handbook focusing specifically on ordinary people's culture (1989). There was thus both epistemological and political convergence among these three researchers, even if there were also differences in emphasis and approach.

The three project directors found common ground in a range of topics while pursuing different avenues for interpreting maroons. All of them believed that the evidence pointed to Palmares being an independent polity, having residents of diverse backgrounds, interacting with colonizers and the broader outside world, and thus offering an alternative to mainstream slave society. In a way, all of these conclusions were already expected at the outset of the archaeological fieldwork. Still, the material remains did seem to indicate that maroons were able to survive quite well for several decades and that Palmares encompassed a diversity of settlers, as witnessed by the presence of a variety of pottery wares.

While different interpretations of Palmares were proposed by Orser, Rowlands, and Funari, these archaeologists' interpretive approaches shared a common concern with democracy, human rights, and social justice—in particular, using archaeology to foster a better society in the present. In the 1990s and 2000s, for instance, Funari and Orser presented interpretations of ethnic and multicultural diversity in Palmares and its meaning to public archaeology (for example, in Orser 1994 and Orser and Funari 2001). This focus on social justice also reflects changes in the discipline of archaeology in Brazil and in Brazilian society, more broadly. Examples of the latter include the 1988 Constitution and, a year later, the first direct elections for president in three decades.

Archaeology itself was undergoing rapid change in the country, as increasing political freedom led to looser control by the archaeological establishment and to closer international contact. Environmental and archaeological legislation began to open new field opportunities and led to a much greater awareness of the social role of the discipline.

Diversification of Brazilian Maroon Archaeology

Research diversification followed these political changes, opening the gates to maroon archaeology and the ongoing quest for a critical and politically committed archaeology. Scott Joseph Allen (1998, 2000, 2001, 2006, 2008) visited Palmares again and focused his interpretations on ethnicity, gender, identity, the diverse uses of the past in the present, contact archaeology, and public archaeology. Since the early 2000s, as a series of policies aiming at diminishing social exclusion and inequalities were put into action, scholarly and social discussion of identity issues has been common. Since the 1990s, diversity has been a key legal framework in Brazil, leading to a multicultural approach to social life and fostering local identity building (Ferreira and Sanches 2011).

Maroons benefited from such political developments. There is increasing legal protection for their lands, sometimes with the active assistance of archaeological and anthropological resource management evaluations. Furthermore, identity politics have been actively engaged in archaeological studies of maroon life; interpretations of Palmares have explored sexuality and polyandry, among other issues (Funari and Carvalho 2012). Archaeological research is thus not only in dialogue with anthropological and historical studies but also and most importantly with social organizations and interest groups such as feminists, gay rights activists, African Brazilian religious groups, and not least of all maroon communities themselves in diverse regional contexts (Carle 2005; Rosa 2009).

There has been growing interest as well in comparative approaches, both in terms of interregional comparisons of maroons and in terms of relating maroon archaeology with the archaeology of slavery (Ferreira 2009). There is now a growing dialogue among Brazilian archaeologists, American scholars, and fellow Latin American archaeologists and increased interest in collaborating with African specialists. South African Martin Hall has worked in cooperation with Brazilians continuously from the early 1990s (Funari and Hall 1999), and several other Africanists have collaborated on a less frequent basis.

Cooperation with other Latin American archaeologists has grown exponentially as well. Despite the language barrier, with Portuguese usually being considered difficult for Spanish speakers, several common research initiatives have been undertaken, and many books and journal articles have been jointly published (Ferreira, Ferreira, and Rotman 2011; Ferreira and Nastri 2010). The archaeological study of maroons is well developed in several countries, most notably Cuba, Colombia, and Venezuela. Brazilians have been cooperating with archaeologists from these countries and have had particularly active joint projects with Cubans (Domínguez and Funari 2008; Ferreira and Corzo 2013; Funari and Domínguez 2005, 2006; Funari, Ferreira, and Domínguez 2006). These collaborations have been important in advancing the discussion of similarities and differences in maroon material culture and in contributing to theoretical debates about such concepts as acculturation, miscegenation, and transculturation. Cooperation with Americans and other English-speaking archaeologists has increased as well, enabling the use of a diverse range of theoretical and empirical research strategies and approaches (Funari and Carvalho 2012).

Contemporary Maroon Identity and Its Relevance to Archaeologies of Modern and Ancient Slavery

The study of maroon communities in Latin America is now well developed, particularly in Brazil. This is due to several reasons, not least the democratic thrust from the late 1970s, as social movements were able to blossom with the decline of dictatorship and the spread of ever more active social movements. This has been mostly a move by anthropologists (O'Dwyer 2007), but archaeologists were able to profit from it in several ways. First, maroon people have produced a plethora of material culture revealing a unique mix of influences and influxes, as in the case of Afro-Brazilian religiosity and the presence of African, Native Brazilian, and European deities, saints, and symbols. This may be very useful for those studying ancient slavery, as this evidence contributes to understanding slave and runaway material culture as a composite. Then again, modern maroons are key social actors using ancient remains (or imagined origins) as a weapon for their own rights. This occurs in several countries and notably in Brazil since restoration of civilian rule in 1985 as maroon land rights have been linked to archaeological remains (Almeida 2012). Such use of maroon material culture is not attested to or even probable in ancient times, but even so, the coalescing role of material culture in shaping a social movement may contribute to understanding how ancient slaves may have used such items as evidence of bondage and of the struggle for freedom at the same time. The uses of palm trees in pipes to refer to a maroon settlement in modern times may lead us to explore counterintuitive ancient evidence such as gladiator weapons to express aspirations of freedom (Garraffoni 2008).

Outlook

Based on the above discussion, it is clear that the potential for further developing maroon archaeologies in Brazil is huge. Maroon communities did not include only people of strictly African descent but a diverse group of people of mixed African, Indian, and European descent, as with the Brazilian population as a whole. Considering their continued relevance in the present, maroons are thus an increasingly important social topic. As Brazil continues to develop economically, paying attention to maroons is part and parcel of the overall process of creating more equal economic, social, political, and cultural relations in the country.

Maroon archaeology in Brazil allows us to examine slavery's continued colonial impact on formerly enslaved people and their descendants living in contemporary maroon communities. The great potential of maroon archaeology in Brazil includes the possibility of promoting social justice, triggering the processes of *quilombagem* in Brazil, according to the perception of Clóvis Moura (2001) as discussed at the beginning of this chapter. As stressed by Hayes and Cipolla (this volume), the collaboration between archaeologists and contemporary stakeholders can amplify communities' narratives and the construction of alternative epistemological perspectives.

Archaeology in Brazil has been increasingly engaging social and power-related issues since the restoration of civil liberties in 1985, and the success of maroon archaeology should be understood as part of this overall trend. The number of archaeologists in the country multiplied at least fourfold in twenty-five years, as did fieldwork activity, conferences, publications, and international collaborations. There is not a single aspect of the discipline left unaffected by the breath of fresh air produced by Brazil's movement toward greater freedom and democracy. The archaeology of maroons is part of democratizing the discipline. Maroon archaeology's influence has been significant outside of Brazil, in other Latin American countries and in the United States. The interregional comparisons now possible contribute to new understandings of runaway slaves as archaeological subjects. Its contribution to a comparative perspective is probably the most important influence of Brazilian maroon archaeology in a global perspective.

But Brazilian maroon archaeology should also contribute to cross-temporal dialogue with classical archaeological studies of slave material culture. Importantly, the study of *instrumentum domesticum* shows how artifacts made or handled by slaves were pervasive in ancient and modern times. Colonoware in the United States as well the pottery associated with the Brazilian maroons were possible to compare with ordinary pottery in the Roman world, also very much a mixed experience in the material world.

The dialogue between archaeologists studying Brazilian slavery and resistance and classical archaeologists could help identify and compare methodological problems such as recognizing material signatures of slavery. Dialogue could promote cross-fertilization between classical archaeologists and Brazilian archaeologists studying slavery and emphasize common research themes such as slave identity and slave sexuality, slave owners' strategies of coercion, vigilance, the built landscapes of slavery, and the processes of slave resistance and formation of runaway slave settlements. Finally, a diachronic approach to the study of slavery could enable archaeologists to analyze the technologies of the slave system and slave agency.

The Brazilian case proves that classical archaeology and historical archaeology can coalesce into creative ways of decolonizing the study of the past. It demonstrates that it is not only the historical archaeology of modern slavery that can inspire classical archaeology, as discussed by Jane Webster (2010), but that Roman graffiti studied as material evidence by scholars in the colonized world may help us understand modern slave struggles. More than that, this approach from scholars living and/or working on similar issues in the Old World may address issues such as sexuality, gender, and identity in innovative ways. There are several reasons this is the case, not least of which is the direct cooperation of scholars with ordinary people and descendant communities. As emphasized by Hodge, Loren, and Capone (this volume) and Mrozowski, Gould, and Law Pezzarossi (this volume), contemporary communities engage with the archaeology of their ancestors while also discussing their own roles and places in contemporary colonial society. In Brazil, our current idea is to take advantage of Brazilian cultural resource management legislation and to compose a policy of protection for maroon archaeological sites. Consequently, we can propose a model of community management of heritage assets based on the local experiences and conceptions in which each family from the community, with our collaboration, would be the stakeholders of the areas historically occupied by their ancestors (Ferreira 2009).

All of these moves and features may serve archaeologists from former colonial powers when dealing with such a delicate subject as slavery. However, it must be said that the traditional disciplinary boundaries limit the spread of those experiences and interpretive interactions. It is still rare to find such a transdisciplinary approach, linking patterns of material culture across disciples of historical archaeology, classical archaeology, and even prehistory. Exceptions like Chris Gosden's (2006) study confirm both the rarity of these attempts and their potential benefits. It is thus possible to say that closer cooperation and exchange of experiences, literature, and much more would benefit archaeologists working on issues of slavery in whatever period or civilization. We are just starting this comparative endeavor, but we consider the outlook for such a project very bright indeed.

Acknowledgments

We owe thanks to Camila Agostini, Scott Allen, Cláudio Carle, Marina Régis Cavicchioli, Lourdes Domínguez, Lourdes Feitosa, Renata Garraffoni, Chris Gosden, Carlos Magno Guimarães, Charles E. Orser Jr., Gabino La Rosa Corzo, and Michael Rowlands. We mention also the support of the World Archaeological Congress, Universidade Estadual de Campinas (Unicamp), Universidade Federal de Pelotas (FPel), Foundation for Research Support of the State of São Paulo (FAPESP), National Council for Scientific and Technological Development (CNPq), and Coordenação de Aperfeiçoamento de Pessoal de Nível Superior (CAPES). The responsibility for the ideas is our own, and we are solely responsible for them.

References Cited

Agostini, Camilla
1998 Resistência cultural e reconstrução de identidades: Um olhar sobre a cultura material de escravos do século XIX. *Revista de História Regional* 3(2):113–137.
2002 *Comunidade e conflito na senzala: Africanos, afrodescendentes e a formação de identidades em Vassouras, 1820–1860.* Unpublished Ph.D. dissertation, University of Campinas, Brazil.

Allen, Scott J.
1998 A "Cultural Mosaic" at Palmares? Grappling with the Historical Archaeology of a Seventeenth-Century Brazilian Quilombo. *Cultura Material e Arqueologia Histórica*, edited by Pedro Paulo Funari, pp. 141–178. Instituto de Filosofia e Ciências Humanas, University of Campinas, Brazil.
2000 Construindo a identidade palmarina. Direções preliminares na arqueologia histórica de Palmares. *Revista de História da Arte e Arqueologia* 3:169–175.
2001 *Zumbi Nunca Vai Morrer: History, the Practice of Archaeology and Race Politics in Brazil.* UMI, Ann Arbor, Michigan.
2006 As vozes do passado e do presente: Arqueologia, política cultural e o público na Serra da Barriga. *Clio* 20:81–101.
2008 Arqueologia na Região Serrana Quilombola: Alagoas, 2008–2009. *Vestígios: Revista Latino-Americana de Arqueologia Histórica* 2:99–101.

Almeida, Fábio G.
2012 *Terra de Quilombo: Arqueologia da Resistência e Etnoarqueologia no Território Mandira, Município de Cananéia/SP.* Unpublished master's thesis, Museum of Archaeology and Ethnology, University of São Paulo, São Paulo.

Baram, Uzi
2008 A Haven from Slavery on Florida's Gulf Coast: Looking for Evidence of Angola on the Manatee River. *The African Diaspora Archaeology Network Newsletter*, April. Electronic document, http://www.diaspora.illinois.edu/news0608/news0608-4.pdf, accessed May 2008.

Behrendt, Stephen D., David Eltis, and David Richardson
2001 The Costs of Coercion: African Agency in the Pre-Modern Atlantic World. *Economic History Review* 54(3):454–476.

Bodel, John
2005 Caveat Emptor: Towards a Study of Roman Slave-Traders. *Journal of Roman Archaeology* 18(1):181–196.

Carandini, Andrea, and A. Ricci (editors)
1985 *Settefinestre: Una villa Schiavistica nell'Etruria Romana.* Modena, Rome.

Carle, Cláudio B.
2005 *A organização dos assentamentos de ocupação tradicional de africanos e descendentes no Rio Grande do Sul, nos séculos XVIII e XIX.* Unpublished Ph.D. dissertation, Pontifical Catholic University of Rio Grande do Sul, Porto Alegre, Brazil.

Cavicchioli, Marina R.
2008 The Erotic Collection of Pompeii: Archaeology, Identity, and Sexuality. In *New

Perspectives on the Ancient World: Modern Perceptions, Ancient Representations, edited by P. P. Funari, R. Garraffoni, and B. Letalien, vol. 1782, pp. 187–194. Archaeopress, Oxford, England.

Costa e Silva, Alberto da

1996 *A enxada e a lança. A África antes dos portugueses.* Editora Nova Fronteira, Rio de Janeiro.

2002 *A manilha e o libambo. A África e a escravidão de 1500 a 1700.* Editora Nova Fronteira, Rio de Janeiro.

2003 *Um Rio chamado Atlântico. A África no Brasil e o Brasil na África.* Editora Nova Fronteira, Rio de Janeiro.

2005 *Das mãos do oleiro, aproximações.* Editora Nova Fronteira, Rio de Janeiro.

Curtin, Philip D.

1969 *The Atlantic Slave Trade: A Census.* University of Wisconsin Press, Madison.

Curto, Jose C., and Paul E. Lovejoy

2004 *Enslaving Connections. Changing Cultures of Africa and Brazil during the Era of Slavery.* Humanity Press, New York.

De Souza, Philip

2011 War, Slavery, and Empire in Roman Imperial Iconography. *Bulletin of the Institute of Classical Studies of the University of London* 54(1):31–62.

Domínguez, Lourdes, and Pedro Paulo Funari

2008 Arqueología de los esclavos africanos e indígenas en Brasil y Cuba. *Revista de História da Arte e Arqueologia* IX:1–20.

Eltis, David, and David Richardson

2010 *Atlas of the Transatlantic Slave Trade.* Yale University Press, New Haven, Connecticut.

Feitosa, Lourdes M. G. C.

2008 Feminine and Masculine in Pompeii: Gender Relations among the Popular Classes. In *New Perspectives on the Ancient World: Modern Perceptions, Ancient Representations*, edited by P. P. Funari, R. Garraffoni, and B. Letalien, pp. 195–203. Archaeopress, Oxford, England.

Feitosa, Lourdes M. G. C., and Renata S. Garraffoni

2010 Dignitas and Infamia: Rethinking Marginalized Masculinities in Early Principate. *Studia Historica Historia Antigua* 28:57–73.

Fentress, Elizabeth

2005 On the Block: Catastae, Chalcidia, and Cryptae in Early Imperial Italy. *Journal of Roman Archaeology* 18:220–234.

2011 Slavers on Chariots. In *Money, Trade, and Trade Routes in Pre-Islamic North Africa*, edited by Amelia Dowler and Elizabeth R. Gavlin, pp. 65–71. The British Museum, London.

Fentress, Elizabeth, Caroline Goodson, and Marco Mauiro

2011 Wine, Slaves, and the Emperor at Villa Magna. *Expedition: The Magazine of the University of Pennsylvania Museum of Archaeology and Anthropology* 53(2):13–20.

Ferreira, Lúcio M.
2009   Arqueologia da escravidão e arqueologia pública: Algumas interfaces. *Vestígios. Revista Latino-Americana de Arqueologia Histórica* 3:7–23.
2010   Arqueología de la Diáspora Africana: Algunas aproximaciones. In *Arqueología Argentina en el Bicentenario: XVII Congreso Nacional de Arqueología Argentina*, edited by J. R. Bárcena and H. Chiavazza, Vol. II, pp. 697–703. Facultad de Filosofía y Letras de Cuyo, Mendoza, Argentina.

Ferreira, Lúcio M., and Gabino la R. Corzo
2013   Símbolo não escolhido: Arqueologia das marcas a ferro em escravos de Cuba. In *Objetos da escravidão: abordagens sobre a cultura material da escravidão e seu legado*, edited by Camilla Agostini, pp. 121–135. Editora 7 Letras, Rio de Janeiro.

Ferreira, Lúcio M, Maria L. M. Ferreira, and Mónica Rotman (editors)
2011   *Patrimônio cultural no Brasil e na Argentina: Estudos de caso*. CAPES/Annablume, São Paulo.

Ferreira, Lúcio M., and Javier Nastri (editors)
2010   *Historias de la arqueología sudamericana*. Fundación de Historia Natural Félix Azara, Buenos Aires.

Ferreira, Lúcio M., and Pedro L. M. Sanches
2011   Arqueologia de contrato e educação patrimonial no Brasil: Algumas provocações. In *Patrimônio cultural no Brasil e na Argentina: Estudos de caso*, edited by L. M. Ferreira, M.L.M. Ferreira, and M. Rotman, pp. 158–168. CAPES/Annablume, São Paulo.

Finley, Moses I.
1980   *Ancient Slavery and Modern Ideology*. Viking Press, New York.

Funari, Pedro P.
1988   *Arqueologia*. Ática, São Paulo.
1989   *Cultura popular na antiguidade clássica*. Contexto, São Paulo.
1993   Graphic Caricature and the Ethos of Ordinary People at Pompeii. *European Journal of Archaeology* 1(2):133–150.
1995   Apotropaic Symbolism at Pompeii: A Reading of the Graffiti Evidence. *Boletim do CPA* (Unicamp) 132:9–17.
1997   European Archaeology and Two Brazilian Offspring: Classical Archaeology and Art History. *Nethistória* (Brasilia) 5(2):137–148.
1999   Historical Archaeology from a World Perspective. In *Historical Archaeology: Back From the Edge*, edited by P. P. Funari, M. Hall, and S. Jones, pp. 37–66. Routledge, London.
2002a Class Interests in Brazilian Archaeology. *International Journal of Historical Archaeology* 6(3):209–216.
2002b Classical Archaeology. In *Encyclopedia of Historical Archaeology*, edited by Charles E. Orser Jr., pp. 108–111. Routledge, London.
2003   Dictatorship, Democracy, and Freedom of Expression. *International Journal of Historical Archaeology* 7(3):233–237.
2006   Conquistadors, Plantations, and Quilombo: Latin America in Historical Ar-

chaeology Context. In *Historical Archaeology*, edited by M. Hall and S. Silliman, pp. 209–229. Blackwell, Oxford, England.

2012   Agencia, teoría social e historicidad: El caso de los cimarrones. In *Reproducción social y creación de desigualdades*, edited by Hope Henderson and Sebastián Fajardo Bernal, pp. 63–78. Encuentro Grupo Editor, Córdoba, Argentina.

2013   Brazilian Archaeology, the Last Two Decades. *Révue de Histoire de l'Art et Archéologie* 7:35–45.

Funari, Pedro P., and Aline V. Carvalho

2005   *Palmares ontem e hoje*. Zahar, Rio de Janeiro.

2012   Gender Relations in a Maroon Community Palmares, Brazil. In *The Archaeology of Colonialism*, edited by B. Voss and E. Casella, pp. 252–269. Cambridge University Press, Cambridge, England.

Funari, Pedro P., and Lourdes Domínguez

2005   La arqueología de Brasil y Cuba, en tiempos de la esclavitud. *Noticias de la Universidad de Tula, Historia y Cultura* 3:79–100.

2006   El método arqueológico en el estudio de la esclavitud en Cuba y Brasil. *Boletín del Gabinete de Arqueología* 5:52–65.

Funari, Pedro P., Lúcio M. Ferreira, and Lourdes Domínguez

2006   *Patrimônio e cultura material*. Instituto de Filosofia e Ciências Humanas, University of Campinas, Campinas, Brazil.

Funari, Pedro P., Renata Garraffoni, and Bethany Letalien (editors)

2008   *New Perspectives on the Ancient World: Modern Perceptions, Ancient Representations*. Archaeopress, Oxford, England.

Funari, Pedro P., Martin Hall, and Sian Jones (editors)

1999   *Historical Archaeology: Back from the Edge*. Routledge, London.

Funari, Pedro P., Andrés Zarankin, and Melisa A. Salerno

2009   Historical Archaeology in South America. In *International Handbook of Historical Archaeology*, edited by T. Majewski and D. Gaimster, pp. 399–408. Springer, New York.

Garraffoni, Renata

2008   Gladiators Daily Lives and Epigraphy: A Social Archaeological Approach to the Roman Munera during the Early Principate. *Nikephoros: Zeitschrift für Sport und Kultur im Altertum* 21:223–241.

2012   Reading Gladiators' Epitaphs and Rethinking Violence and Masculinity in the Roman Empire. In *The Archaeology of Colonialism: Intimate Encounters and Sexual Effects*, edited by B. L. Voss and E. C. Casella, pp. 214–231. Cambridge University Press, New York.

Garraffoni, Renata S., and Pedro P. Funari

2009   Reading Pompeii's Walls: A Social Archaeological Approach to Gladiatorial Graffiti. In *Roman Amphiteatres and Spectacula, a 21st c. Approach*, edited by T. Wilmott, pp. 185–193. Archaeopress, Oxford, England.

2012   The Uses of Roman Heritage in Brazil. *Heritage and Society* 5:53–76.

Gorender, Jacob

1980   *O escravismo colonial*. Ática, São Paulo.

Gosden, Chris
2006 *Archaeology and Colonialism: Cultural Contact from 5000 BC to the Present.* Cambridge University Press, Cambridge, England.

Guimarães, Carlos M.
1992 Esclavitud, rebeldia y arte. *Arte Rupestre Colonial y Republicano de Bolivia y Paises Vecinos* 1:212–219.
1996 Mineração, quilombos e Palmares. In *Liberdade por um fio: História dos quilombos no Brasil*, edited by J. J. Reis and F. dos Santos Gomes, pp. 139–163. Companhia das Letras, São Paulo.

Guimarães, Carlos M., and Ana L. D. Lanna
1980 Arqueologia de quilombos em Minas Gerais. *Revista de Antropologia* 31:23–28.

Karasch, Mary
2000 *A Vida dos escravos no Rio de Janeiro (1808–1850).* Companhia das Letras, São Paulo.

Leite, Ilka B.
2008 O projeto político Quilombola: Desafios, conquistas e impasses atuais. *Estudos Feministas* 16(3):965–977.

Linebaugh, Peter, and Marcus Rediker
2008 *A Hidra de muitas cabeças: Marinheiros, escravos, plebeus e a história oculta do Atlântico revolucionário.* Companhia das Letras, São Paulo.

Mattoso, Kátia M. de Queirós
1987 *Ser escravo no Brasil.* Brasiliense, São Paulo.

Menezes, Ulpiano Bezerra de
1967 *O eterno presente (Brochura da I Bienal de Ciências e Humanidades).* Conselho Nacional de Desenvolvimento Científico e Tecnológico, São Paulo.

Miller, Daniel, and Michael Rowlands
1989 *Domination and Resistance.* Routledge, London.

Miller, Joseph C.
2012 *The Problem of Slavery as History.* Yale University Press, New Haven, Connecticut.

Ministério da Educação
2005 Programa Brasil Quilombola. Secretaria Especial de Políticas de Promoção de Igualdade Racial-Seppir, Brasília.

Moura, Clóvis A.
2001 Quilombagem como expressão de protesto radical. In *Os quilombos na dinâmica social do Brasil*, edited by C. Moura, pp. 102–117. Editora da Federal University of Alagoas, Maceió, Brazil.

O'Dwyer, Eliane C.
2007 Terras de quilombo: Identidade étnica e os caminhos do reconhecimento. *Tomo* 11:43–58.

Orser, Charles E.
1988 *The Material Basis of the Postbellum Tenant Plantation: Historical Archaeology in the South Carolina Piedmont.* University of Georgia Press, Athens.

1994 Toward a Global Historical Archaeology: An Example from Brazil. *Historical Archaeology* 28:5–22.

1996 *A Historical Archaeology of the Modern World*. Plenum Press, New York.

Orser, Charles E. Jr., and Pedro P. Funari
2001 Archaeology and Slave Resistance and Rebellion. *World Archaeology* 33(1):61–72.

Reis, João J., and Flávio dos Santos Gomes
1996 Introdução. In *Liberdade por um Fio: História dos quilombos no Brasil*, edited by J. J. Reis and F. dos Santos Gomes, pp. 9–25. Companhia das Letras, São Paulo.

Rosa, João H.
2009 *Entre alagados e penhascos: O ouro da liberdade nas resistências quilombolas do século XVIII na capitania de Mato Grosso—região mineradora guaporeana*. Unpublished master's thesis, University of São Paulo, São Paulo.

Rowlands, Michael, and Jean-Pierre Warnier
1988 Sorcery, Power, and the Modern State in Cameroon. *Man*, New Series, 23(1):118–132.

Schmitt, Alessandra, Maria C. M. Turatti, and Maria C. P. de Carvalho
2002 Atualização do conceito de quilombo: Identidade e território nas definições teóricas. *Ambiente e Sociedade* 5(10):1–6.

Singleton, Theresa
1999 Introduction. In *"I, Too, Am America": Archaeological Studies of African American Life*, edited by T. Singleton, pp. 1–17. University Press Virginia, Charlottesville.

Singleton, Theresa, and Marcos A. T. de Souza
2009 Archaeologies of African Diaspora: Brazil, Cuba, and United States. In *International Handbook of Historical Archaeology*, edited by T. Majewski and D. Gaimster, pp. 449–469. Springer, New York.

Small, David (editor)
1995 *Methods in the Mediterranean: Historical and Archaeological Views on Texts and Archaeology*. Brill Press, Leiden, Netherlands.

Souza, Marcos A. T. de
2007 Uma outra escravidão: A paisagem social no engenho de São Joaquim, Goiás. *Vestígios* 1(1):59–92.

Souza, Marcos A. T. de, and Luís C. P. Symanski
2009 Slave Communities and Pottery Variability in Western Brazil: The Plantations of Chapada dos Guimarães. *International Journal of Historical Archaeology* 13:513–548.

Stahl, Ann B.
2008 The Slave Trade as Practice and Memory: What Are the Issues for Archaeologists? In *Invisible Citizens: Captives and Their Consequences*, edited by Catherine M. Cameron, pp. 25–56. University of Utah Press, Salt Lake City.

Symanski, Luís C. P.
2007 O domínio da Tática: Práticas religiosas de origem africana nos engenhos da Chapada dos Guimarães. *Vestígios* 1(2):9–36.

Thompson, F. Hugh
2003 *The Archaeology of Greek and Roman Slavery.* Duckworth, London.
Webster, Jane
2005 Archaeologies of Slavery and Servitude: Bringing "New World" Perspectives to Roman Britain. *Journal of Roman* Archaeology 18(1):161–179.
2008 Less Beloved: Roman Archaeology, Slavery, and the Failure to Compare. *Archaeological Dialogues* 15(2): 103–123.
2010 A Distant Diaspora: Thinking Comparatively about Origins, Migration, and Roman Slavery. *African Diaspora Archaeology Newsletter*, March. Electronic document, http://www.diaspora.uiuc.edu/news0310/news0310-3.pdf, accessed August 1, 2013.
Weik, Terrance M.
2008 Mexico's Cimarron Heritage and Archaeological Record. *African Diaspora Archaeology Network Newsletter*, June. Electronic document, http://www.diaspora.illinois.edu/news0608/news0608.html#3, accessed May 2008.
2009 The Role of Ethnogenesis and Organization in the Development of African–Native American Settlements: An African Seminole Model. *International Journal of Historical Archaeology* 13:206–238.
Wiedemann, Thomas
2005 *Greek and Roman Slavery.* Routledge, London.

Part II

LOOKING BACK, MOVING FORWARD

Comparative Colonialism and the Future

11

Comparative Colonialism and Indigenous Archaeology

Exploring the Intersections

STEPHEN W. SILLIMAN

Studies of comparative colonialism—the explicit comparison of colonialism in different geographic, temporal, or historical contexts for purposes of improving broader understandings of it and fine-tuning its applications in specific contexts—have placed archaeologists around the world in conversations about colonies, colonization, colonialism, postcolonialism, cultural entanglement, empire, indigeneity, power, and the very fundamentals of culture change and continuity (Alcock et al. 2009; Dietler 2010; Gosden 2004; Jordan 2009; Lightfoot 2005, 2012; Lightfoot et al. 2013; Silliman 2005, 2009; Stein 2005; van Dommelen 2006; Voss and Casella 2012). It is an unprecedented conversation for the discipline, and comparative analysis brings with it significant promise for intellectual and political advancement as well as potential perils.

For many—but certainly not all—archaeologists studying these topics, whether locally or comparatively, the commitment to understanding colonialism and its effects has made them keenly aware of the legacies and ongoing manifestations of colonialism in the contemporary world in which they work. In other words, colonialism is not just a phenomenon to study in the past but rather a long-standing, multifaceted process that links past and present. This has been most acutely felt in settler nations such as the United States, Canada, and Australia where indigenous archaeologists, nonindigenous archaeologists and the indigenous communities with whom they work have tackled head-on some of colonialism's persistent presence in the political world in which archaeology operates and in the disciplinary practice of the field itself. The former has involved archaeology in issues pertaining to historic preservation efforts, land title in Australia, federal acknowledgment in the United States, the U.S. Native American Graves Protection and Repatriation Act, associated repatriation practices with respect to human remains and sacred objects, and more. The emphasis on the discipline itself has conjoined two elements: a focus on community-based archaeology that attends to the needs of indigenous descendent communities (Atalay 2012; Colwell-Chanthaphonh and Ferguson 2008; Silliman, ed. 2008; Watkins and Ferguson 2005) and attention to the decolonization of language in the conceptual and methodological realms of practice (Ferris 2009; Jordan 2009; Liebmann 2008; Silliman 2005, 2009; Watkins 2004, 2005).

This edited volume presents a unique and ambitious effort to combine aspects of both of these trends: studying colonialism in a comparative archaeological context and examining the relevance of those colonial aspects to the world today inhabited by archaeologists, descendants, and various heritage publics. As the editors articulate in the introduction (Hayes and Cipolla, this volume), studying colonialism without talking with indigenous communities and others who have less-than-privileged positions as a result of that colonialism will leave us in the predicament of actually not understanding colonialism or its long-term and ongoing effects. Therefore, the editors required that contributors try to speak to each of these components, which proved to be quite natural for some who have been looking at that intersection for many years and a bit novel for others who previously may have found the temporal distance too far or the contemporary communities too removed.

The intentional entangling of New World and ancient Mediterranean colonialism in the volume raises important issues. At the same time, it begs the larger question of how recently colonialism needed to happen (begin? end?) for it to still have interpretive and heritage resonance, or whether its resonance is more a matter of how we narrate it now vis-à-vis political issues among stakeholders. For settler nations, colonialism can be made simultaneously distant, when talked about in the context of national identity and settler politics or even the so-called contact period, and palpably recent, when talked about by indigenous people who still feel its effects. In other sociopolitical contexts, such as nations in western Europe, colonialism as a collective memory, national heritage, and academic project usually takes on a different valence. Hingley (this volume) demonstrates how Britain used its Roman colonial past in the sixteenth through nineteenth centuries to justify its own civilization (an ironic nod of gratitude to having been colonized) and to advocate its own ambitions in Wales, Ireland, Scotland, and the Americas (a direct importation of the model of colonization). The latter highlights how the mobilizing or silencing of colonial pasts is an active heritage project with great political import and not just an academic preference. Unlike settler nations of the past few centuries, these Old World colonial pasts had to be reintroduced into the lexicon of Renaissance Europe since they did not form a continuous thread of heritage and connection following the collapse of previous Greek or Roman colonial efforts (Dietler 2005; Hingley, this volume; contra Wells, this volume).

Overall, the outcomes in these chapters produce positive and revealing results, and these cases can help to guide future such studies meant to be concerned with both the past and the present of colonialism. However, my charge in one of the paired concluding chapters is not to examine each chapter individually for its successes in that joint project but rather to set these chapters and issues into a broader context of "indigenous archaeology" and comparative colonialism. Lightfoot (2012) prepared a similar contextualization of comparative colonialism and collaborative archaeology to conclude a recent edited volume on comparative colonialism and indigenous histories (Oland, Hart, and Frink 2012); I do not want to simply repeat what he offers elegantly there but rather try to build upon his insights. Performing that task for this volume has made me see powerful points of overlap and complementarity but also divergences that deserve some reflection as we move forward in these various intellectual and political projects.

Indigenous Archaeology

Active for less than fifteen years as an identifiable realm of the discipline, indigenous archaeology has been defined primarily through a set of inclusive prepositions, as an archaeology of, with, for, and by indigenous communities (Atalay 2012; Nicholas 2008, 2010; Silliman, ed. 2008; also Bruchac, Hart, and Wobst 2008; Watkins 2000). Pertinent to this edited volume, the practice and outcomes of this kind of archaeology have frequently been deeply engaged with the nature of colonialism and its effects (Lightfoot 2012). As I have noted before (Silliman 2008:3), "The intersections of colonialism, sovereignty, dispossession, and anthropology's tainted history with indigenous people make collaborative indigenous archaeology a unique enterprise." Rather than offer a summary already provided by those cited above, I want to comment on the current uncertain state of indigenous archaeology before talking about its relationship to comparative colonialism research. By "uncertain," I do not mean that those archaeologists practicing various forms of it have changed course or given up on its important objectives, for this is far from the case. Rather, I mean that its unique drawing together of archaeology, politics, and community engagement is undergoing critique from outside (Holtorf 2009; McGhee 2008; Stump 2013) and expansion from within to include more kinds of local community engagement (Atalay 2006, 2012).

The former aspect, critique from the outside, appears to pose little threat to the overall agenda of those who have advocated for an indigenous archaeology. McGhee's (2008) critique of indigenous archaeology as compromising science, homogenizing indigenous people, and demonstrating few tangible results has fallen flat, as evidenced by the commentaries to his original article (Colwell-Chanthaphonh et al. 2010; Croes 2010; Silliman 2010; Wilcox 2010), as well as by the increasing numbers of those who work with indigenous communities and produce quality archaeology (Atalay 2012; Lyons 2013). Stump (2013) has followed suit with a different critique of indigenous archaeology, which he instead calls "hybrid archaeology." Although he is considerably more sympathetic to community-based archaeologies than McGhee, despite erroneously claiming "local" and "indigenous" to be interchangeable terms (Stump 2013:271), Stump argues that this "hybrid" model of combining Western standards of knowledge production and indigenous perspectives has not met any of its lofty ambitions and does not have viability without a major revolution in archaeological epistemology. Yet, contrary to these recent concerns by archaeologists like McGhee and Stump, indigenous archaeologies now thrive, showing not only the coexistence but also the mutual constitution of community-based indigenous archaeology and rigorous archaeological research, all set in the acknowledgement of colonialism's impact on archaeologists and community members alike.

The other critique of indigenous archaeology looks at broader political heritage issues rather than outdated models of archaeological science (Holtorf 2009). In this version of critique, Holtorf argues that privileging an indigenous archaeology—meaning a prioritization of or value-giving to the archaeology of those people considered "first" in an area—could prove politically damaging to latecomers in a particular region. I agree completely that we must be very cautious about the application of "indigenous archaeology" in this way, particularly in European cases where the nonindigenous referent would apply to more recent immigrants, those frequently powerless within a nationalist context. One can imagine the complexities of defining and doing this in places like Israel and Palestine as well where the very definition of who was first and when is highly contested along political and national lines and has changed over time (Abu El-Haj 2001). However, this condition is explicitly not what indigenous archaeology addresses for those who practice it in settler nations, as it is primarily in the context of settler colonialism that a notion of "indigeneity" and its associated "indigenous archaeology" have meaning. Those who have practiced this kind of archaeology have sought to reposition indigenous histories within overarching colonial ones, indigenous viewpoints alongside and in conversation with academic perspectives, and indigenous people with respect to a professional and disciplinary undertaking that has repeatedly colonized and appropriated their histories. Moreover, advocates do not suggest that it must replace all other kinds of archaeology, especially those projects that do not work with or study indigenous people. This does not mean that "indigenous" presents a noncontested and undebated term, however, as witnessed by Hayes's chapter in this volume, the various engagements with indigeneity excerpted in Bruchac, Hart, and Wobst (2008), and even in Strump's (2013) cautionary statement about the lack of salience for this term in many African cases.

The real change to indigenous archaeology will not come from these external critiques but from its own practitioners who refine and expand their craft. Sonya Atalay's 2012 book, *Community-Based Archaeology: Research with, by, and for Indigenous and Local Communities*, illustrates this nicely. In the book she explicitly positions her commitments within (and arising from) indigenous archaeology to inform a broader community-based sense of activism and engagement. This means that she continues her dedication to indigenous communities, but she also expands that vision to include other "local" communities as well. In fact, she has taken her own North American indigenous perspective and applied it on the other side of the world in ancient Turkey (Atalay 2006). For her, the objective in these projects is upsetting power differentials, giving voice to structural silences, finding relevance through community-based participatory research, and challenging archaeology's status quo. Ironically, then, her application of "indigenous archaeology" in European cases worried over by Holtorf (2009) could translate into "immigrant archaeology" or simply "local archaeology," as it might assist those struggling within overarching powerful nation-states to have their voices and their heritages heard and properly understood. Or perhaps her perspective would align with Hingley's (this volume) and advocate for listening to the stories of communities living along Hadrian's Wall in northern England. It would certainly apply to the progressive political efforts in postdictatorship Brazil as the origins and fate of the *quilombo* maroon communities and associated collaborations were linked explicitly to the outcomes of contemporary social justice (Ferreira and Funari, this volume).

Therefore, the state of indigenous archaeology remains unclear. Its tenets and commitments may, as some have hoped, become simply the way archaeology is practiced with indigenous communities and later require no specific label (Nicholas 2010; Silliman 2008). The danger, of course, is then that these origins in indigenous struggles and experiences might become lost in a greater narrative of archaeology's history, making it appear as though archaeologists—many of whom were not indigenous people during the period of its ascendance—somehow brought about this transformation from a merely intellectual or professional place without the participation and activism of indigenous people inside and outside of the discipline itself. We need to maintain that disciplinary heritage intact to avoid such an outcome. Alternately, indigenous archaeology may continue to join the ranks of other community-engaged, participatory, applied-research archaeology projects that work with a variety of stakeholding communities, some descendent and some simply local (Colwell-Chanthaphonh and Ferguson 2008; Nicholas 2010). These make good allies with shared activist goals. However, we do not want to lose sight of the differences between indigenous communities and others while simultaneously recognizing their similarities. Furthermore, we have to recognize that working on behalf of some kinds of local communities may put projects and archaeologists at odds with local indigenous communities. This could be especially true in contexts with more volatile colonial heritages.

Comparative Colonialism and Indigenous History

Regardless of the tautness of connection to indigenous communities and collaborative archaeology, one of the challenges of conducting studies of comparative colonialism in archaeology or other disciplines is the very definition of colonialism itself. Most authors in this volume dodge that issue, although Hayes (this volume) considers some of the complexities of the term "colonialism" and its associated ideas of indigeneity and diaspora. Some authors assume a colonial context rather than apply colonialism as an analytical lens (Mullins and Ylimaunu, this volume), choosing instead to orient their research to one of impoverishment. Others redefine certain interactions as "cultural colonialism" to not require colonization but merely the convincing by powerful elites of distant elites to buy into their ideologies and material practices (Wells, this volume). I am not sure this latter use actually expands our scope and analytical sharpness. It seems to remove agency from Iron Age societies at the periphery of these Mediterranean colonial systems by suggesting that the Greeks culturally colonized them into accepting and valuing their elite goods rather than asking how these Iron Age society elites may have encouraged or adopted these objects and material symbols on their own terms. That is, sometimes expansion of colonial fronts comes not at the expense, initially, of elite residents but rather at their request and for their benefit. The Spanish missionary expansions into parts of La Florida provide pertinent examples (Scarry and McEwan 1995).

Yet despite these ambiguous research parameters, the authors in this volume have mobilized a healthy suite of approaches for looking at those being colonized and asserting themselves and their identities. Cipolla (this volume) draws on notions of consumption, developed and applied adeptly by Mullins (2004, 2011) over recent years. Cornell (this volume) deals with ideas about social innovation and the creation of new cultural formations in colonial contexts even without the adoption of European material objects. Mrozowski, Gould, and Law Pezzarossi (this volume:123) advance understandings of indigenous people in New England with careful attention to their own generational trajectories and the nondichotomous nature of "tradition and innovation, habit and ingenuity, replication and modification, and memory and anticipation." Hodge, Loren, and Capone (this volume:157) outline how Native American students negotiated their position in the "unique inflection of Puritan colonialism, which privileged literacy and anxiously evaluated bodies and souls" at Harvard University's Indian College in the early seventeenth century. They join others (among them Bragdon 2010) in making a point about the ways that literacy formed both a context of colonialism and a mechanism of cultural production and navigation of new circumstances for New England's Algonquian people.

In that larger context, the growing corpus of work on comparative colonialism, in and outside this volume, has given archaeologists broadened perspectives and enhanced conceptual tools for tackling large and small issues in colonialism. As a comparative project, its goals tend to be quite academic and intellectual in scope. The work seeks to expand the global material from which to mobilize archaeological and historical interpretations in specific contexts, and it often strives to establish overarching models of colonialism that draw from the outcomes and processes identified in similar or disparate localities around the world. Hayes and Cipolla (this volume:3) note quite correctly, "These disciplinary and scalar tensions reflect that a comparative approach can identify common concepts and categories but can also be used to deconstruct common (received) concepts and categories." As such, studies of comparative colonialism work laterally. They take colonialism as the critical analytical and processual link between geographical and cultural locales. Comparative colonialism as a research program has spaces for collaborative and community-based research within the local studies, but I have noticed that the approach easily slips into an academic-only space once the broader comparisons are set in motion.

Concurrent with the expansion of comparative studies of colonialism has been a growing parallel focus among archaeologists on long-term indigenous histories (Oland, Hart, and Frink 2012; Scheiber and Mitchell 2010; Schmidt and Mrozowski 2014). I suggest here that despite many points of overlap with comparative colonialism studies and often many of the same practitioners pursuing the two approaches, a tension remains. Studies of long-term indigenous histories have grounded their approach in the recognition that understanding indigenous people affected by colonialism requires interpreting native histories up to, through, and beyond different manifestations of colonialism. Colonialism appears as one inflection point, albeit a significant one, in long-term cultural and historical engagements by native peoples in their homelands. In contrast to the lateral approach of comparative study, long-term indigenous history approaches offer distinctly longitudinal and diachronic investigations, ones designed to elucidate trajectories rather than models. Furthermore, these approaches to native histories can and should rely fundamentally on involvement with descendant indigenous communities, for these groups comprise only the latest incarnation of those changes, continuities, intersections, and entanglements.

Herein lies the tension: How do we study comparative colonialism in ways that do not set long-term indigenous histories adrift in an interpretive sense, and how do we ensure that studies of long-term indigenous histories do not become insular and disconnected from broader anthropological understandings? One way to balance these tensions is to use colonialism as an analytical pivot point, swiveling perspectives back and forth between the long *durée* of cultural histories and the short *purée* of colonial entanglements (Silliman 2010). Similarly, we can use this swivel to counter narratives of inevitability that have been embedded in many archaeological studies of colonialism, as demonstrated by several chapters in this volume (Cipolla; Hayes and Cipolla; Mrozowski, Gould, and Law Pezzarossi) and beyond (Jordan 2009; Silliman 2009). Rather than assuming the outcome and finality of colonialism as we may see it from our present position looking back, it has proven helpful to decouple some of those historical outcomes from the actions of those embroiled in the formative moments and making decisions based on their own pasts and uncertain futures. We may know how these events lead to "colonialism," but the individuals in the past—even those we call colonizers—may not have, especially if we consider them engaged with "colonial projects" (Thomas 1994).

At the same time, how do we conduct comparative colonialism studies, including finding our way through the various opinions on how to define and study colonialism, while staying connected to local communities and their ancestors who lived them? Many communities may want archaeologists to acknowledge the harsh realities of the colonial process, from beginning to end, to accentuate their current political positions or their struggles to persist. Alternately, some may grow weary of having their cultures today always anchored in the moments of disruption and dislocation of colonialism rather than in the longer trajectories of indigenous histories. This is a real tension, felt not only by indigenous communities but also African diasporic ones. Unlike many other communities who might work with archaeologists, indigenous ones are those that feel the brunt of these historical narratives and political realities.

More seriously, some contemporary indigenous communities may recoil from archaeological attributions of colonialism to their own ancestors that some comparative studies have proposed or entertained in their attempts to find the limits of colonization and colonialism. The passing mention of the Pequot in Hayes and Cipolla (this volume) as potential colonizers in their own right before the English arrived in the early seventeenth century would likely not find resonance with Pequot people today, especially since we have little archaeological information to even support it. Another chapter in this volume proposes an inversion, stating that the Indian students at Harvard University in the early seventeenth century may have colonized the Indian College rather than simply the opposite: "In a sense, these Native American students colonized Harvard" (Hodge, Loren, and Capone, this volume:153). Admittedly, these authors seek to advance an argument that gives Native American students agency and ability to chart their way through this early university setting and the complexities of Christianity and literacy, but I have to wonder whether this kind of inversion is appropriate. Giving the "colonized" the opportunity to be colonizers themselves, either before or within the context of expanding European colonial powers, is tricky narrative business. Does this rhetoric grant a wrong kind of agency that attributes to them the same kinds of motives as to those who waged military and cultural war against them? If so, this starts to undermine the real struggles of agency in colonial contexts and begins to make "colonialism" what everyone can do, almost as an aspiration. This redirects attention away from its unique forms and its lopsided power and legacy.

Not all cases are so ambiguous and fraught with difficulty. For example, descendant communities and academics may not find a problem with talking about colonialism in other "premodern" contexts, as might be the case for obvious imperial actions and ambitions of Peruvian and Mesoamerican polities in the centuries before Spanish arrival in the sixteenth century and their descendants' engagements with that historical reality. Yet, these kinds of claims would not work for most North American groups whose pasts may have been characterized by migration, territorial contests, and interpersonal and intercultural conflicts—some of which bear similarities with colonialism—but decidedly unlike the acts of imperial expansion, city-state polities, and aggressive eradication of others' claims to territory or to cultural practices. The connection forged with local indigenous communities as we do our archaeologies of colonialism should give us pause, not to achieve a kind of "politically correct" interpretation that does not offend contemporary communities but rather to make sure that we do not start to inscribe loaded legacies of the post-Columbian era onto the autochthonous communities of settler nations without careful consideration of what that means for the past and present.

Of course, "finding" versions of colonialism in pre-European contexts in the Americas does not translate inherently into a deflation of the significance of European colonialism and might offer some interesting points of comparison if conducted critically and carefully. We do know, for instance, that some Native Americans groups allied militarily with colonizers at times to leverage against neighboring enemies, which in effect furthered a colonial project that would ultimately not benefit them. However, we already have instances in which the use of "comparative colonialism" supports a particular narrative for undermining indigenous heritage and political claims rather than outlines an analytically sophisticated analysis. For example, in his critique of indigenous archaeology, McGhee argues that indigenous people's experience of colonialism deserves no special attention or archaeological sensitivity since "the accumulated evidence of history demonstrates that all of our ancestors have at some point lost their homelands, taken over the homeland of others, mixed with other societies and changed beyond recognition over time" (2008:583). Such a perspective does not encourage the critical comparison proposed by authors of this volume but rather the apologetic leveling of historical outcomes. The former proposes to treat people with equity and attentiveness to their historical origins; the latter merely claims that everyone is somehow the same in order to more easily recast historical events and dilute responsibility among those in contemporary positions of privilege.

In light of these complex issues, we have to mind the gap that could be produced while we analytically swivel. We cannot lose the broader vision offered by comparative colonial studies, nor can we afford to ignore the local ties and understandings produced by indigenous archaeologies that study colonialism. Archaeologists must also be attentive to cases in which the "indigenous community" is not so clear and perhaps actually formed in the heritage process itself, much as Hingley (this volume) has hinted for Hadrian's Wall and Roman colonization in ancient England. In other words, archaeologists do not always work with communities that already have a strong heritage connection; their efforts at decolonization and engagement with communities are making a space for those connections to be better forged. This can have quite different outcomes for indigenous communities in settler nations versus subcultural elements in larger nation-states, and we need to be attentive to archaeologists' roles in these processes.

We might even have to reconsider some of what we find as the most fundamental in our studies. Mullins and Ylimaunu (this volume:50) make a provocative observation: "Poverty offers a powerful archaeological metaphor rooted in a concrete material reality and an aesthetic and corporeal experience. Therefore, it is one of the few dimensions of colonial life over the past half millennium that may offer a truly global interpretive framework." If we take this charge seriously, then perhaps colonialism is a mechanism, and one of many, of impoverishment. At least this might be the case for the past half millennium, Mullins and Ylimaunu assert: "A global picture provides a rigorous analysis of impoverishment that places poverty at the heart of life in the past five hundred years yet recognizes it has been experienced in many different forms" (43). Comparative colonialism would be approached quite differently if impoverishment was taken as a core feature and as outlined above and in their chapter (Mullins and Ylimaunu, this volume), either tactic requires expanded, comparative scopes of analysis anchored in local, material conditions.

Multiethnic and Shared Histories

One of the key realizations of comparative colonialisms over the past twenty years has been that of the complex mixes of backgrounds present in our no-longer-so-distinct silos of the colonized and the colonizer. For studies conducted on the past five hundred years, these colonizer/colonized binaries were usually assumed to be easily rendered as "European" for the colonizers and "indigenous" for the colonized, and we fashioned our analytical categories for artifacts and sites to parallel those assumptions. However, plenty of research has revealed the error in these assumptions and the complexities of participants in colonial projects, thanks in large part to the early, inspired studies by Thomas (1994), Stoler (1989), and others. For example, Voss (2008) has demonstrated how the "colonizers" in Spanish colonial San Francisco were not simply Spanish but actually Spanish, *criollo*, Mexican, African, and Native American. King (2012) similarly uses the diverse array of identities (Spanish, Zapotec, Aztec, African, and more) in Oaxaca, Mexico, to better nuance the cultural and political negotiations under study. Once these complexities are acknowledged, we can turn attention to how identities are created, not simply manifested inherently, as part of the colonial process.

Yet, one aspect that has only recently received attention has been the mixtures of peoples and heritages on the side of the colonized during the colonial process. Some studies have foregrounded this, such as Lightfoot's studies of Russian colonization in California (Lightfoot 2005; Lightfoot, Martinez, and Schiff 1998), a process that involved the importation of Alaskan Native peoples into California Indian territory in the early nineteenth century, or Weisman's studies (2007) of the development of the Seminole in Florida, but others have only recently explored what this might mean. For example, Cipolla (2013, this volume) examines a powerful case of the Brothertown Indians, a group formed from the amalgamation of Samson Occom's followers drawn from several Native communities in southern New England, and their movements to New York and then Wisconsin that structured their genesis as a new community.

Hayes (2013, this volume) also explores the coming together of heritages on Shelter Island, New York, as Native Americans and Africans worked side by side as laborers. In doing so, she follows through with a concern that I raised years ago (Silliman 2005:64, 68) about the disconnect in project perspectives and even terminology between archaeologists who work on Native Americans in colonial contexts (previously known as the "contact period") and archaeologists of the African diaspora. I am pleased to see more work on this topic, especially given the complex mixtures of Native Americans and people of African descent in the eastern half of the United States (Weik 2009). If we want to study colonialism and its impacts on people, then we have to look at the intersections of different peoples, similar experiences of labor, and novel situations created by diaspora and colonial settlement. This will necessitate more attention to the entanglement of Native American and African peoples and cultures.

Research on maroon communities in Brazil makes this point boldly (Ferreira and Funari, this volume; Funari 2006; Orser and Funari 2001). Here archaeologists face a unique situation that turns understandings of captivity, colonialism, communities, and collaboration on their head. Typical models of captivity and enslavement do not apply here, as these

Africans broke free from their bondage and established communities outside the reach of the colonial powers in Brazil. In doing so, they allied with and incorporated indigenous people into their society. They cannot be studied by archaeologists by using a simple presence or absence of African cultural elements; instead, they have to be studied as the result a complex ethnogenesis drawing on various heritages and historical constraints and opportunities. As Ferreira and Funari (this volume) explain, archaeological work to date has been particularly attuned to the political needs of these extant communities. In a sense, work with them could be placed beneath the umbrella of indigenous archaeology, for they have almost become a kind of indigenous community, forged in diaspora and colonialism, and definitely would fit comfortably in a variety of community-based archaeology projects.

Hayes (this volume) argues with respect to handling these complex mixtures that we need to parse out colonialism into its constituent processes for those most (adversely?) affected by it: indigeneity and diaspora. These offer helpful anchors for comparative and local work. That said, though, the viability of diaspora to link the experiences of colonized and colonizer in Australia, for example (Lilley 2006), remains to be seen. Lilley joins the calls in Australian archaeology and historiography to consider a notion of "shared histories" that invests both Aboriginal people and Anglo settlers in joint uses of materials, spaces, and landscapes (Byrne 2003; Harrison 2004; Murray 2004). Yet, his diaspora perspective may take too much off the edge of colonialism. Archaeologists might agree that some experiences of dislocation and unsettling could occur with both colonizer and colonized in a case like this, but feeling unsettled marks a noticeably different experience for those who are settled upon than those who do the settling.

Conclusion

The projects of comparative colonialism and indigenous archaeology share many objectives and can find common ground, especially when practiced jointly by the same archaeologist or collaborative group of archaeologists. In particular, both realms of archaeological practice want to understand the complexities of colonialism, past and present, and to find answers to questions that matter not only for historical communities but also for contemporary ones living in the legacies or ongoing currents of colonialism. Expansions of colonial studies to set up comparative potential across time and space (Greeks, Romans, British, Spanish, Inca, and others) have great potential to reveal the problems and possibilities of our conceptual frames of reference, terminology, and overall understanding of historical process. Similar expansions in the communities affected by colonialism and worthy of contemporary collaborative engagement to include not only indigenous communities but also diasporic ones—and instances when those communities have both components (Cipolla, this volume; Ferreira and Funari, this volume; Hayes, this volume)—will better position archaeologists to study realistic cultural interactions and cultural productions in the colonial past and to account for those resonances in communities today.

Concurrently, though, we have to monitor the tendency for comparative projects to drift from their local constituencies and collaborative partners in indigenous communities. These critical swivel points need careful articulation to keep them from starting to stick too much, especially on the comparative side at the expense of the community one. In addition, we need more archaeologists of indigenous descent, broadly defined, to conduct research not only on long-term indigenous histories, as is most commonly done, but also on comparative cases of colonialism, even those far removed from their own communities' historical experiences. Just as Atalay has brought exciting new approaches to archaeology of ancient Turkey courtesy of her Anishinaabe background and academic training (2010, 2012), we need examples like this in studies of comparative colonialism. To want this is not a result of essentializing indigenous experiences (contra McGhee 2008) or an assertion that such scholars will always think about everything differently than a nonindigenous person or will impart only "indigenous knowledge" to their study subjects (although they frequently will, which we should welcome) but rather to acknowledge the value of situated cultural experiences and diversity in our attempts to better archaeological practice. This could not be truer than in the study of colonialism itself, a multitemporal, transgeographical process that has resulted in some of the very categories of difference that inform or plague us today. Think of the interesting redirections in intellectual and disciplinary practice that might result if a Maya anthropologist studied French colonization in Canada, if a Hopi scholar studied Roman colonization in England, if an Australian Aboriginal person studied Russian colonization in Alaska, if a Native Hawaiian archaeologist researched Greek colonization in southern France, and if a Quechua archaeologist from Peru studied the Norse colonization of Iceland. Some versions of these configurations are perhaps already ongoing in new, unpublished work by indigenous scholars and graduate students, but I suspect numbers are few and far between. Even if we cannot achieve this "practitioner" result quickly, archaeologists of comparative colonialism would still benefit from the voices of indigenous communities from other places and histories to offer sources of inspiration or redirection, not as an appropriative tool but an inclusive one.

To recognize the value of this kind of entangling of past and present, of contexts near and far, recommended in this volume is to recognize how deeply entangled these histories and legacies already are. As a result, as advocated in this volume, we need to keep talking—across regions, about time, along trajectories, among archaeologists, and between communities.

References Cited

Abu El-Haj, Nadia
2001   *Facts on the Ground: Archaeological Practice and Territorial Self-Fashioning in Israeli Society*. University of Chicago Press, Chicago.
Alcock, Susan E., Terence N. D'Altroy, Kathleen D. Morrison, and Carla M. Sinopoli (editors)
2009   *Empires: Perspectives from Archaeology and History*. Cambridge University Press, Cambridge, England.
Atalay, Sonya
2006   Indigenous Archaeology as Decolonizing Practice. *American Indian Quarterly* 30(3–4):280–310.
2010   "We Don't Talk about Çatalhöyük, We Live It": Building Community Capacity through Archaeological Research Using a Community-Based Participatory Research (CBPR) Methodology. *World Archaeology* 43(1):419–429.
2012   *Community-Based Archaeology: Research with, by, and for Indigenous and Local Communities*. University of California Press, Berkeley.
Bragdon, Kathleen J.
2010   The Pragmatics of Language Learning: Graphic Pluralism on Martha's Vineyard. *Ethnohistory* 57(1):35–50.
Bruchac, Margaret M., Siobhan M. Hart, and H. Martin Wobst (editors)
2008   *Indigenous Archaeologies: A Reader in Decolonization*. Left Coast Press, Walnut Creek, California.

Byrne, Denis
2003   The Ethos of Return: Erasure and Reinstatement of Aboriginal Visibility in the Australian Historical Landscape. *Historical Archaeology* 37(1):73–86.
Cipolla, Craig N.
2013   *Becoming Brothertown: Native American Ethnogenesis and Endurance in the Modern World*. University of Arizona Press, Tucson.
Colwell-Chanthaphonh, Chip, and T. J. Ferguson (editors)
2008   *Collaboration in Archaeological Practice: Engaging Descendant Communities*. AltaMira Press, Lanham, Maryland.
Colwell-Chanthaphonh, Chip, T. J. Ferguson, Dorothy Lippert, Randall H. McGuire, George P. Nicholas, Joe E. Watkins, and Larry J. Zimmerman
2010   The Premise and Promise of Indigenous Archaeology. *American Antiquity* 75(2):228–35.
Croes, Dale R.
2010   Courage and Thoughtful Scholarship = Indigenous Archaeology Partnerships. *American Antiquity* 75(2):211–216.
Dietler, Michael
2005   The Archaeology of Colonization and the Colonization of Archaeology: Theoretical Challenges from an Ancient Mediterranean Colonial Encounter. In *The Archaeology of Colonial Encounters: Comparative Perspectives*, edited by Gil Stein, pp. 33–68. School for Advanced Research Press, Santa Fe, New Mexico.
2010   *Archaeologies of Colonialism: Consumption, Entanglement, and Violence in Ancient Mediterranean France*. University of California Press, Berkeley.
Ferris, Neal
2009   *The Archaeology of Native-Lived Colonialism: Challenging History in the Great Lakes*. University of Arizona Press, Tucson.
Funari, Pedro Paulo
2006   Conquistadors, Plantations, and Quilombo: Latin America in Historical Archaeology Context. In *Historical Archaeology*, edited by Martin Hall and Stephen W. Silliman, pp. 209–229. Blackwell, Oxford, England.
Gosden, Chris
2004   *Archaeology and Colonialism: Cultural Contact from 5000 BC to the Present*. Cambridge University Press, Cambridge, England.
Harrison, Rodney
2004   Shared Histories and the Archaeology of the Pastoral Industry in Australia. In *After Captain Cook: The Archaeology of the Recent Indigenous Past in Australia*, edited by Rodney Harrison and Christine Williamson, pp. 37–58. AltaMira Press, Walnut Creek, California.
Hayes, Katherine
2013   *Slavery before Race: Europeans, Africans, and Indians at Long Island's Sylvester Manor Plantation, 1651–1884*. New York University Press, New York.
Holtorf, Cornelius
2009   A European Perspective on Indigenous and Immigrant Archaeologies. *World Archaeology* 41(4):672–681.

Jordan, Kurt A.
2009   Colonies, Colonialism, and Cultural Entanglement: The Archaeology of Postcolumbian Intercultural Relations. In *International Handbook of Historical Archaeology*, edited by Teresita Majewski and David Gaimster, pp. 31–59. Springer, New York.

King, Stacie M.
2012   Hidden Transcripts, Contested Landscapes, and Long-Term Indigenous History in Oaxaca, Mexico. In *Decolonizing Indigenous Histories: Exploring "Prehistoric/Colonial" Transitions in Archaeology*, edited by Maxine Oland, Siobhan M. Hart, and Liam Frink, pp. 230–263. University of Arizona Press, Tucson.

Liebmann, Matthew
2008   Postcolonial Cultural Affiliation: Essentialism, Hybridity, and NAGPRA. In *Archaeology and the Postcolonial Critique*, edited by Matthew Liebmann and Uzma Z. Rizvi, pp. 73–90. AltaMira Press, Walnut Creek, California.

Lightfoot, Kent G.
2005   *Indians, Missionaries, and Merchants: The Legacy of Colonial Encounters on the California Frontiers*. University of California Press, Berkeley.
2012   Lost in Transition: A Retrospective. In *Decolonizing Indigenous Histories: Exploring "Prehistoric/Colonial" Transitions in Archaeology*, edited by Maxine Oland, Siobhan M. Hart, and Liam Frink, pp. 282–298. University of Arizona Press, Tucson.

Lightfoot, Kent G., Antoinette Martinez, and Ann M. Schiff
1998   Daily Practice and Material Culture in Pluralistic Social Settings: An Archaeological Study of Culture Change and Persistence from Fort Ross, California. *American Antiquity* 63:199–222.

Lightfoot, Kent G., Lee M. Panich, Tsim D. Schneider, Sara L. Gonzalez, Matthew A. Russell, Darren Modzelewski, Theresa Molino, and Elliot H. Blair
2013   The Study of Indigenous Political Economies and Colonialism in Native California: Implications for Contemporary Tribal Groups and Federal Recognition. *American Antiquity* 78(1):89–104.

Lilley, Ian
2006   Archaeology, Diaspora, and Decolonization. *Journal of Social Archaeology* 6(1):28–47.

Lyons, Natasha
2013   *Where the Wind Blows Us: Practicing Critical Community Archaeology in the Canadian North*. University of Arizona Press, Tucson.

McGhee, Robert
2008   Aboriginalism and the Problems of Indigenous Archaeology. *American Antiquity* 73(4):579–597.

Mullins, Paul
2004   Ideology, Power, and Capitalism: The Historical Archaeology of Consumption. In *A Companion to Social Archaeology*, edited by Lynn Meskell and Robert W. Preucel, pp. 195–211. Blackwell, Malden, Massachusetts.

2011   The Archaeology of Consumption. *Annual Review of Anthropology* 40:133–144.
Murray, Tim
2004   The Archaeology of Contact in Settler Societies. In *The Archaeology of Contact in Settler Societies*, edited by Tim Murray, pp. 1–16. Cambridge University Press, Cambridge, England.
Nicholas, George P.
2008   Native Peoples and Archaeology (Indigenous Archaeology). In *The Encyclopedia of Archaeology*, Vol. 3, edited by Deborah Pearsall, pp. 1660–1669. Elsevier, Oxford, England.
2010   Seeking the End of Indigenous Archaeology. In *Bridging the Divide: Indigenous Communities and Archaeology into the 21st Century*, edited by Caroline Phillips and Harry Allen, pp. 233–252. Left Coast Press, Walnut Creek, California.
Nicholas, George P. (editor)
2011   *Being and Becoming Indigenous Archaeologists*. Left Coast Press, Walnut Creek, California.
Oland, Maxine, Siobhan M. Hart, and Liam Frink (editors)
2012   *Decolonizing Indigenous Histories: Exploring "Prehistoric/Colonial" Transitions in Archaeology*. University of Arizona Press, Tucson.
Orser, Charles E. Jr., and Pedro Paulo Funari
2001   Archaeology and Slave Resistance and Rebellion. *World Archaeology* 33(1):61–72.
Scarry, John F., and Bonnie G. McEwan
1995   Domestic Architecture in Apalachee Province: Apalachee and Spanish Residential Styles in the Late Prehistoric and Early Historic Period Southeast, *American Antiquity* 60(3):482–495.
Scheiber, Laura L., and Mark D. Mitchell (editors)
2010   *Across a Great Divide: Continuity and Change in Native North American Societies, 1400–1900*. Amerind Studies in Archaeology. University of Arizona Press, Tucson.
Schmidt, Peter, and Stephen A. Mrozowski (editors)
2014   *The Death of Prehistory*. Oxford University Press, Oxford, England.
Silliman, Stephen W.
2005   Culture Contact or Colonialism? Challenges in the Archaeology of Native North America. *American Antiquity* 70(1):55–74.
2008   Collaborative Indigenous Archaeology: Troweling at the Edges, Eyeing the Center. In *Collaborating at the Trowel's Edge: Teaching and Learning in Indigenous Archaeology*, edited by Stephen W. Silliman, pp. 1–21. Amerind Studies in Archaeology 2. University of Arizona Press, Tucson.
2009   Change and Continuity, Practice and Memory: Native American Persistence in Colonial New England. *American Antiquity* 74(2):211–230.
2010   The Value and Diversity of Indigenous Archaeology: A Response to McGhee. *American Antiquity* 75(2):217–220.
2012   Between the Longue Durée and the Short Purée: Postcolonial Archaeologies of Indigenous History in Colonial North America. In *Decolonizing Indigenous*

Histories: Exploring "Prehistoric/Colonial" Transitions in Archaeology, edited by Maxine Oland, Siobhan M. Hart, and Liam Frink, pp. 113–132. University of Arizona Press, Tucson.

Silliman, Stephen W. (editor)
2008 *Collaborating at the Trowel's Edge: Teaching and Learning in Indigenous Archaeology*. Amerind Studies in Archaeology 2. University of Arizona Press, Tucson.

Stein, Gil J. (editor)
2005 *The Archaeology of Colonial Encounters: Comparative Perspectives*. School for Advanced Research Press, Santa Fe, New Mexico.

Stoler, Ann
1989 Rethinking Colonial Categories: European Communities and the Boundaries of Rule. *Comparative Studies in Society and History* 31:134–161.

Stump, Daryl
2013 On Applied Archaeology, Indigenous Knowledge, and the Usable Past. *Current Anthropology* 54(3):268–298.

Thomas, Nicholas
1994 *Colonialism's Culture: Anthropology, Travel, and Government*. Princeton University Press, Princeton, New Jersey.

van Dommelen, Peter
2006 Colonial Matters: Material Culture and Postcolonial Theory in Colonial Situations. In *Handbook of Material Culture*, edited by Christopher Tilley, Webb Keane, Susan Küchler, Michael Rowlands, and Patricia Spyer, pp. 104–123. Sage, London.

Voss, Barbara L.
2008 *The Archaeology of Ethnogenesis: Race and Sexuality in Colonial San Francisco*. University of California Press, Berkeley.

Voss, Barbara L., and Eleanor Conlin Casella (editors)
2012 *The Archaeology of Colonialism: Intimate Encounters and Sexual Effects*. Cambridge University Press, Cambridge, England.

Watkins, Joe E.
2000 *Indigenous Archaeology: American Indian Values and Scientific Practice*. AltaMira Press, Lanham, Maryland.
2004 Becoming American or Becoming Indian? NAGPRA, Kennewick, and Cultural Affiliation. *Journal of Social Archaeology* 4(1):60–80.
2005 Through Wary Eyes: Indigenous Perspectives on Archaeology. *Annual Review of Anthropology* 34:429–449.

Watkins, Joe E., and T. J. Ferguson
2005 Working with and Working for Indigenous Communities. In *Handbook of Archaeological Methods*, edited by Herbert D. G. Maschner and Christopher Chippendale, pp. 1371–1405. AltaMira Press, Walnut Creek, California.

Weik, Terrence M.
2009 The Role of Ethnogenesis and Organization in the Development of African-Native American Settlements: An African Seminole Model. *International Journal of Historical Archaeology* 13:206–238.

Weisman, Brent R.
2007   Nativism, Resistance, and Ethnogenesis of the Florida Seminole Indian Identity. *Historical Archaeology* 41(4):198–212.

Wilcox, Michael
2010   Saving Indigenous Peoples from Ourselves: Separate but Equal Archaeology Is Not Scientific Archaeology. *American Antiquity* 75(2):221–227.

12

Comparative Colonialism

Scales of Analysis and Contemporary Resonances

AUDREY HORNING

Colonialism matters today. No matter how far back into time we cast our glance, be it the Iron Age Mediterranean, Roman Britain, or seventeenth-century Harvard College, the present is never far away in terms of the reach and relevance of colonialism, lending urgency and immediacy to historical and archaeological discussions. Over the past twenty years, comparative studies of colonialism have increased exponentially in recognition of this entanglement of the present in the past. But there are serious risks in adopting broad perspectives on disparate engagements. Historical archaeologists typically approach global experiences in the period after 1600 through prioritizing capitalism as at the center of all colonial affects and effects (Orser 1996). But what happens when we toss the ancient world into the mix (Gosden 2004) without capitalism as a unifying element? What grounds our discourse? Or, following Michael Dietler (2010:22–23), would we do better to ask whether it is even possible to understand colonialism in the modern world without understanding its earlier expressions? After all, as he notes, "while the huge geographic extent of capitalist expansion is undeniable, it is well to recall that, for example, the Roman Empire lasted far longer than any modern empire and, in many ways, its colonial practices had even more profound cultural and social consequences than more recent examples."

While one might query the second part of Dietler's assertion, one of the profound impacts of the Roman Empire was the manner in which early modern colonial theorists routinely invoked Roman achievements and policies as they set out their plans for expansion and conquest, as discussed by Hingley (2000, this volume). For example, English efforts to plant colonies in sixteenth-century Ireland were explicitly based upon readings of Roman history by individuals like Sir Thomas Smith, whose unsuccessful attempt to plant the Ards Peninsula in County Down was sophisticated in his use of Roman models but woefully naïve in his understanding of the existing Irish political and cultural landscape (Curran 2002; Hill 1873; Kewes 2011; Morgan 1985). Resonances from ancient colonialism may be felt in other, less direct ways. Peter Wells (this volume) argues that the positive character of contemporary European attitudes toward the antiquities of Greece may be rooted as far back as the late Iron Age, when northern and central Europeans placed considerable value on the acquisition of Greek material culture in a process Wells considers to be colonial, albeit without colonization.

Ancient or modern, what are we actually talking about when we speak of colonial encounters and colonial legacies? Anyone engaged in comparative colonialism struggles with selecting the key points of convergence for examination. Violence, death, poverty, marginality, destruction, and displacement are attendant upon all colonial experiences to varying degrees, given that the one element of colonialism that remains true through time and space is the operation of unequal power relations. So should we concern ourselves primarily with illustrating the "power to" held by colonial and imperial overlords or the "power not to" tentatively maintained by subjects? Or perhaps we should instead focus on the less harmful and even creative elements emerging from colonial encounters, examining and celebrating the ways in which individuals and communities negotiate and strategize their own existence within the constraints of oppressive colonial systems. But ultimately, if we can say anything at all about colonialism in different spaces and places and times—whether it be Roman Britain, Puritan New England, or Spanish Argentina—it is that colonialism was and is ugly, unfair, violent, and disfiguring. In seeking to understand colonialism and how it reverberates and is still being enacted around the world, we cannot and must not lose sight of that essential fact. As noted by the historian James Sweet (2011:212), "Cultural mixture and ethnogenesis were rarely neutral exchanges among peoples of equal power, and it was through these hierarchies of power that collective identities emerged and evolved."

Compelled by colonial inequities to engage, Native peoples in North America clearly acted strategically to preserve their own interests. As demonstrated by Christina Hodge, Diana Loren, and Patricia Capone in this volume, English literacy was empowering for the handful of Indian scholars at Harvard, as they gained knowledge that would allow them to both better understand the actions of whites and manipulate white understandings of Native peoples. However, we should not forget that the English language itself was a powerful colonial weapon. Here I am particularly reminded of the seventeenth-century Gookin family. Daniel Gookin Jr. worked alongside the Reverend John Eliot. Eliot, also discussed in this volume by Stephen Mrozowski, Rae Gould, and Heather Law Pezzarossi, is best known for translating the Bible into Algonquian to aid his efforts to convert Massachusetts Natives. Gookin himself was acutely aware of the politics of language, having been raised in the Munster Plantation in County Cork, Ireland. There, his uncle Vincent gained a reputation for the virulence of his dislike for the Irish, routinely castigating his English planter neighbors for learning the Irish tongue and insisting that he would "not so much as suffer my children to learn the language" (Gookin 1903 [1633]:184–185). English planters who learned Irish, in Gookin's estimation, risked their very civility and undermined their claims to superiority. But the English in Munster were far outnumbered by their Irish counterparts, making communication essential. Perhaps absorbing lessons from his youth, Daniel Gookin Jr. also took a pragmatic approach to his intercultural dealings with the Algonquian peoples of Massachusetts. But as major general for the Massachusetts Colony, Gookin was in no danger of diluting his English identity or undermining his political power through strategically employing the Algonquian language. And just because Caleb Cheeshahteaumuck and Wowaus, or James Printer, learned English (and in Wowaus's case, the trade of printing) precisely because they also understood that language was a powerful weapon does not blunt the force with which it could be wielded against them.

As illustrated by the politics of the Harvard Indian College, the struggle between structure and agency lies at the root of our concerns. So too, do issues of scale, as addressed by Craig Cipolla in this volume. In considering the material engagements of the Brothertown Indians, Cipolla seeks to, in his terms, "flatten out" the macro and micro scales. His argument directly challenges approaches that prioritize the macroscalar processes of inequality attendant upon colonialism and capitalism by exposing the rootedness of the macro in the micro. How one does this without appearing to argue that "others" such as the Brothertown Indians are complicit in their own oppression requires careful balance, which he achieves through acknowledging that Brothertown survival strategies were consciously founded upon the calculated engagement with the dominant white society.

Several of the chapters, including Cipolla's, inevitably raise the specter of George Quimby (1966; Quimby and Spoehr 1951) and his acculturation equation, whereby the greater the percentages of Euro-American goods on an indigenous site, the greater the quantifiable loss of "authentic" Native identity. Cipolla suggests more nuanced ways of considering the meaning of material culture in sites associated with New England Native groups and the Brothertown community. His argument for longer-term maintenance of ideologies about the dead and their treatment, as reflected in a time lag in the adoption of commercially carved headstones by comparison to the adoption of Euro-American manufactured household goods, is simple and logical. Of course, very few people could afford or chose to buy such headstones, and I know from my own experience that in the close-knit Euro-American communities of the Virginia Blue Ridge (Horning 2004), unmarked fieldstone graves were the norm well into the 1930s—after all, everyone knew who was buried and where, without needing their names to be commemorated. To need the name presumes an expectation of forgetting. But to make this case—that it was not unusual for white communities to also eschew expensive carved headstones—is to completely miss the point.

We don't need to find difference in material culture and archaeological assemblages to prove indigenous identity if we start by acknowledging indigenous identity and then looking to see what the assemblages say about individuals, households, and communities. For the Brothertown Indians, the adoption of Christianity and the use of selected consumer items served to protect and preserve their Indian identity through not only projecting conformity (for example, through the use of mass-produced "familiar" headstones) but also by providing the means for communication and the grounds for negotiation. Mrozowski, Gould, and Law Pezzarossi (this volume) take this argument one step further in relation to the Praying Indian communities of colonial New England, noting that the acquisition and use of new forms of material culture and the acceptance of new forms of religious worship should not be interpreted as a priori evidence of the catastrophic loss of Native cultural identities but should instead be viewed as evidence for the centrality of innovation and dynamism in the formulation, expression, and maintenance of Native community identities—characteristics of Native life that long preceded the arrival of Europeans.

Colonized peoples everywhere ordered their lives through similar strategic negotiations. In so doing, they were dealing with daily realities and necessities, operating without the gift of foresight to know that at some point in the future, judgment might be passed on the "authenticity" of their indigenous or other identities based upon the choices they made. I am reminded of the exasperated comments of the Harvard anthropologist Carl Seltzer, sent by the Bureau of Indian Affairs to North Carolina in the 1930s, to determine the "true" identity of the Robeson County Indians through cranial measurement. Seltzer decided that only twenty-two out of one hundred volunteers possessed any Indian ancestry, and he complained, "Our task was made difficult at the outset by the fact that these people did not have a clear understanding of the term Indian. . . . They considered anybody who lived in their community as one of them" (in Oakley 2005:50). Tales of trauma and cultural loss in the past disenfranchise descendant communities in the present. Are they not who they know themselves to be because their ancestors coped with oppression through adopting Christianity and engaging in consumer behavior, in a pattern of adaptation and innovation that Mrozowski, Gould, and Law Pezzarossi (this volume) argue long predates the arrival of Europeans in the Americas?

Debates over authenticity are not merely academic for Native communities in the United States who lack the necessary paper trails to readily attain federal recognition. A case in point are the Indian communities of Virginia. Eleven groups possess state recognition, but none enjoys federal recognition—although the existing Pamunkey and Mattaponi Reservations were established by treaty in the 1640s. Proving the continuity of community identity for the recognized Virginia groups is hampered by legislated racism in the twentieth century. The 1924 Racial Integrity Act, devised by Walter Plecker, registrar of the Virginia Bureau of Vital Statistics from 1912 to 1946 and an outspoken white supremacist, designated any person claiming Indian heritage as "colored." As expressed by Rappahannock Chief Anne Richardson, "We were not allowed to be who we are in our own country, by officials in the government" (in Moretti-Langholtz and Daniel 2005: chapter 7; also discussed in Cook 2003; Smith 1993; Waugaman and Moretti-Langholtz 2000). Six of Virginia's tribes, the Chickahominy Indian Tribe, the Chickahominy Indian Tribe Eastern Division, the Upper Mattaponi Tribe, the Rappahannock Tribe Inc., the Monacan Indian Nation, and the Nansemond Indian Tribe, opted to strategically employ their involvement in the 2007 Jamestown four-hundredth anniversary as a catalyst for a direct petition to Congress for recognition. In May 2007, coinciding with the visit of Queen Elizabeth II to Jamestown, the House passed the Thomasina Jordan Indian Tribes of Virginia Federal Recognition Act H-1294, but it stalled in the Senate. In May 2013 a revised version of the act (HR 2190) was again referred to a House committee for consideration, and in April 2014 it was finally sent to the Senate for consideration (S 1074). In October 2014 the passage of the bill had a prognosis of 20 percent. The momentum of 2007 has long ebbed away. That the House committee in charge of deciding the fate of this bill is the Natural Resources Committee is just another reminder of the lasting power of the colonial tropes that classified indigenous people as part of the natural rather than cultural world. The strength of the American colonial metanarrative may be waning in the face of changing economic and demographic realities, but the alternative narratives of the Virginia Indians hold little sway.

History in the United States still appears agreed upon, with little room for new stories. This is not the case in Northern Ireland, where I live and work. Here, one is never very far away from the past. Understandings (and misunderstandings) of the character of the relationship between Britain and Ireland lie at the root of today's contemporary dichotomous identities (Protestant/Unionist on the one hand, Catholic/Nationalist on the other). Different understandings of the actualities and legacies of the past not only inform but also are foundational to contemporary identity and contemporary conflict, and they inevitably cause impact upon how archaeologists do or do not engage with the material remains from contested periods (Horning 2013). Everyone in Northern Ireland is, one way or another, entangled in some form of colonial narrative. Of course, this is true everywhere—yet it feels far more visceral in Northern Ireland because no single narrative is dominant. History is not agreed upon, as it can appear to be in lands where the power differential is so much more asymmetrical. In the United States the term "colonial" usually means something wholesome and homespun that you can buy in a craft market. In Northern Ireland, any use of the term is instantly divisive and as such unlikely to sell any product to any buyer.

By contrast, the term "colonial" has little currency of any kind in Great

Britain, either positive or negative. Unlike in Northern Ireland, there are very few historic monuments that people contest or that mean radically different things to different groups of people. This is certainly not to say there are no colonial legacies—the diverse population of British cities is in itself a testament to the afterlife of empire, as are the continuing and often acrimonious debates over immigration. But the local roots of such histories seldom spark much popular debate or even interest. Even the 2007 anniversary of the ending of the slave trade, notwithstanding some exhibitions and critical commentaries (Wilson 2008), was publicly greeted as the story of someone else's problem solved by heroic British abolitionists, having little to do with contemporary Britain or even past Britain. So I am particularly inspired by the call of Richard Hingley (this volume) for new and critical forms of engagement with Britain's older colonial legacies. Why do English people like the Romans so much? Or, as Hingley asks, do they really? What conversations about the present involvement of Britain in the affairs of non-Western nations might occur in the shadow of Hadrian's Wall, were a more nuanced and participative form of public education undertaken?

I am encouraged by this quest to engage the public in postcolonial critiques of Roman Britain. Like Hingley, I think nonarchaeologists are quite capable of grasping nuance and may be less frightened of drawing parallels with the present than are many practitioners. And what about the potential of an archaeology of Romano-British slavery? When it comes to comparisons of ancient-world slavery with that of the early modern world, I have also been struck by the lack of self-reflexivity employed by ancient-historians drawing on the American slave experience. More conversations among scholars of the African diaspora, who long have recognized the dangerous and dehumanizing power of academic verbiage, are needed. I think particularly of the centrality of studies of maroon settlements in Brazil to the contemporary fight for social justice as discussed by Lúcio Menezes Ferreira and Pedro Funari in this volume. As they also demonstrate, in Brazil the impetus for understanding the historical archaeology of enslavement came from scholars like Funari who were trained in classical archaeology. As such, the integration of classical and historical approaches in Brazil stands as a useful exemplar for the development of more critical, comparative studies of slavery elsewhere, as also advocated by Jane Webster (2008).

Hingley (this volume) raises critical issues about public presentations of colonial violence, noting the sanitized version of Roman military life proffered by re-enactment groups. The same can be said of many living-history museums particularly in North America that attempt to balance education with entertainment. Here I can draw upon my own experience as an employee in the 1980s at the Jamestown Settlement Museum, working alongside Virginia Indians as a costumed historical interpreter presenting Powhatan life during the first two decades of the Jamestown colony. The job was challenging, as the vast majority of visitors possessed little to no knowledge about Native society and particularly not of eastern Native society. Rather than focus upon the violence of encounter, or indeed very many elements of encounter at all, we instead concentrated efforts on demonstrating noncontested, basic aspects of early-seventeenth-century daily life: stone tool and pottery production, hide tanning, horticulture, cooking. The principal messages we were concerned about conveying were, one, Virginia was not an empty land when the English arrived; two, yes, it was possible to lead a fulfilling life without metal implements; and three, there are still Virginia Indians (but yes, they drive automobiles like anyone else).

When living-history museums do take risks in presenting violence in the past, the backlash can be fierce. In 1994 the Colonial Williamsburg Foundation decided to re-enact a slave auction. This decision was not taken lightly by the African American Interpretation and Presentations department, which developed the plan: "We knew that while Virginia's gentry debated liberty at their favorite taverns, at those same places they would buy and sell human beings as casually as a piece of land or a horse" (Matthews 1997:109). Despite the involvement of prominent African American scholars and historical interpreters in the project, when word leaked out the public outcry was immediate and angry, sparking protest by the state NAACP (although the local chapter, familiar with the efforts of the museum, was supportive). The event went ahead anyway on October 10, 1994, notwithstanding a crowd of more than two thousand, including many vocal protesters. In the end, all were silenced by the horrors being dramatized, as acknowledged by one of the chief protesters, Jack Gravely of the NAACP: "I would be lying if I said I didn't come out with a different view . . . The presentation was passionate, moving, and educational" (Krutko 2003:32; Associated Press 1994). While arguably a successful event in achieving its educational purpose, the auction took its toll on all involved and all who were witnesses: "You take yourself back in time . . . where people were once sold as property. This experience leaves part of you right where you stood. The impact is hard to describe" (Robert Watson Jr., quoted in Jones 1994). The auction re-enactment has not been repeated.

Re-enacting unresolved histories is very difficult indeed, but so, too, is writing about them when an ill-thought-out word choice can inadvertently misdirect understandings. For example, what value are terms like "diaspora" and "indigenous"? These two terms are problematic because they were and are political. As demonstrated by Katherine Hayes (this volume), these terms both constrain and frame our interpretive contexts. Indigeneity and diaspora are not mutually exclusive states of being, as she notes, nor is it helpful to entirely separate or segregate Native versus African American experiences of colonial asymmetries. The contemporary separation of Native and African American histories is political and is ahistorical. As scholars, we can follow her lead and argue for a breaking down of the boundaries. What is ahistorical about the segregation is the reality of mixed or creole communities throughout the Americas, as also demonstrated by the complexity of the Palmares maroon settlement and by extension the whole of Brazilian society, as considered by Ferreira and Funari in this volume. But recognition of the ways in which gene pools as well as identities are entangled works against the interests of Native communities in the present who must dance the dance of strategic essentialism, as pointed out by Mrozowski, Gould, and Law Pezzarossi (this volume) in their consideration of the Nipmuc and underscored by the lasting and deleterious effects of the 1924 Racial Integrity Act in Virginia, as discussed above. Native communities in the American South continue to fight against the legacy of these racial codes where one could only be black or white, not Indian. For some Indian peoples, this makes the issue of African heritage within their communities highly problematic, particularly for those now seeking federal recognition. This is a particularly ugly legacy of colonialism. The Brazilian situation, however, reminds us that multicultural identities emerging from the forces of colonialism can also serve as a unifying and useful element of contemporary society (Ferreira and Funari, this volume).

Diaspora and indigeneity are also problematic because of racism and, as noted by Paul Mullins and Timo Ylimaunu (this volume), racism and poverty are inextricably entwined in North America. But how do we approach poverty and marginalization in the archaeological record? Their analysis of poverty in Finland highlights the limits of imposing any all-encompassing model to address the materiality of poverty. Instead, their study teases out the specifics of perception, reality, and meanings of material culture in this locale and particularly how marginalized individuals, families, and communities struggling with poverty both managed and strategically manipulated their consumption patterns in ways that were often incomprehensible to outside observers (themselves governed by xenophobia) but that were following a logic for survival. Marginality is not only in the eye of the beholder. Perceptions of marginality are key to contemporary identity in Northern Ireland, where the Protestant and Catholic communities, approximately equivalent in number, individually define themselves as marginal within the specific context there. The Protestant and Unionist communities who have been up in arms since December 2012 (McKeown 2012) over the issue of the perennial flying of the Union flag are marginal in numbers on the island of Ireland but not in the context of the United Kingdom—although, that said, they probably are in the minority in their fervent adherence to the notion of the United Kingdom, given the relatively narrow defeat of the Scottish independence referendum in 2014 and the current call for Welsh independence.

Just as the operation of asymmetrical power hierarchies is a defining feature of colonialism through space and time, so is the reality that no one was left unchanged by colonial experiences, including—and perhaps especially—those in power. For example, anxiety emerges as the principal characteristic of colonial rulers in Martin Hall's influential characterization (2000) of colonial elites in South Africa and Virginia. One perennial cause of anxiety in colonial settings, reflected in Vincent Gookin's aforementioned rejection of the Irish language, is the manner in which the cultures and practices of the powerless insinuated themselves into the practices of the dominant. The consideration by Per Cornell (this volume) of the emergence of the Spanish American colonial town is a case in point. As he powerfully argues, the urban character of Tenochtitlán—far more ordered and sizable than any contemporary Spanish city—had a considerable impact upon the form and the ideology of subsequent Spanish colonial settlements. Such an indigenous legacy is seldom acknowledged and must have been a cause for significant anxiety among colonial planners. A parallel would be the dispersed settlement pattern of the colonial Chesapeake, where plantations were built all along the many navigable rivers of the region. Usually attributed to the tobacco economy, the vast majority of these early settlements were in fact deliberately placed atop and in some cases within Native villages (Hatfield 2003, 2004). Here the most obvious material manifestation of colonial power—the colonial settlements themselves—are in effect a forgotten transcript of Native influence.

Colonialism did not only happen to the marginalized. It affected everyone in its grasp. The few, of course, prospered obscenely from its inequalities. One can see this perhaps most clearly in the seemingly uncontested English landscape, with its estates and manor houses built on exploitation around the globe. There are many lessons left to learn and many injustices to rectify. But to not consider the human capacity for joy, creativity, and communal spirit demonstrated by even the most marginalized and oppressed groups is perhaps the greatest injustice of all. This contention is not the result of a naïve or "single-minded" application of a "culturalogical approach" that ignores "the reasons why struggle and resistance is necessary," as Charles Orser (2011:539) insists. Instead, it fully acknowledges the inequities and constraints placed on past people, as this is the context within which individuals and communities developed and implemented whatever strategies they could devise to get through the day. If we do not seek to understand their actions on their own terms while also highlighting the operation of broader colonial power structures, then we do no favors for anyone—least of all to the descendant communities who still struggle against the same forces that in some cases compelled their ancestors to go into hiding.

While the chapters in this collection take a very wide-ranging and comparative view of colonialism through space and time, they do so in a manner that showcases rather than mutes the value of locally rooted, textually and materially informed case studies. Most significantly, each of the chapters contributes to the whole in dealing explicitly with the contemporary resonances and ongoing legacies of colonial encounters in the twenty-first century, individually and collectively highlighting the reality and continuing importance of human experiences through as well as in spite of colonial entanglements.

References Cited

Associated Press
1994   NAACP rejects Official's Remarks: Political Action Head Praised Slave Auction. *Daily Press* (Hampton, Virginia), October 13.

Cook, Samuel R.
2003   Anthropological Advocacy in Historical Perspective: The Case of Anthropologists and Virginia Indians. *Human Organization* 62(2):191–201.

Curran, John E.
2002   *Roman Invasions: The British History, Protestant Anti-Romanism, and the Historical Imagination in England, 1530–1660.* University of Delaware Press, Newark, New Jersey.

Dietler, Michael
2010   *Archaeologies of Colonialism: Consumption, Entanglement and Violence in Ancient Mediterranean France.* University of California Press, Berkeley.

Gookin, Vincent
1903 [1633]   Letter to Lord Deputy Wentworth. In *Calendar of State Papers of Ireland 1647–1660*, edited by Robert Pentland Mahaffey, pp. 181–186. H.M. Stationery Office, London.

Gosden, Chris
2004   *Archaeology and Colonialism: Cultural Contact from 5000 BC to the Present.* Cambridge University Press, Cambridge, England.

Hall, Martin
2000   *Archaeology and the Modern World: Colonial Transcripts from South Africa and the Chesapeake.* Routledge, London.

Hatfield, April Lee
2003   Spanish Colonization Literature, Powhatan Geographies, and English Perceptions of Tsenacommacah/Virginia. *Journal of Southern History* 69(2):245–282.
2004   *Atlantic Virginia: Intercolonial Relations in the Seventeenth Century.* University of Pennsylvania Press, Philadelphia.

Hill, George
1873   *The MacDonnells of Antrim.* Glens of Antrim Historical Society, Belfast.

Hingley, Richard
2000   *Roman Officers and English Gentlemen: The Imperial Origins of Roman Archaeology.* Routledge, London.

Horning, Audrey
2004   *In the Shadow of Ragged Mountain.* Shenandoah Natural History Association, Luray, Virginia.
2013   Exerting Influence? Responsibility and the Public Role of Archaeologists in Divided Societies. *Archaeological Dialogues* 20(1):19–29.

Jones, Tamara
1994   Living History or Undying Racism?: Colonial Williamsburg's "Slave Auction" Draws Protest, Support. *Washington Post*, October 11, sec. A, p. 1.

Kewes, Paulina
2011   Henry Savile's Tacitus and the Politics of Roman History in Late Elizabethan England. *Huntingdon Library Quarterly* 74(4):515–551.

Krutko, Erin
2003   Colonial Williamsburg's Slave Auction Re-Enactment: Controversy, African

American History, and Public Memory. Master's thesis, American Studies, College of William and Mary, Williamsburg, Virginia.

Matthews, Christy
1997 Where Do We Go From Here? Researching and Interpreting the African American Experience. *Historical Archaeology* 31(3):107–113.

McKeown, L. A.
2012 Violence Flares after Controversial Belfast Vote over Union Flag, *The Independent*, December 4.

Moretti-Langholtz, Danielle, and Angela Daniel
2005 A Study of Virginia Indians and Jamestown: The First Century. Report prepared for Colonial National Historical Park. http://www.nps.gov/history/history/online_books/jame1/moretti-langholtz/chap7.htm.

Morgan, Hiram
1985 The Colonial Venture of Sir Thomas Smith in Ulster 1571–1575. *Historical Journal* 27:261–278.

Oakley, Christopher
2005 *Keeping the Circle: American Indian Identity in North Carolina 1885–2004*. University of Nebraska Press, Lincoln.

Orser, Charles E.
1996 *An Historical Archaeology of the Modern World*. Plenum, New York.
2011 The Archaeology of Poverty and the Poverty of Archaeology. *International Journal of Historical Archaeology* 15:533–543.

Quimby, George
1966 *Indian Culture and European Trade Goods*. University of Wisconsin Press, Madison.

Quimby, George, and A. Spoehr
1951 Acculturation and Material Culture. *Fieldiana: Anthropology* 36(6):107–147.

Smith, J. David
1993 *The Eugenic Assault on America: Studies in Red, White, and Black*. George Mason University Press, Fairfax, Virginia.

Sweet, James H.
2011 The Quiet Violence of Ethnogenesis. *William and Mary Quarterly* 68(2):209–214.

Waugaman, Sandra, and Danielle Moretti-Langholtz
2000 *We're Still Here: Contemporary Virginia Indians Tell Their Stories*. Palari, Richmond, Virginia.

Webster, Jane
2008 Less Beloved: Roman Archaeology, Slavery and the Failure to Compare. *Archaeological Dialogues* 15(2):103–149.

Wilson, Ross
2008 Representing the Diaspora: Performances of "Origin" and "Becoming" in Museums. *African Diaspora Archaeology Network Newsletter*, March. Electric document, http://www.diaspora.illinois.edu/news0308/news0308-8.pdf, accessed May 2, 2014.

Contributors

Patricia Capone is associate curator at the Harvard Peabody Museum.

Craig N. Cipolla is curator of North American archaeology at the Royal Ontario Museum and member of the Anthropology Department at the University of Toronto.

Per Cornell is professor in the Department of Historical Studies, University of Gothenburg, Sweden.

Lúcio Menezes Ferreira is professor of anthropology and archaeology at the Federal University of Pelotas, Brazil.

Pedro Paulo A. Funari is professor of historical archaeology at the University of Campinas, Brazil.

D. Rae Gould works for the Advisory Council on Historic Preservation, Office of Native American Affairs, and is a member of the Nipmuc Nation in Massachusetts.

Katherine H. Hayes is associate professor of anthropology and affiliate faculty in American Indian studies and heritage studies and public history at the University of Minnesota, Twin Cities.

Richard Hingley is professor of archaeology at the University of Durham, England.

Christina J. Hodge is academic curator and collections manager of the Stanford University Archaeology Collections, California.

Audrey Horning is professor of archaeology and head of the School of Geography, Archaeology, and Palaeoecology, Queen's University Belfast, Northern Ireland.

Heather Law Pezzarossi is a Ph.D. candidate in anthropology at the University of California, Berkeley.

Diana D. Loren is associate curator at the Harvard Peabody Museum.

Stephen A. Mrozowski is professor of anthropology at the University of Massachusetts Boston.

Paul R. Mullins is professor of anthropology at Indiana University–Purdue University, Indianapolis.

Stephen W. Silliman is professor of anthropology at the University of Massachusetts Boston.

Peter S. Wells is professor of anthropology at the University of Minnesota, Twin Cities.

Timo Ylimaunu is senior lecturer in historical archaeology at the University of Oulu, Finland.

Index

Academia, 137, 162, 180, 183, 193–194, 196, 215, 217, 220, 222, 227, 238, 240
Acerbi, Joseph, 40–42, 44–45, 47, 51
Affluence, 41–45, 47, 50–51
African American, 241; archaeologies of, 54–56, 225–226, 242; consumption, 33
diaspora 59–60, 63, 69–70, 222, 240, 242
African Burial Ground site, 69–70
Agency, 3, 6, 8–10, 20, 86, 201, 219, 222, 236
Algonquian, 4, 9, 21, 31, 56, 57m, 58, 68, 147–148, 236; language 144–145, 152, 236
Ancient history, 10, 19, 92, 172–173, 175–176, 191, 193–194, 196, 223, 235
Andes, 104, 111
Anishinaabe, 56, 58–59, 64–65, 67, 227
Architecture, 24–25, 76–77, 79, 84, 87, 89–90, 92, 112, 129, 135, 147, 149, 155
Atalay, Sonya, 217–218, 227
Athens, 78, 83
Authenticity, 7, 19, 103, 122–123, 134–135, 148, 150, 153, 237–238

Bhabha, Homi, 102, 113, 147–149, 153
Black Atlantic, 60
Boston, Sarah, 124, 131–133, 133f
Braudel, Fernand, 100
Brazil, 70, 190–202, 218, 225–226, 240, 242

Britain, 10, 44, 93, 127, 161–162, 164–165, 165m, 167–168, 170–172, 174–177, 179–181, 215, 234–235, 239–240
British Museum, 92
Bronze Age, 86
Brothertown Indians, 8, 17, 22, 26, 27f, 28–29, 30–35, 63, 137, 225, 236–237

Capitalism, 19, 100–102, 151, 235–236
Christian Indians, 17, 21, 28, 33, 124–126, 147–148, 151–152, 237–238
Civil Rights Movement, 54–55
Class, 17, 40, 70, 133–134
Classical archaeology, 194–195, 201–202, 240
Client kings, 77, 87
Colonial: difference, 33, 41, 102, 112, 147, 227, 237; futures, 2, 4, 7, 8, 20, 55, 93, 123, 131, 137, 154
Colonialism: comparative analysis of, 1–11, 19, 55, 64, 157, 191–195, 198, 201, 213–228, 234–244; cultural, 54–70, 219, 235; Dutch, 56; English, 20–22, 57, 122, 126–132, 143, 147–150, 164, 222, 234–236, 241, 244; French, 56–59, 64–65; Greek, 10, 19, 76–93, 112, 215, 219, 235; narratives, 2, 8, 10, 35, 42, 70, 131, 168, 175, 183, 221–222; Roman, 10, 19, 77, 93, 161–183, 191, 193–202, 215, 223, 234–235, 240–241; Spanish, 9, 99–114, 124, 219, 222, 224–225, 243; Swedish, 40–51

Community-based archaeology, 146, 214, 216–218, 220, 226
Consumption, 8, 17–39, 43, 45, 51, 86, 219, 243
Creolization, 172, 256
Critical geographies, 4, 5, 9, 11, 62
Critical temporalities, 4, 7–9, 102, 123, 130

Daily life, 5, 101, 121, 124, 126, 131, 137, 149, 152, 241
Decolonization, 11, 58, 101, 157, 161, 183, 201, 214, 224
Derrida, Jaques, 102, 103, 114
Diaspora, 4, 9, 54–56, 59, 60–64, 69–70, 101, 167, 192–193, 195, 222, 225–227, 240, 242
Dietler, Michael, 19, 20, 234
Displacement, 55, 60, 62–63, 68, 235
Domination, 68, 131, 143, 197

Eastern Pequot Reservation, 21–23, 131, 134
Eliot, John, 20–21, 126–127, 128f, 144–145, 147, 150, 236
Enslaved Africans, 54, 56, 59–60, 69
Entanglement, 4, 7, 10, 21, 35, 56, 68, 147, 149, 152, 154, 213, 221, 225, 228, 234, 239, 242, 244
Epistemology, 9, 193, 197, 200, 216
Ethnicity, 17, 43–44, 62–63, 67, 110–112, 195, 197, 224
Ethnography, 162, 179–183
Etruscans, 78–79, 83, 85–89, 92

Federal Recognition, 2, 7, 34–35, 58, 122, 137, 238–239, 242
Feudalism, 100, 102
Finland, 40–51, 42m, 46f, 243
Finley, Moses, 191, 194

Germany, 78–80, 88, 91–92, 182
Globalization, 5, 10, 19, 43

Grafenbuhl burial, 81m, 83, 85–87
Great Britain, 10, 56, 93, 127, 145, 161–183, 163m, 165m, 166m, 170f, 178f, 179f, 215, 234–235, 239–240
Greek colonies, 10, 19, 76–93, 112, 215, 235
Greeks, 2, 79, 82, 85, 86, 89, 92–93, 219, 227

Hadrian's Wall, 157, 162–165. 163m, 165m, 169, 177, 179, 180–183, 218, 223, 240
Hall, Martin, 198, 243
Harvard College, 127, 143–154, 157
Harvard Indian College, 143–157, 155f, 183, 219–220, 222, 236
Hassanamesit, 124–127, 125m, 129, 131–136, 132m, 133f, 136f, 145
Heritage, 2, 5–6, 8–10, 42–43, 57, 61, 70, 146, 156, 162, 167, 173–176, 179–183
Historical archaeology, 3, 40, 42, 45, 55, 124, 164, 190–191, 193–195, 197, 201–202, 234, 240
Hochdorf burial, 80–82, 81m, 84–87
Homeland, 4, 22, 55, 59, 60, 79, 220, 223
Horning, Audrey, 3, 10
Human Rights, 64, 173–174, 196–197
Hybridity, 113, 129, 135–137, 143, 148–150, 153–154, 167, 172, 216

Identity, 6, 8, 10, 34, 43, 55–56, 58–61, 63, 86, 88, 92, 121, 124, 131, 134, 136–137, 150, 156, 172, 192, 198–199, 201, 214, 235, 237–238, 243
Ideology, 148, 150, 243
Inca, 107–108, 110, 227
Indigenous voices, 172, 218, 228
Indigeneity, 10, 54–75, 101–102, 157, 213, 217, 219, 226, 242
Indigenous archaeology, 7, 61, 137, 172–173, 213–218, 223, 226–227
Inequality, 6, 42–43, 236
Inevitability, 4–5, 55, 123, 131, 134, 137, 168, 221

Innovation, 4, 9, 101, 106, 110, 113–114, 121, 123–124, 130, 134–135, 149, 168–169, 219, 237–238
Ireland, 164, 171, 215, 235–236
Iron Age, 9, 78–93, 99, 111–113, 169–170, 174–176, 183, 219, 234–235

King Philip's War, 126–127, 144–145, 148

Labor, 50, 55–57, 68, 225
Landscape, 4, 9, 24, 26, 44, 58, 60, 62, 64–66, 68–69, 77, 79, 135, 157, 174, 176, 181, 183, 201, 226, 235, 244
Latin America, 9, 100–101, 105–106, 113, 198–199, 201
Latour, Bruno, 5, 17, 19
Lightfoot, Kent, 3, 6, 34, 35, 215
Little Round Hill site, 64–67, 66f, 67f, 70

Magunkaquog, 21, 124–131, 125m, 128f, 134
Manhanset, 68–69
Marginality, 43, 235, 243
Maroon, 9, 70, 113, 191–192, 194–202, 218, 225, 240, 242
Mashantucket Pequot Reservation, 21–25, 28, 30
Materiality, 5, 23, 34, 43, 124, 131, 133, 148, 154, 190, 243
Matthews, Christopher, 6
Mattingly, David, 167, 172
Mediterranean, 9, 76–80, 83–84, 86–93, 99, 111, 164, 167, 182, 195, 214, 219, 234
Memory, 8, 10, 31, 33, 55, 123, 131, 133–134, 136, 155–156, 214, 219
Mesoamerica, 99–120, 222
Mesopotamia, 76
Metacom's Rebellion. *See* King Philip's War
Middle ground, 58, 64, 113, 152
Mimicry, 147, 153

Modernity, 10, 193
Morgan, Lewis Henry, 123
Mosher, Belva, 17, 22, 33–35
Mullins, Paul, 5, 8–9, 18, 25, 33, 224, 242
Multivocality, 183

Native American, 1–2, 6, 9, 19–24, 28, 32, 54–56, 59, 64, 121–124, 127–137, 143–157, 155f, 219, 222–223, 225, 237, 241–242
Native American Graves Protection and Repatriation Act, 1, 55, 122
Neoliberalism, 3, 69
New England, 20, 24, 28, 31, 33, 121–126, 130–131, 135, 137, 143–147, 151–152, 157, 219–220, 225, 235, 237
New York, 4, 6, 17, 22, 26, 28–30, 32–33, 44, 56, 57m, 68, 70, 225
Nipmuc, 8, 124, 126, 130–135, 137, 145–146, 156, 242
Nordic War, 49
North America, 5–6, 8, 18–20, 33–34, 42–43, 78, 124, 126, 137, 145, 152, 173, 217, 222, 235, 241–242
Northern Ireland, 3, 239–240, 243

Occom, Samson, 32, 35, 225
Other, 102–103, 236

Palmares, 70, 195–198, 242
Pays d'en haut, 58, 62, 64, 68
Peabody Museum of Archaeology and Ethnology, 146, 155–156
Pequot Indians, 4–5, 8, 21–26, 28–30, 35, 69, 131, 134, 222
Plurality, 1, 8
Postcolonial, 2, 102, 121, 161, 164, 167, 172–173, 182, 213, 240
Postcolonial Roman archaeologies, 161–162, 167–169, 172, 183
Poverty, 5–6, 9, 40–44, 50–51, 62, 224, 235, 242–243

Power, 3–5, 8, 10, 18, 43, 45, 101, 103, 123, 131, 151, 197, 200, 213, 217, 222, 235–236, 239–240, 243–244
Prehistory, 48, 82, 89, 101, 121–124, 130–131, 134, 173–176, 202
Probate, 45, 47
Public, 6–7, 10, 78, 92, 146, 154, 156–157, 162, 164, 171–172, 174–175, 179–180, 183, 214, 240, 241
Puritanism, 143–144, 148, 150–153, 219, 235

Quimby, George, 237

Race, 7, 44, 54, 57, 63–64, 70, 133, 152–153
Réaume Post site, 64–68, 70
Religion, 20, 48, 79, 123–124, 126, 130, 144–145, 151–153, 174–176, 198–199, 237
Renaissance, 91–92, 105, 215
Resistance, 5, 68, 121, 191–192, 197, 201, 244
Ritual, 48, 59, 82, 85–88, 151, 177
Roman Britain, 10, 93, 161–183, 163m, 165m, 215, 234–235, 240
Romans, 77, 162, 168, 171, 175–176, 227, 240
Romanization, 10, 162, 164–165, 168

Sámi, 48–49
Scale, 2–3, 5, 18–19, 23, 61, 90, 113, 131, 154, 157, 168, 170, 220, 236
Scandinavia, 41, 48
Silliman, Stephen, 10, 23–25, 30, 131
Slavery, 4–5, 9, 54, 56–60, 63, 69–70, 89, 100, 113, 164, 167–169, 171, 190–202, 225, 240, 241
Society for Propagation of the Gospel, 143–145

Sovereignty, 6–7, 34–35, 61, 63–64, 69, 121, 147, 149, 153–154, 195, 216
Spivak, Gayarti Chakravorty, 102
Stakeholders, 150, 156–157, 200, 202, 214, 219
Status, 32, 40, 47, 50, 54, 57, 77, 82, 88, 123, 151, 169, 195
Sweden, 40, 45, 49, 106, 112
Sylvester Manor, 56, 58f, 60, 68–69
Symbolism, 21, 29, 35, 41, 49, 70, 156–157, 173, 182, 197, 199, 219
Symposion, 82, 85–86

Tableware, 22, 24, 40, 45f, 133
Temporality, 1–2, 4, 8, 59, 70, 124, 183, 201, 213, 214, 227. *See also* Critical temporalities
Terminology, 17, 19, 225, 227
Theory, 2, 19, 99–100, 102, 114, 121, 161–162, 164, 172, 197, 199, 234
Third Space, 102, 113
Time, 4, 19, 22, 51, 102–103, 114, 227, 228, 234, 235, 243, 244
Time Team, 168–170, 172
Tornio, 45–49, 46f

Uruk, 76

Vix burial, 78, 82–87, 92

Western narratives, 41–42, 56, 122–123, 131
White, Richard, 58–59, 113
Witgen, Michael, 58–59, 62, 64
World Archaeological Congress, 194